2049.
SJ9/09

Crime Reduction and the law

This innovative and pioneering new book explains the multifaceted links between crime reduction and the law and how current British legislation works to improve or hinder crime reduction.

Providing a detailed and sustained analysis, *Crime Reduction and the Law* offers a thorough guide to many of the most contemporary and pressing concerns in the field of crime reduction. It considers social policy, politics and the legislation that surrounds and drives the crime reduction agenda and how specific legislation and the setting of performance targets aids or undermines attempts at crime reduction. This includes consideration of the creation of 'safe environments' through town and country planning legislation, the role of local authorities in crime reduction initiatives, the effectiveness of police performance targets, the concept of crime as pollution, the role of the national offender management service, paedophilia legislation and programmes to control crime committed by the mentally disordered.

Bringing together the work of internationally renowned experts in this field, this book will be highly useful to students of criminology and sociology, as well as crime prevention and reduction practitioners, police officers and community safety partnership professionals.

Kate Moss is Lecturer in Criminology at Loughborough University. Her research specialisms are crime prevention and community safety and she has recently undertaken work for the Home Office on information sharing to reduce crime and also the development of a risk index for domestic burglary.

Mike Stephens is Senior Lecturer in Criminology and Social Policy at Loughborough University. He has specialised in policing and criminal justice matters for a number of years and he has published widely in these fields. Recently, he has been interested in the role of the police in the handling of those with acute mental health problems.

Crime Reduction and the Law

Edited by Kate Moss
and Mike Stephens

Routledge
Taylor & Francis Group

LONDON AND NEW YORK

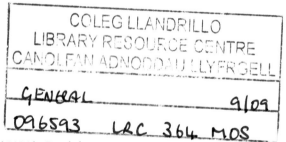

First published 2006 by Routledge
2 Park Square, Milton Park, Abingdon, Oxon, OX14 4RN

Simultaneously published in the USA and Canada
by Routledge
270 Madison Ave, New York, NY 10016

Routledge is an imprint of the Taylor & Francis Group

© 2006 Edited by Kate Moss and Mike Stephens

Typeset in Sabon by Taylor & Francis Books
Printed and bound in Great Britain by
TJ International Ltd, Padstow, Cornwall

British Library Cataloguing in Publication Data
A catalogue record for this book is available from the British Library

Library of Congress Cataloging in Publication Data
Crime reduction and the law / edited by Kate Moss and Mike
Stephens.-- 1st ed.
    p. cm.
  Includes bibliographical references and index.
  ISBN 0-415-35144-8 (pbk.) -- ISBN 0-415-35143-X (hard cover)
1. Crime--Government policy--Great Britain. 2. Crime prevention--
Great Britain. 3. Criminal law--Great Britain. I. Moss, Kate. II.
Stephens, Mike.

HV6947.C734 2006
364.4--dc22

2005011246

ISBN10: 0–415–35144–8 ISBN13: 978-0-415-35144-7 (pbk)
ISBN10: 0–415–35143–X ISBN13: 978-0-415-35143-0 (hbk)

Taylor & Francis Group is the Academic Division of T&F Informa plc.

For my parents, Graham and Pauline, and my children, Gemma and Christopher.

For my brother and very good friend, Mark, who gave me his only rugby ticket for the Millennium Stadium where Wales beat Ireland for the Grand Slam. 'Greater love hath no man ….'

Contents

Notes on contributors

Dr Stephen Brookes QPM is the Home Office Director for the Government Office for the East Midlands. He has been in post for four and a half years. For three years prior to this he was a member of Her Majesty's Inspectorate of Constabulary at Cambridge and, in the last 12 months, led, on behalf of the Regional Inspector, the national review of crime reduction that was published as 'Calling Time on Crime'. He has been a police officer for 29 years and has a wide range of experience in relation to crime reduction activity and partnership working. In 1996, as an Area Commander in Leicestershire, he was directly involved in the introduction of problem-oriented policing working alongside Professor Nick Tilley. This concept is now a nationally accepted approach to policing in general and partnership working in particular.

As the Home Office Director, he has taken a lead role in a number of national projects, including information exchange and analysis between partnerships, and developing a process for assessing the effectiveness of partnership working. In November 2004 he was conferred with a Ph.D. at Nottingham Trent University. His thesis sought to identify the conditions that help or hinder the development of Community-Based Policing and Partnerships. He was awarded the Queen's Police Medal in the Jubilee Birthday Honours in June 2002, for distinguished police service.

Dr Steve Everson is the former head of crime reduction in the West Yorkshire Police. He is now an independent researcher affiliated to the Applied Criminology Group at the University of Huddersfield and also a director of a crime reduction consultancy, Design Out Crime Limited (steve.everson@designoutcrime.com). He has written articles and spoken throughout the United Kingdom on repeat victimization and designing out crime. He was a founder member of the Home Office Crime Reduction College User Group and sat for many years as a member of the ACPO N.E. Region Crime Prevention Sub-Committee.

Armitage, R. and Everson, S. (2003) 'Building for Burglars?' *Crime Prevention and Community Safety: An International Journal,* 5(4), 15–25.

Everson, S. (2003) 'Repeat Victimisation and Prolific Offending: Chance or Choice?', *International Journal of Police Science and Management*, 5(3), 180–94.

Graham Farrell Ph.D. (University of Manchester) is Professor of Criminology in the Department of Social Sciences, Loughborough University. He has previously worked at the University of Cincinnati, Rutgers University, and the Police Foundation (Washington, DC) in the United States, for the United Nations in Vienna, and at the University of Oxford and the University of Manchester. His research is mainly in the areas of crime reduction and repeat victimization as well as drug policy but includes various other areas of criminal justice. Publications and a full *curriculum vitae* are online at: http://www-staff.lboro.ac.uk/%7Essgf/index.htm

Dr Steve Goode was Chief Probation Officer of Derbyshire until December 2004, after which he took up the post of Regional Offender Manager for the West Midlands for the National Offender Management Service. He was awarded the CBE in December 2002, for Services to the Probation Service.

Dennis Howitt is a Reader in Applied Psychology in the Department of Social Sciences, Loughborough University. His research career began with the study of mass communications but has developed into a broader interest in the application of psychology to social issues. As such, his primary research areas include the effects of mass communications, especially with reference to crime, violence and pornography, racism and the profession of psychology, paedophiles and sex offenders, and forensic psychology. He is a chartered (forensic) psychologist and a Fellow of the British Psychological Society. Selected publications include:

Howitt, D. (1995) *Paedophiles and Sexual Offences against Children*, Chichester: Wiley.

Howitt, D. (1998) *Crime, the Media and the Law*, Chichester: Wiley.

Howitt, D. (2002) *Forensic and Criminal Psychology*, London: Prentice Hall.

Howitt, D. and Cramer, D. (2005) *Introduction to Research Methods in Psychology*, Harlow: Prentice Hall.

Cramer, D. and Howitt, D. (2004) *Sage Dictionary of Statistics*, London: Sage.

Dr Kate Moss is a Lecturer in Criminology and Director of the M.Sc. course in Criminology in the Department of Social Sciences, Loughborough University. She gained an M.Phil. in Criminology at the Institute of Criminology, Cambridge, and obtained her Ph.D. from the University of Manchester. She also has an LL.B. degree. She has conducted extensive research and consultancy work for a wide range of institutions including the police, the Home Office and Centrex. Her main current research interest is crime prevention and in this capacity she has recently been appointed as a consultant to the Government Office for the East Midlands.

Ken Pease is Visiting Professor at the Department of Social Sciences, Loughborough University and at the Jill Dando Institute of Crime Science, having previously been Professor of Criminology at Manchester University. He was head of the Home Office Policing and Reducing Crime Unit and has been an adviser on crime prevention to the United Nations and to the Council of Europe. In 1998 he was awarded the OBE for services to crime prevention, on which topic he has published extensively.

Herschel Prins has over 50 years' experience of working with, writing and teaching about offenders and offender-patients. His early career was spent in the probation and psychiatric social work services, in the Home Office (Probation Inspectorate), and latterly in full-time university teaching (Leeds, Department of Psychiatry and Leicester, School of Social Work and Medical School). He has served on various government and voluntary sector bodies such as the Parole Board, the Mental Health Review Tribunal, the Mental Health Act Commission and NACRO (Mental Health Advisory Committee). He has chaired three committees of inquiry into mental health issues, and is the author of some 11 books (two co-authored), and over 150 papers in academic and professional journals. He sits on the editorial boards of five journals. The third edition of *Offenders, Deviants or Patients?* was published in February 2005. He is External Professor in the Department of Social Sciences, Loughborough University, and Honorary Professor, School of Psychology, Birmingham University.

John Roman is a Senior Research Associate at the Justice Policy Center of the Urban Institute in Washington, DC. Among his publications in the area of criminal justice are various studies of the theory, method and application of cost–benefit analysis. These include evaluations of various drug courts, including the Washington, DC Superior Court, studies on cost estimation and the application of cost–benefit analysis for the modelling of graduated sanctions, criminal justice evaluations and crime reduction.

Martin Seddon studied geology at the University of Nottingham and started his career in local government at Rotherham MBC, moving to Wakefield MDC where he spent most of his career working on reclamation, mineral and waste planning and environmental conservation and improvement. He was Environmental Planning and Development Control Manager until 2002, when he started his own consultancy, working on a wide range of planning cases and Best Value inspection. He has held interim management posts at City of York Council and Staffordshire Moorlands DC and has particular experience of working with police Architectural Liaison Officers on aspects of crime prevention and design.

Dr Mike Stephens is a Senior Lecturer in Criminology and Social Policy in the Department of Social Sciences, Loughborough University, where he teaches a number of criminological modules. He gained his D.Phil. in civil law from the University of Oxford. Since then, his research interests have turned towards criminological issues and include police training and community policing, and the role of the police in first encounters with those experiencing acute mental health problems. He has been a Visiting Professor at the School of Law, University of Wisconsin – Madison, and at the European University Institute, Florence.

Stephens, M. (2000) *Crime and Social Policy*, Eastbourne: The Gildredge Press.

Preface

There is a well-established, if relatively recent, literature on crime reduction. The innovative and unique aspect of *Crime reduction and the law* is
that it provides a detailed and sustained analysis of how specific legislation
and the setting of performance targets aids or undermines attempts at
crime reduction. Moreover, the book has been written and edited by a
combination of internationally renowned academics and criminal justice
practitioners. *Crime reduction and the law* offers a thorough and analytical guide to many of the most pressing and contemporary concerns in the
field of crime reduction. It is a pioneering work and one that could not be
more timely.

A changing world and mounting political and public pressures upon
criminal justice agencies and other public bodies with crime prevention
responsibilities have signalled a change in the delivery of crime prevention
and community safety initiatives. Added to this, traditional styles of crime
prevention are no longer appropriate for the twenty-first century. For
example, it has taken over 150 years for crime prevention to be viewed as
one of the most important tasks for the police. As the police are no longer
viewed as the sole primary crime prevention agents, there is now also a
realization that they will be more effective in detecting and reducing crime
if they ally themselves with other agencies in taking forward a partnership
approach to reducing crime. An informed discussion of a range of such
innovative crime reduction strategies and developments is therefore timely.
It is these developments that this book seeks to explore.

In the first chapter, Kate Moss sets out the clear potential of crime
reduction legislation, such as the Crime and Disorder Act 1998, but also
shows how much of that potential has been undermined or ignored.
Despite patchy implementation of this Act, Moss argues convincingly that
crime reduction strategies are nevertheless a new and exciting trend and
that they can have an impact on the work of the police, local authorities
and other agencies. Steve Everson, however, shows how other demands on
the police are pulling them in alternative directions. Growing pressures on
police resources have led them to concentrate more time and effort on a
narrow band of activities; namely, the performance targets set for them by

the Home Office. While this has helped to reduce crime in certain (measured) areas, it has also increasingly marginalized many activities previously felt to be fundamental features of UK policing by consent. However, reducing repeat victimization offers the police an opportunity both to meet key performance indicators and to provide consensual policing through which to improve crime reduction.

Extensive change is also happening within other criminal justice agencies in relation to the management of offenders. For example, the probation service was once about befriending and helping offenders subject to community-based sentences. In recent times, this philosophy has given way in large measure to a much greater emphasis on risk assessment, control over offenders, and the administration of community punishments. Government initiatives have heralded yet more change for the probation service, not least the recent merger with the prison service. The chapter by Steve Goode and Stephen Brookes highlights just how the probation service is coping with these changes and with the new demands now expected of it by central government. Goode and Brookes also examine how inter-agency policies to target persistent offenders can have a crime reductive effect. In addition to such local initiatives, the chapter describes the organizational merging of the prison and probation services within the National Offender Management Service whose primary aim is the effective management of offenders to ensure further crime reduction outcomes.

Just as the police and probation services have undergone significant change, the same can be said of local government. This is reflected in the chapters by Martin Seddon and by Stephen Brookes which respectively highlight the role of planning laws and procedures and the partnership approach to reducing crime. Seddon shows how environmental factors impact on crime and how planning controls and guidance may be effectively used to reduce crime and to produce safer environments. Brookes focuses on partnership working and how it can encourage the police and local authorities, in conjunction with appropriate legislation, to improve community safety and to tackle anti-social and alcohol-fuelled behaviour and youth crime. He also uncovers existing problems that hinder effective partnership working and, finally, he emphasizes the critical need for community leadership.

Two further areas which traditionally lead to public concern are crimes committed by the mentally ill generally and those committed by paedophiles specifically. These are sensitive topics, but both Herschel Prins in his chapter describing the mentally disordered and Dennis Howitt in his chapter on child molestation set out very clearly and dispassionately exactly where and how the law may intervene to lessen the harm caused by the mentally disordered and by paedophiles. Prins reveals how governmental concerns for public safety (often fuelled by moral panics) in respect of crimes committed by the seriously mentally ill have produced draft proposals which many mental health practitioners and others consider unjust and unworkable. He also tellingly highlights just how complex and tentative is the relationship between criminality and mental disturbance, which in itself places certain limits on policies and practices which may be expected to reduce crimes committed by the mentally disordered. Similarly complex and tentative is the debate about paedophiles and what to do with them, not least – as Howitt points out – because of the generally poor state of accurate data in this area. What Howitt's chapter conveys well is the sense of how difficult it is to police paedophiles and their activities, despite the undoubted advances made by recent legislation. Moreover, even when paedophiles are known to the authorities, problems remain in relation to inconsistent sex offender treatment programmes in prison, and less than perfect risk assessment and risk management procedures for child sex offenders under official scrutiny in the community.

Crime reduction and the law has a wide coverage, not least the extent to which it deals with current and pressing issues in an imaginative fashion. Nowhere is this more evident than in the separate chapters by Ken Pease, and by Graham Farrell and John Roman. Pease offers an insightful analysis about how to close down opportunities for and pathways into criminal activity. Personal path choices or dispositions interact with affordance perceptions and may lead to crime. An understanding of disposition-affordance interactions has policy implications for crime reduction. Such policies include a more effective use of section 17 of the Crime and Disorder Act 1998, and more accurate targeting of prolific and persistent offenders. Farrell and Roman write controversially about the need to make 'crime polluters' pay rather than the costs of such preventable crime falling on the victim or society in general. They examine crime as a form of pollution and argue cogently that one way to effect greater crime reduction would be to adopt market-based incentives to encourage manufacturers and other firms to improve their products' designs or organizational policies in order to reduce criminal opportunities. This is a radically different philosophy to that based traditionally on punitive approaches to crime control and reduction.

In the final chapter, Kate Moss reprises many of the themes and lessons set out in the preceding chapters. More importantly, Moss goes on to stress the need for academics, practitioners, the government and the public to take greater responsibility for crime and crime reduction. She argues the need for all of us to change the manner in which we think about crime reduction, and outlines a number of innovative ways in which the future of crime reduction may be taken forward.

In conclusion – and to draw an analogy with the medical profession – in spite of its spectacular expertise and knowledge in saving lives and curing illness, the health care system currently places more and more emphasis on policies and public education to maintain good health through preventive measures. Something similar is happening in the criminal justice system. It is not that we are banishing the traditional work of criminal justice agencies anymore than we are abandoning surgery and innovative drug treatments. It is that we no longer have to depend on traditional approaches to crime alone. We have alternatives even if they are not yet fully formed nor fully embraced in every quarter. This book highlights many of those alternatives and how they can have an impact upon the future reduction of crime.

Mike Stephens
Loughborough
March 2005

1　Crime prevention as law: rhetoric or reality?

Kate Moss

This chapter focuses on a recent trend that has changed the emphasis from legislating to create new crimes in order to keep ahead of the criminal, to legislating in order to facilitate a greater sharing of the responsibility to reduce crime. It will highlight how this has been achieved, whom it affects and how successful or otherwise this move has been. The radical and innovative nature of this trend will be discussed alongside the nature of its uptake and its implementation by the agencies it affects. Seven years on from the implementation of the legislation which initially brought this idea to us – the Crime and Disorder Act 1998 – this chapter will contend that both the understanding and uptake of this type of legislation as a tool for the reduction of crime have been patchy. The rhetoric is good; the reality is that it has not worked well thus far. Poor articulation and a lack of guidance upon implementation have contributed to this. The Home Office's current undertaking to amend the legislation, which is of prime importance to this change in emphasis, will also be discussed.

The chapter also focuses on the background to legislating to reduce crime; what crime is, and the notion of sharing responsibility for crime reduction implemented by the Crime and Disorder Act 1998. Two examples will then be used to demonstrate how this principle is supposed to work in practice. The first concerns the implementation of section 17 of the Crime and Disorder Act 1998 (hereinafter referred to as 'CDA'), which sought to legislate to spread the responsibility for reducing crime. The second addresses the implementation of the Data Protection Act 1998 (hereinafter referred to as 'DPA'), which has also sought to assist agencies in reducing crime by facilitating the lawful sharing of data to reduce crime alongside section 115 of the CDA. Some of the difficulties in the implementation and use of these crime reductive tools will be highlighted in order to particularize the chapter's general contention of imperfect implementation.

Crime prevention is not a new idea but interest and relevant research have increased in volume and quality over the last 30 years. The 'idea' of preventing crime predates this period by a substantial amount. In his Statute of Winchester 1285, the reforming medieval English King Edward I tried to control highway robbery by forcing property owners to clear the verges of highways (by cutting down trees and bushes alongside them) so that robbers would have nowhere near the road to hide, from which to surprise passers-by. Property owners who failed to do this were held legally liable for any robberies which occurred along their uncleared verges. So the idea of legislating for crime reduction has a long history. What have changed over the years (alongside the nature of crime itself) are the methods employed to give effect to crime reduction and ideas about who should be responsible for it.

Before embarking on the promised examples, it is pertinent to ask two questions: 'What is a crime?' and 'What is meant by crime prevention?' As regards a definition of crime prevention, Ekblom (1994: 1) argues that: 'Crime prevention involves the disruption of mechanisms which cause crime events.' This is not as simple as it sounds, for a number of reasons. It presumes clarity about what constitutes a crime. A crime comes into existence when a government legislates to make something a crime. This differs from jurisdiction to jurisdiction although there are, of course, some overlaps. Definitions of crime change over time alongside changes in society. Some acts which used to be crimes are no longer, such as consensual adult homosexual acts, whilst new crimes derive from new opportunities and ways of behaving afforded by advances in technology. Internet grooming under the Sexual Offences Act 2003 provides one recent example. Because crime changes over time, the scope of crime prevention changes too. Ekblom's definition is not prescriptive in terms of *how* crime events should be disrupted and can vary from capital punishment of suspects to redesign of attractive targets. There is certainly no suggestion that to disrupt a crime requires police or criminal justice intervention. It is just as well that crime prevention does not only seek legal intervention but also concentrates on a much more diverse range of disruptive techniques because, as Pease (1998: 963) states: 'A society in which more crime is prevented is not necessarily a more pleasant society. The burdens and restrictions imposed on people to prevent crime must be balanced against the harm caused by the crime prevented.'

There are two basic aspects to legislating to reduce crime. The traditional way has been to prescribe punishments so that people are deterred from committing acts that were crimes already. The second way is demonstrated by the more recent return to legislating to enable a sharing of the responsibility for reducing crime. This has included legislating to enable the sharing of information about crimes and in some cases about criminals themselves and is embodied in sections 17 and 115 of the CDA 1998, and in the DPA 1998. These two pieces of legislation seek to act as crime reductive tools. They will be used as the basis for the discussion in this chapter.

The last decade has seen major shifts in thinking about who should be responsible for preventing crime. Traditionally, the police had been assigned primary responsibility for that task. More recently, however, the Morgan Report 1991 sought to allocate responsibility for crime reduction to local authorities. A less radical option was legislated in the CDA 1998. Under section 17, local authorities and the police were designated as jointly responsible. Section 17 specifically imposes a duty on each local authority to exercise its functions with due regard to the need to do all that it reasonably can to prevent crime and disorder in its area.

The Home Office Consultation Document 'Getting to Grips with Crime: A New Framework for Local Intervention' (1997: chap. 3, para. 33) stated that the purpose was to 'give the vital work of preventing crime a new focus across a very wide range of local services … It is a matter of putting crime and disorder at the heart of decision making …'.

In the midst of an Act which contained many radical innovations, arguably section 17 could be perceived as one of the most radical, producing as it did the notion of shared responsibility for crime reduction across a wide range of local authority services. It should be acknowledged that section 17 was primarily conceived as an 'enabling device' for the promotion of effective crime reduction in the everyday activities of the police and local authorities. How has section 17 influenced practice on the ground?

Moss and Pease (1999) argued that the potentially far-reaching nature of this section of the 1998 Act appeared not to have been recognized even within government and amongst local authority officials. They speculated that this was due in part to the compartmentalization of thought which besets most discussions of crime and criminality, with the problem of crime popularly being reduced to the problem of what do to about the criminal, whereby the relevance of much local decision-making (for example in planning decisions) would be overlooked. The public debate continues, in spite of the CDA 1998, to be characterized by compartmentalization, which is reflected in the over-representation of 'people-processing' departments in local groups taking the implementation of the Act forward.

Whilst it is the case that the more proactive local authorities arranged specific training in respect of section 17, this has not been, and is still not being mainstreamed. Agencies affected by this legislation remain largely unaware of the issues that section 17 covers. In fact, it would be easier to ask to what section 17 does not extend, since almost every decision that could be made by a local authority could potentially have implications in terms of this section. For example, Moss and Pease (1999: 16) argue that:

> Because [these] crime drivers pervade every sphere of local authority responsibility, it is difficult to conceive of any decision which will remain untouched by s.17 considerations. Do you want to close a road? Crime patterns respond to such closures. Do you want to undertake or permit the building of new homes? Unless you ensure they are built to 'secured by design standards' they will be burgled more. Unless you can ensure rapid repair of council homes which have been burgled, they are liable to be burgled again. …

In spite of the fact that the range of issues to which it potentially extends is enormous, and in spite of the fact that a subsequent Home Office Briefing Note (11/00) (2000: 1) stated that: 'Section 17 was primarily conceived as an "enabling device" for the promotion of effective crime reduction in the everyday activities of police and local authorities', it remains poorly articulated and implemented with perhaps one exception. From the author's extensive experience of working nationally with the police, planners and local authorities, it had become clear that in relation to planning legislation it was perceived as a means of effectively reducing crime. Unfortunately, section 17 did not have the impact in this sphere that was hoped. Why was this so?

Subsequent to the enactment of the CDA 1998 and in line with the requirements of section 17, some police forces and local authorities endeavoured to implement this in the decision-making processes which concerned planning. Specifically, section 17 was seen by some of the more proactive architectural liaison officers and crime prevention design advisers as an enabler to incorporating more crime prevention measures in town-centre planning applications or change of land usages where that use was specifically related to restaurant, bar or club use, with all the potential attendant crime problems in 'attractive nuisances'. It is probably true to say that section 17 was seen initially as a godsend by worried police officers and local authorities contending – alongside changes in licensing laws – with the push for a 24-hour-a-day, seven-day-a-week town or city centre economy. The hope was that given the move towards a shared responsibility for crime reduction under this section, all agencies would come together to 'sing from the same hymn sheet' in relation to creating a balanced economy in the town centres of the UK which could be well planned and adequately policed. Against this background, developers were aware that this sort of move in the licensing laws signalled a potentially lucrative period for them and many moved in on town and city centres across the country to develop franchised nightclubs and to request permissions for changes to the classification of existing premises to class A3, which indicates use for a pub or club. In the cases where a change of use or a request for planning permission was denied at the local level on the ground of crime prevention under section 17, some developers were prepared to appeal that decision to the Planning Inspectorate, a central government department. What is particularly interesting, given the reason for the enactment of section 17 in the first place as a crime reductive tool, is the outcome of these cases and the reasons given for the decisions which in most instances went against the local agencies and led to the Planning Inspectorate stating quite firmly that section 17 – the very basis under which the planning applications had been refused in the first place – was not a factor it was prepared to take into consideration. Indeed, to the Inspectorate, section 17 was not even a material consideration in its decision-making processes. It is relevant to describe some examples of this in order to explain how and why this could occur, and, in doing so, to elucidate one of the main reasons why section 17 has so far failed as an enabling device for the promotion of effective crime reduction in the planning context.

The case of *Aquarium Entertainments Ltd* v. *Brighton and Hove Council* (2000) is famous (or infamous) for two reasons. First, it was the first case of its kind. Second, it was not unusual in the trend it set in decision-making in relation to the use of section 17 as an enabler for crime reduction. In this case, a developer (Aquarium Entertainments) had applied for and was granted planning permission for a nightclub develop-ment for up to 900 people. The developers then applied for permission to extend this initial development into two adjacent units which would house a maximum of 1,740 people. After consultation with the police and local residents, and mindful of the new statutory duty that section 17 had recently placed on them to 'exercise their functions with due regard to the need to do all they reasonably could to prevent crime and disorder', Brighton and Hove Council refused the second application. The developers appealed this decision and the appeal was upheld by the Planning Inspectorate. Some important issues can be teased out of this decision.

Without doubt, the local council and the police in this case felt that they were acting (and indeed were) within the boundaries of the statutory responsibility which had so recently been imposed upon them in the form of section 17. They had interpreted this responsibility (quite correctly) as enabling them to act in ways which would reduce crime in their locality and protect citizens from the types of nuisance, crime and disorder that are associated with the nightclub culture and an extended night-time economy. This has been evidenced most recently by Finney (2004). In the face of this, to receive such a decision was, to say the least, a disappoint-ment and it is worth looking in more detail at the reasons given for the Inspector's decision. The Inspector accepted that licensed premises had a connection with crime and disorder and that the council and the residents were right to be concerned about crime and to prevent it wherever possible; she also demonstrated that she was aware that recent statistics had shown that violent crimes in Brighton were at that time twice the national average per head of population. In spite of this, she implied that section 17 was not relevant to this particular appeal. How could this be the case? The explanation is simple. In the drafting of section 17, the responsibility it imposed on local authorities to reduce crime had simply not been extended to central government in any way and so the Planning Inspectorate, representing an arm of central government, was simply not bound by the same criteria as local government departments. Therefore, in hearing the appeal it was under no compunction to apply section 17 criteria. This represented (and still does, since this Act has not been amended) a legal loophole which had unfortunately not been foreseen and inadvertently had created a situation between central and local govern-ment which could best be described as 'do as I say rather than do as I do'.

Recommendations for the extension of the section 17 duty to central government have been made, for example by the second Foresight Crime Prevention Panel Report (2000), but these recommendations have yet to be implemented formally.

In making her decision on the basis that section 17 did not apply to the Planning Inspectorate, the Inspector in this case could be deemed to be correct. However, several other issues were not taken into consideration. Section 17 actually emphasized the legally binding principles of a previous Home Office Circular, namely No. 5 of 1994: 'Planning out Crime' (referred to as 5/94) which had established that crime prevention was capable of being what is called a 'material consideration' and one to which the Inspector should have given weight. Circular 5/94 acknowledges that successful crime prevention depends on a wide range of co-ordinated measures which, used together, can work to discourage anti-social behaviour and make it harder for criminals to find targets. It also encourages sensitive use of the planning system and its guidelines to urge developers to take into account the security of both people and their property when decisions concerning the siting of new residential, commercial or leisure developments are made. Where there was potential to reduce crime, as demonstrated by the *Aquarium Entertainments* case, this rightly featured in the discussions that the authority had with the developers and the local police. It is also something which should have been taken into consideration in the appeal process. In this particular case, the local authority and the police were mindful of their statutory duty under section 17 to 'consider crime prevention in all their decision-making processes' and felt duty bound to get this right. What they did not foresee – nor could they reasonably have done – was that this would be at odds with the guidelines to which the Planning Inspectorate would continue to operate. Understandably, this made many people operating at the local level feel that the Inspectorate was putting 'development' firmly before security, safety, community and partnerships.

In a letter to Brighton and Hove Council following the appeal decision, the Inspectorate contended that the CDA was not material to its decision. Its legal advisers informed the Inspectorate that section 17 was not in itself a material planning consideration. Having established that the Inspectorate was not under the same duty imposed by section 17, it remains pertinent to draw attention to exactly what constitutes a material consideration and why section 17 should already have been construed as such, rendering immaterial the fact that the Inspectorate was not specifically bound by the section itself.

Moss (2000) outlines that crime prevention is one of the social considerations to which regard must be given in development plans and highlights that it is important that crime prevention schemes are designed to meet specific security needs on a location basis. The *Aquarium Entertainments* case, like many such cases since, demonstrates that in every town or city there are particular trouble spots, highly vulnerable to opportunistic crime, for which effective and simple crime prevention measures are available. The people best placed to determine what these are, are the police working in partnership with local councils and the community. So when the Inspectorate states that section 17 is not a 'material consideration' this is a very narrow view, particularly since case law already exists which determines what types of crime and disorder issues can be material.

Whilst it is true that there is still no case law specific to the CDA itself, as any self-respecting lawyer will tell you, it is not the subject matter of a particular case which is important, but the legal principle embodied in that decision. Cases such as *Stringer* v. *Minister for Housing and Local Government* (1970) and *Ladbroke Rentals Ltd* v. *Secretary of State for the Environment* (1981) established some time ago what sorts of crime and disorder issues are capable of being material. These include issues impacting on a greater need for policing; on residents; on the feasibility of policing at key times; on the considerations of health and safety and law and order; and on amenities with attendant law and order problems.

Because these are all crime and disorder issues and material considerations, according to existing precedent, it could realistically be argued that it is neither appropriate nor legally correct to suggest that the crime prevention issues raised by section 17 are not similarly material. It would also be logical to suggest that section 17 serves to emphasize these requirements and if not taken into account, this could be *ultra vires* on the ground of unreasonableness, as established in *Associated Provincial Picture Houses* v. *Wednesbury Corporation* (1948).

So what is the impact of this interpretation of section 17 on its feasibility as a legislative crime reductive tool? Decisions such as the *Aquarium Entertainments* case, and others such as that in *Warrant Investments* (2000) have demonstrated that whilst many police forces and local authorities nationally have endeavoured to implement section 17 of the CDA in line with government policy, they have been frustrated in their attempts to do this effectively by the Planning Inspectorate. As an arm of central government, the Inspectorate is not itself bound by this statutory requirement and has maintained that section 17 is not a material consideration in spite of legal precedent which justifies numerous crime and disorder issues as material. This interpretation of the statute by the Inspectorate has created a bizarre situation whereby local authorities make decisions based on the crime and disorder criteria they are bound by statute to consider but if these are appealed the Inspectorate is at liberty to claim that these criteria are irrelevant because it is not operating to the same guidelines.

Moss and Seddon (2001: 25) highlighted that:

> Whilst it is true that some initial appeal decisions were not favourable to the use of section 17 as a crime and disorder material consideration, more recent decisions have been more supportive of this trend. Crime

prevention is capable of being a material planning consideration – but is probably not being given the profile it deserves in planning decision-making. Using crime prevention considerations as a reason, or supplementary reason, for refusing planning permission ultimately develops case law through the appeal system. Recent appeal decisions support this.

For example, in the *Jackson's Farm* case (2001) an appeal was made against the requirement for lighting on a public driveway. The appeal was dismissed because the Inspector agreed that the condition had been imposed in the interests of crime prevention and community safety. Similarly, in the *Grove Vale Depot* case (2000) the main issue concerned a residential development of 93 houses and whether the design and layout would provide a safe and attractive environment for future residents. The Inspector noted that a through route for pedestrians and cyclists would permit access for strangers; that underground parking would produce a gloomy and unsafe atmosphere; and that overall there were substantial shortcomings in crime prevention and defensible space which were sufficient to dismiss the appeal. It has also been established in a number of cases (such as *Gateshead MBC* v. *Secretary of State for the Environment* (1994) and *West Midlands Probation Committee* v. *Secretary of State for the Environment* (1997)) that the fear of crime can be a material planning consideration.

Whilst problems of interpretation have prevailed in relation to section 17, the main guidance that has been used in respect of crime prevention and planning has been Home Office Circular 5/94 'Planning out Crime', which did give some advice about crime prevention. However, problems of interpretation and the anomalous situation with regard to section 17 led in part to a recent revision of the guidance in Home Office Circular 5/94. However, it has been argued (Moss 2003) that the drafting of this has still not given priority to crime prevention issues. Neither has it rectified the fact that whilst local government is still bound by section 17, central government remains unbound. The current situation remains such that there is still a lack of awareness of section 17 on the ground and still a need for further training for local authorities on its merits and potential implications. Perhaps the most unfortunate drawback is that the anomalous situation highlighted here and the lack of will to rectify this sooner has meant that section 17 has not had the impact that it could have had in terms of being a radical and innovative crime reductive tool.

The second way in which the CDA has sought to emphasize the potential for legislation to act as a crime reductive tool is through section 115. We have already seen that the same Act charges responsible authorities with devising and implementing strategies for community safety. Responsible authorities in this case comprise the police and local authorities working as crime and disorder reduction partners. The rhetoric of the

Act emphasizes partnership and in line with this, section 115 allows the disclosure of personal information to the police, local authorities, probation committees and health authorities for any legitimate activity associated with the reduction of crime. Specifically, it allows any person to disclose information, either to a relevant authority or to a person acting on behalf of such an authority, where that disclosure is necessary or expedient for the purpose of any provision of the Act. According to Brookes *et al.* (2003: 8): 'In essence, s 115 provides a statutory gateway for information flow. It gives [crime reduction] partners the legal power to exchange.'

As such, the CDA appears to provide legal authority for the exchange or disclosure of certain types of information, although it should be remembered that this must be read alongside other statutory or common law restraints on disclosure, including areas such as breach of confidence, human rights and administrative law. In practice, partnerships have experienced problems in reaching agreements about what data can legitimately be shared and on what basis, with police data protection officers varying greatly in how they interpret the statute and senior officers or managers not taking active roles in promoting data sharing – possibly because of a lack of knowledge of the issues. The result of this in most cases has been a presumption *against* the sharing of data – which is disappointing given the innovative nature of this trend. It is more disappointing when we remember the recent problems of data exchange highlighted by the Ian Huntley case and the fact that poor data-sharing mechanisms enabled Huntley's appointment as caretaker at Soham College which in turn enabled the murders of Holly Wells and Jessica Chapman. This more than anything else clearly demonstrates the importance of the need for information sharing. However, it is also pertinent to point out that appropriate data sharing is important for other reasons. For example, our knowledge of repeat victimization and the predictive nature of this, by now well established by Pease (1998), shows that we can prevent more crime by sharing disaggregated victimization data. Again, the rhetoric of this idea, embodied as it is in legislation, is innovative but, as with section 17, the reality of the practice of data sharing does not match the rhetoric. The CDA, therefore, does provide legal authority for the sharing of information but should be read alongside other countervailing rights which necessarily may bring with them uncertainty. These include other statutory or common law restraints on disclosure and human rights issues as well as the principles of administrative law which state that any authority exercising a statutory power must do so for the purpose the statute specifies.

For example, the DPA 1998 exists to ensure that personal data is used properly through the use of protocols. This does not prevent data sharing and should not be perceived as doing so but unfortunately this appears to have been the perception within many crime and disorder partnerships. According to Schedule 1 to the Act, eight principles of data protection are designed to ensure acceptable data exchange by stating that data must:

1. be fairly and lawfully processed;
2. not be further processed in a manner incompatible with the purpose for which it was obtained;
3. be relevant, adequate and not excessive;
4. be accurate;
5. not be kept longer than is necessary;
6. be secure;
7. not be transferred to other countries without adequate protection;
8. be processed in accordance with the data subject's rights.

Partners who exchange data have also to be mindful of their obligations under common law, many aspects of which have developed specifically to protect individual liberty or privacy, such as the common law tort of breach of confidence. With the current propensity within crime reduction to 'name and shame', this is an aspect which needs to be considered, but perhaps not 'over-considered' as the case of *Hellewell* v. *Chief Constable of Derbyshire* (1995) demonstrates. This case concerned the legitimate use of a 'mug shot' which had been circulated to shopkeepers. The photograph was of a plaintiff who had 32 previous convictions. He claimed that the use of his photo was a breach of confidence by the police. The court found that the police had in fact acted in good faith since they had only circulated the photo to shopkeepers and not more generally. Whilst it is important to be mindful of these issues, it is even more important that they do not stifle data sharing to reduce crime. Unfortunately, both these and other reasons which cross the boundaries of cultural, political and practical limitations are often given for the inability to share data. But are these real reasons not to share?

Legally, there are no constraints on sharing data, provided that it is done on the basis of reducing crime. Although section 115 of the CDA provides a statutory gateway for information flow, giving partnerships the legal power to exchange, excuses are often made not to share. One way in which this could be overcome is to agree objectives between partners based on the most recent crime audit, and to sign a regularly revised data-sharing protocol in respect of this. Embarrassment about the condition or state of an agency's data can also be a limiting factor. Exchanging it also means losing control of that data and this could be potentially embarrassing for the owner if the data presents as 'dirty', unflattering or ambiguous. Cleaning such data also adds an extra cost to the process of analysis. Sometimes there is a lack of analytical capability to undertake the kind of collection and analysis that is meaningful, although recent fieldwork by the author which has already been referred to earlier in this chapter suggests that this is less the case now than it was formerly. However, perhaps the most significant hindrance to sharing data to reduce crime has been highlighted by Brookes *et al.* (2003: 12) where a study of best practice in data sharing within the East Midlands region established that:

The most common problematic themes which emerged from the research were related to issues of focus, communication and leadership. In terms of focus, most CDRPs [Crime and Disorder Reduction Partnerships] over-emphasized the need for populating systems with data without focusing on what could be achieved with that data or how it could be used to solve problems.

The findings of this research led to a pilot study in which data sharing and analysis specifically based upon risk was carried out in two residential areas within Nottingham city. Based on this study, Moss and Pease (2004) outlined the difficulties highlighted by Brookes *et al.* (2003) in relation to data sharing to reduce crime and proposed an approach which minimized formal data sharing whilst maximizing relevance to crime reduction. The approach they described is based upon a schedule of contingent actions whereby the agreement is *not* to share data routinely, but to act in agreed ways in circumstances designated by partner agencies – an approach they feel has advantages over blanket agreements to share data.

Notwithstanding this, the bottom line with modern crime reductive legislation has been to recognize that agencies other than the police routinely make decisions with crime consequences and that they should therefore all be involved in crime reduction by a co-location of responsibility for community safety. The legislation looked at within this chapter is a radical repositioning of responsibility for crime and does require some trade-offs between crime reduction and privacy. However, what is needed above all is an emphasis on agreement which would afford a level playing field for all the agencies involved in these processes. The fact that this has not been made clear has hindered the progress that might have been otherwise made.

Let us return now to the question initially posed: is legislating to reduce crime rhetoric or reality? Section 115 of the CDA makes it very clear that the government's view is that exchanging data, within the formal guidelines, could help to reduce crime and disorder. It is vital, therefore, that this sort of approach does not become sidelined, not least because of the links that it has with the statutory obligations encapsulated in section 17. CDRPs should mainstream an approach to data sharing to underpin these obligations but at the same time the government must realize that data sharing is not a 'quick fix', requiring as it does, time, commitment, effort and money. Most of all, what current research, highlighted by Brookes *et al.* (2003) and Moss and Pease (2004), shows is that there must be focus regarding why people want to share data and what sharing it will achieve in terms of reducing crime. As with section 17, a better 'steer' from central government about this may well improve upon the reluctance that many agencies still have about sharing data. Specifically, partnerships need to be reassured that it *is* legally possible; that it *can* help them to concentrate on the issues that are really problematic; and that this consequently might allow them to spend more time thinking about *why* they should share data and what to do about the presenting relationships between crime and data.

What can be drawn from all of this? The drafting of legislation is complex and mistakes can be made but it remains important to respond to any mistakes or inadvertent anomalies quickly in order for that legislation not to become meaningless or impossible to respond to. Practitioners and all those involved in issues such as these have to respond to many demands on their time and to many changes in legislation and policy which necessarily affect their working lives and the ways in which they operate. For new ideas to be successful, they must be implemented with sufficient guidance and must be seen to apply to all, rather than just those working at the local level. Successful implementation of what are, in essence, innovative and ground-breaking ideas with the potential to change the face of crime reduction altogether also depends on those on the ground having the certainty that everyone is 'singing from the same hymn sheet'.

The Home Office has recently accepted that the anomalies which remain with regard to the CDA and the DPA merit another look at the legislation with a view to amending it in some way. However, it remains to be seen, given the generalist nature of the Home Office and in particular of career civil servants who may be tasked to take the lead on this, whether future amendments, if made by non-specialists in the field, will amount to any significant and meaningful changes.

Bibliography

Aquarium Entertainments Ltd v. *Brighton and Hove Council*, Appeal Ref. T/APP/Q1445/A/99/1025514/P2, 22 February 2000, 1–2 and 15–18.

Associated Provincial Picture Houses v. *Wednesbury Corporation* [1948] 1 K.B. 223.

Brookes, S., Moss, K. and Pease, K. (2003) 'Data Sharing and Crime Reduction: The Long and Winding Road', *Crime Prevention and Community Safety: An International Journal*, 5(4), 7–14.

Ekblom, P. (1994) 'Proximal Circumstances: A Mechanism-Based Classification of Crime Prevention', in Clarke, R. (ed.) *Situational Crime Prevention Studies*, NY: Monsey.

Finney, A. (2004) 'Violence in the Night Time Economy: Key Findings', *Home Office Key Research Findings No. 214*, London: HMSO.

Foresight Crime Prevention Panel (2000) 'Turning the Corner', London: DTI.

Gateshead MBC v. *Secretary of State for the Environment* [1994] JPL 432.

Grove Vale Depot case, Appeal Ref. APP/A5840/A/00/1041744 (Grove Vale Depot, Vale End, East Dulwich), 25 October 2000.

Hellewell v. *Chief Constable of Derbyshire* [1995] 1 W.L.R. 804.

Home Office (1994) Circular No. 5 'Planning out Crime', London: Home Office.

Home Office (1997) 'Getting to Grips with Crime: A New Framework for Local Intervention', London: Home Office.

Home Office (2000) 'Anticipating the Impact of Section 17 Crime and Disorder Act 1998', Briefing Note 11/00, London: Home Office.

Jackson's Farm case, Appeal Ref. APP/E2530/A/00/1054000 (Land adjoining Jackson's Farm, off Middle Street, Skillington, Lincolnshire NG33 5ER), 28 February 2001.

Ladbroke Rentals Ltd v. *Secretary for State for the Environment* [1981] J.P.L. 454.

Maguire, M., Morgan, R. and Reiner, R. (2002) *Oxford Handbook of Criminology* (3rd ed.), Oxford: Oxford University Press.

Morgan Report (1991) 'Safer Communities: The Local Delivery of Crime Prevention through the Partnership Approach', London: Home Office.

Moss, K. (2000) 'Crime Prevention v Planning: Section 17 of the Crime and Disorder Act. Is it a Material Consideration?', *Crime Prevention and Community Safety: An International Journal*, 3(2), 43–8.

Moss, K. (2003) 'The Good, the Bad or the Ugly? What will the new Planning out Crime Guidance be Like and What Should it be Like?', *Community Safety Journal*, Vol. 2, Issue 1, January 2003.

Moss, K. and Pease, K. (1999) 'Crime and Disorder Act 1998: Section 17. A Wolf in Sheep's Clothing?', *Crime Prevention and Community Safety: An International Journal*, 1(4), 15–19.

Moss, K. and Seddon, M. (2001) 'Crime Prevention and Planning: Searching for Common Sense in Disorder Legislation', *Crime Prevention and Community Safety: An International Journal*, 3(4), 25–31.

Moss, K. and Pease, K. (2004) 'Data Sharing in Crime Prevention: Why and How', *Crime Prevention and Community Safety: An International Journal*, 6(1), 7–12.

Pease, K. (1998) 'Repeat Victimisation: Taking Stock, Crime Detection and Prevention' Paper No. 90, London: Home Office.

Stringer v. *Minister for Housing and Local Government* [1970] 1 W.L.R. 1281.

Warrant Investments Ltd v. *Newcastle-under-Lyme Borough Council*, Appeal Ref. T/APP/P3420/A/00/1036269/P2, 3 May 2000.

West Midlands Probation Committee v. *Secretary of State for the Environment* [1997] J.P.L. 323.

2 Law and the management of places

Martin H. Seddon

Introduction

This chapter refers to the growing body of research, theory and practice concerning the influence of environmental factors on levels of crime and fear of crime. It explores the origins of contemporary planning controls and guidance which influence the places where we live, work and play and how these can be used to help create a safer environment. The roles of planners, the police, developers and the community are critical in the process of achieving significant reductions in crime and disorder by applying best practice at the local level.

Crime and the environment

There is a long historical link between the design and management of places and crime prevention in its broadest sense. The need to defend settlements from invading forces often influenced their original siting. The use of high ground allowed surveillance of the surrounding area to identify the oncoming enemy and gave a positional advantage. The construction of ditches and ramparts and city walls in Roman times and the building of Norman castles were extreme forms of 'target hardening'. Defensive structures such as these were mainly applied to existing settlements, but occasionally a new fortified town was created, such as Palmanova in eastern Italy. This star-shaped settlement was built in the 1590s by the rulers of Venice to protect the rural neighbourhood from attack by the Ottoman Empire (Watkin 2000: 280).

In referring to political and military developments in Italy during the Renaissance, Eaton (2002: 56) notes that:

> The walls of medieval towns may have looked impressive but they offered little resistance to modern technology. New, deep fortifications were required to stand up to the evolving situation and the sixteenth century produced a rash of military designs which took on but compromised the notion of the ideal city, not just in aesthetic terms, but also in that of ambition, reducing it to a large fortress.

More recently, the threat of terrorism has caused authorities to look more closely at the design of public buildings and places and how they can be reinforced and provided with security measures and personnel to limit their vulnerability. Often, for government and local authority buildings, there is a trade-off between security and freedom of access for the public. In some new residential estates there has been a desire to restrict access through gating and fencing as a response towards a fear of crime. UK town and city centres have experienced a growth in the use of solid steel shutters for shop fronts as an anti-burglary measure, with associated aesthetic drawbacks, particularly in historic areas. Closed circuit television (CCTV) has also been introduced, backed by government funding through the Home Office, to improve surveillance in city centres.

Whilst there is an obvious link between fortification and defence against the threat of warfare and crime, there are subtleties in the way in which a particular environment may help or hinder crime and disorder. For example, an unlit underpass presents an opportunity for assault, or a footpath at the rear of houses may provide an easy access and escape route for burglars. Late-night opening hot food take-aways can act as a focus for groups to congregate after public houses have closed, with potential for noise, disturbance and conflict. Understanding the influence of local environmental factors can inform the process of planning new developments and contribute towards safer places.

An important early work which explored crime and the urban environment was Jane Jacobs's book (1961) *The Death and Life of Great American Cities*. It was an attack on city planning and re-building which was current at that time. She looked at how cities worked in real life and what kinds of city streets are safe or unsafe. In this respect she put forward the idea of the 'stranger' as central to the understanding of safety in the urban context and that a person must feel secure on the street amongst all the strangers. She identified three key safety attributes for city streets:

- First, there must be a clear demarcation between what is public space and what is private space. Public and private spaces cannot ooze into each other as they do typically in suburban settings or in projects.
- Second, there must be eyes upon the street, eyes belonging to those we might call the natural proprietors of the street. The buildings on a street equipped to handle strangers and to ensure the safety of both residents and strangers must be oriented to the street. They cannot turn their backs or blank sides on it and leave it blind.
- And third, the sidewalk must have users on it fairly continuously, both to add to the number of effective eyes on the street and to induce the people in buildings along the street to watch the sidewalks in sufficient numbers.

(Jacobs 1961: 44–5)

This approach has contemporary expression through environmental campaign organizations such as 'Living Streets' which considers that 'in large part, improving community safety depends on designing environments that facilitate the self-policing effect of the public using those streets and public places' (Connolly 2002: 16).

The concept of the 24 hour city is also relevant; i.e. bringing life to town and city centres through mixed developments and uses and community and recreational facilities, rather than such centres being dominated by central business districts which are empty in the evenings and at weekends. However, the concentration of pubs, clubs and ancillary uses which has resulted in many UK towns and cities has brought with it a particular set of social problems and resource demands for the police.

The ideas of surveillance and defensible space were developed by Oscar Newman in the USA. He was especially critical of high-rise apartment towers which created an environment where it was impossible to recognize strangers. A large number of unsupervised access points in housing projects also made it easier for criminals to enter and escape. He criticized the location of housing schemes in high crime areas and their stigmatizing appearance. Three criteria were identified that increased the rate of crime in any residential block:

- first, anonymity through people not knowing who their neighbours were;
- second, lack of surveillance through the absence of windows on internal corridors, hidden entrances and stairwells, making it easier to commit a crime unseen;
- third, the availability of escape routes for criminals.

'Defensible space' was defined as 'a living residential environment which can be employed by inhabitants for the enhancement of their lives, whilst providing security for their families, neighbours and friends' (Newman 1973: 3). Newman identified the following key aspects of defensible space:

- territoriality – the capacity of the physical environment to create perceived zones of territorial influences;
- natural surveillance – the capacity of physical design to provide surveillance opportunities for residents and their agents;
- image and milieu – the capacity of design to influence the perception of a project's uniqueness, isolation and stigma;
- geographical juxtaposition – safe and unsafe activity areas.

Newman's work was extremely influential and the issues of access and permeability, surveillance and private/public space remain as important design considerations. This can be seen in an approach known as 'Crime Prevention Through Environmental Design' (CPTED). The main thrust of CPTED is that:

The physical environment can be manipulated to produce behavioural effects that will reduce the incidence and fear of crime, thereby improving the quality of life. These behavioural effects can be accomplished by reducing the propensity of the physical environment to support criminal behaviour.

(Crowe 1991: 29)

The three overlapping strategies of the approach are territorial reinforcement, natural access controls and natural surveillance. A more recent development has been termed 'Situational Crime Prevention/2nd Generation CPTED' (Colquhoun 2003). This extends defensible space and CPTED ideas to include social and economic strategies and a more holistic attitude towards crime prevention and community safety. Here, the ideas of 'community' and the more recent concept of 'sustainable community' are important as they underpin current UK government crime and disorder and planning initiatives, for example in the government's White Paper 'Building Communities, Beating Crime' (H.M. Government 2004). The term 'sustainable community' has been defined thus:

Sustainable communities are communities which succeed economically, socially and environmentally and respect the needs of future generations. They are well designed places where crime and disorder, or the fear of crime, doesn't undermine quality of life or community cohesion.

(ODPM/Home Office 2004: 7)

It is important, in my opinion, to question any idealised concept of 'community'. The days when UK residents could leave their doors unlocked and open to calling neighbours have long since gone. Communities which grew around the traditional industries of mining, steel and textiles have fragmented, with industrial and social change, including increased mobility. With this fragmentation, 'policing' by the communities themselves has also broken down. In my view, it is important to abandon assumptions about communities and to look at the specific social characteristics of each individual locality.

The developing theories regarding the influence of the environment on crime and the fear of crime inform the work of police crime prevention officers and architectural liaison officers (ALOs) – known as Crime Prevention Design Advisors (CPDAs) in some forces, including the Metropolitan Police. Their key role is advising on local town and country planning policies and proposed developments, which are usually in the form of a planning application. They are well placed to use local knowledge about the social characteristics of specific localities and have access to pertinent crime statistics. Much of their work is underpinned by the principles of Secured by Design (SBD). SBD is an award scheme which is run by the Association of Chief Police Officers and aims to design out crime in a wide range of land uses. It particularly concentrates on reducing domestic burglary, but extends to a range of building and land uses including car parks. The key issues in this approach are physical security, surveillance, access and egress, territoriality, and management and maintenance.

Evidence has emerged that SBD is generally successful in reducing the incidence of burglary. Armitage (2000) carried out an evaluation of the impact of SBD on housing estates in West Yorkshire. The analysis took place on three distinct levels:

- refurbished estates – pre- and post-SBD certification;
- new build estates – comparison with non-SBD estates;
- residents' crime survey.

On refurbished estates it was found that crime rates had been 67 per cent and 54 per cent higher pre-SBD certification. Comparisons of recorded crime figures were made for 25 SBD and 25 non-SBD estates. Overall, there were 26 per cent fewer crime events per dwelling in the SBD sample. There was almost twice the number of burglaries in the non-SBD sample (0.42 compared with 0.24 per household). Vehicle crime was also lower in the SBD sample. The key findings were that on both new build and refurbished SBD housing estates the incidence of recorded crime was considerably lower than on the non-SBD counterparts. More recently developed SBD estates showed consistently lower rates of burglary compared with those built in the mid-1990s. There was no evidence to suggest that reductions in burglary had resulted in increases in alternative offences, such as vehicle crime, on SBD estates. Results of the residents' survey also indicated that fear of crime was lower amongst those living on SBD estates.

Planning decisions are based upon legislation and guidance which has evolved in the UK over the last 150 years. It is important to examine how this has developed in relation to crime and disorder issues and to gain an appreciation of how the success of the work of ALOs and planners may be aided or limited by current law and planning procedures.

Town and country planning legislation

Legislation to control and influence the management of places in England and Wales arose in the nineteenth century (Cherry 1974). It was primarily a response to the problems created by the rapid growth in population, and by industry and urban development. Lack of control led to housing with poor standards of construction and ineffective sanitation, often mixed with workshops and factories with associated noise, air and water pollution. Town and Country Planning legislation has its origins in the Public Health Acts 1848 and 1875, along with the Nuisances and Disease Prevention Act 1848, which was replaced by the Nuisances Removal Act 1855. The trigger for the introduction of regulations was the serious outbreak of cholera and typhoid in the 1830s and 1840s and the need for intervention to protect the health of the population. A power was introduced to pass byelaws to control the size of rooms, space around houses and width of streets. This led to the uniform streets and housing rows that became a characteristic feature of many of the residential areas of towns and cities. The incidence of crime was not a prominent causal factor in this, or later measures, to control the built environment. However, even in the late eighteenth century the novelist and Bow Street magistrate, Henry Fielding, had commented that:

> whoever ... considers the cities of London and Westminster with the late vast addition of their suburbs, the great irregularity of their buildings, the immense number of lanes, alleys, courts and byeplaces must think that, had they been intended for the very purpose of concealment, they could scarce have been better contrived.
>
> (Emsley 1987: 78)

Powers under the Public Health Acts were supplemented by housing legislation to deal with individual unsanitary houses through the Artisans and Labourers Dwelling Act 1868 and by powers in 1875 to carry out slum clearance. Local government was reformed in 1888 and 1894 and in 1890 measures were introduced to build houses for the working classes. By the end of the century there was an effective system of local government with a raft of legislation for public health and housing.

The possibility of building planned new developments was exemplified through the projects carried out by industrial philanthropists at New Lanark, Bourneville, Port Sunlight and New Earswick. In 1898 Ebeneezer Howard wrote *Garden Cities of Tomorrow* which set out a vision which led to the creation of Letchworth and later inspired the New Town movement. Whilst Garden Cities and New Towns were perhaps practical attempts at social engineering, with the objectives of relieving urban congestion and creating harmonious communities in a pleasant environment, the connection between crime and design was not directly made. However, many of the developments which took place would have involved houses with their own enclosed gardens and defensible space with good surveillance characteristics.

The first Planning Act was passed in 1909 and authorized the preparation of planning schemes by local councils for any urban or suburban land which was in the course of development or which appeared to be likely to be used for building. This was for the purpose of good sanitary conditions, amenity and convenience. The Town and Country Planning Act 1932 extended the powers to prepare schemes for any land in England and Wales. This was supplemented by the Restriction of Ribbon Development Act 1935.

The growth in road transport, utilities and industrial change led to the Barlow Report of 1940 on the distribution of industry and industrial population and the Scott Report on Land Utilization in Rural Areas of 1942. These reports formed the rationale for the Distribution of Industry Act 1945 and the New Towns Act 1946. The modern planning system was effectively established by the Town and Country Planning Act 1947. This introduced a system of development plans to succeed the planning schemes. Plans were to be prepared following a survey of the area and would be reviewed every five years. The Act also introduced the process of development control whereby developers had to seek permission before carrying out a project. The system was further refined through the Town and Country Planning Acts 1968, 1974 and 1990. Consideration of the relationship between crime and the design of development does not feature overtly in this legislation. Whilst the Acts were not specific in this respect, they did allow policies for crime prevention measures to be written into development plans. This facility gained increased importance with the introduction of section 54A of the Town and Country Planning Act 1990 under the provisions of the Planning and Compensation Act 1991. Section 54A states that: 'Where, in making any determination under the Planning Acts, regard is to be had to the development plan, the determination shall be made in accordance with the plan unless material considerations indicate otherwise.' Essentially, this introduced a presumption in favour of adopted development plan policies and land allocations in those plans. Any policies in an adopted plan concerning crime prevention could therefore be used to support or refuse a development proposal.

Increasing concern about the global effects of industrialization and population growth has led to the concept of sustainable development being introduced into planning legislation. The most widely used definition of sustainable development is that drawn up by the Brundtland Commission in 1987; i.e. development that meets the needs of the present without compromising the ability of future generations to meet their own needs.

Whilst sustainable development initially had an environmental emphasis, it has now been widened in a town planning context to include economic and social considerations, including community safety. The government has set out four aims for sustainable development in its strategy 'A Better Quality of Life – A Strategy for Sustainable Development in the UK'. These are:

1. Maintenance of high and sustainable levels of economic growth and employment.
2. Social progress which recognizes the needs of everyone.
3. Effective protection of the environment.
4. The prudent use of natural resources.

(H.M.Government 1999)

Allied to this strategy is a set of indicators for sustainable development and the quality of life. These include vehicle and related theft, the total number of crimes reported by the police and fear of crime. All these indicators show a positive outcome in recent years, with a downward trend since the early 1990s.

The Planning and Compensation Act 2004 introduced a radically new system for development plans. The development plan is to comprise the Regional Spatial Strategy prepared by the regional planning body (Spatial Development Strategy in London) and Development Plan Documents prepared mainly by district and unitary authorities. Local Development Frameworks will set out a portfolio of local development documents consisting primarily of the Local Development Scheme, Statement of Community Involvement and Annual Monitoring Report.

Paragraph 1.13 of 'Planning Policy Statement 12: Local Development Frameworks' (ODPM 2004b) states that local development documents should include policies that set out strategic design and access objectives in line with 'Planning Policy Statement 1' and objectives in line with 'By Design, Safer Places and Planning and Access for Disabled People' (ODPM 2005). The new system places greater emphasis on the involvement of the local community and community groups, and should provide a firm basis for crime and design issues to be brought into the debate.

The Building Act 1984

The Building Regulations 1991 are made under powers conferred by section 1 of the Building Act 1984. The Regulations cover aspects of construction such as structural matters, fire safety and energy conservation. Building security is currently not an issue which is subject to any specific detailed control.

The Crime and Disorder Act 1998

The Crime and Disorder Act has raised the profile of crime prevention in relation to the role of local government and local planning authorities (Scanlan 1998). The government's objective in promoting the new Act was to enable people to enjoy the most basic of human rights; i.e. the right to live free from fear and crime. The Act was also intended to help re-build communities and to tackle social exclusion. Two specific parts of the Act are relevant to planning. Sections 5–7 cover crime and disorder reduction strategies and section 17 concerns a general duty for local authorities to prevent crime and disorder in their areas. The Act also introduced the concept of anti-social behaviour orders.

The need for multi-agency approaches to crime prevention had been recognized in Circular 1/84 (DoE 1984) and reinforced by the Morgan Report (1991). The new Act gave extra impetus to this approach and placed an emphasis on the role of local authorities. Sections 5 and 6 of the Act require local authorities to formulate and implement strategies for the reduction of crime and disorder in their areas, in consultation with the public. The strategies are to be based upon a review of levels and patterns of crime and disorder and an analysis of that review. The resultant report has then to be the subject of consultation with relevant individuals and bodies. Regard must be taken of their views in preparing the strategy. The strategy must be kept under review whilst it is being implemented in order to monitor its impact and make any necessary changes. Local planning authorities and police ALOs are usually represented on partnership forums, thereby creating a link between the community and opportunities for preventing crime in new developments and regeneration projects.

Section 17 of the Act complements the duty to formulate crime and disorder strategies. A local authority has a duty to: 'Without prejudice to any other obligations imposed on it ... exercise its functions with due regard to ... the need to do all it reasonably can to prevent crime and disorder in its area.' This has implications for the town and country planning function, as local planning authorities, if challenged, would now need to be able to demonstrate that they have met the requirements of section 17 in determining planning applications for development in their area and in formulating planning policies. The potential for litigation brought about by the Act has led to it being described as 'a wolf in sheep's clothing' (Moss and Pease 1999: 15).

The introduction of warden schemes has been a key development in the management of places to reduce crime and disorder. The neighbourhood warden programme was launched in 2000. A street warden programme was separately managed and the police have initiated a complementary scheme of police community support officers to work in partnership with wardens (Edwards 2004: 22). Warden schemes provide a valuable local presence which can provide feedback to community safety partnerships. The initiative can be seen as part of the process of re-building and strengthening local communities by having a local point of personal contact to whom residents can relate.

This theme continues in the government's White Paper 'Building Communities, Beating Crime' which was issued in November 2004. This gives ten commitments to citizens, including to be and feel safe in their homes and community and to know who their local police officer, community support officer and wardens are and how they can be contacted. The White Paper also proposes a review of partnership arrangements under the Crime and Disorder Act 1998, with a view to making partnerships more effective and truly accountable, with local authorities playing an increasing role both as partners and scrutineers (H.M. Government 2004).

The Human Rights Act 1998

The Human Rights Act gave further effect in domestic law to the rights enshrined in the European Convention on Human Rights (Chandran 1999).

The Convention is an international treaty signed in 1950 under the auspices of the Council of Europe. The Act imposes an express duty on public authorities, including the police and local planning authorities, to comply with the Convention's rights, and authorities' decisions can be open to challenge if they do not comply. The Act has been central in planning enforcement cases where dwellings have been erected and occupied without planning permission or where gipsies have settled on land. Article 8 of the Act, the right to respect for family and private life, is particularly relevant:

> Everyone has the right to respect for his private and family life, his home and his correspondence.

> There shall be no interference by a public authority with the exercise of this right except such as is in accordance with the law and is necessary in a democratic society in the interests of national security, public safety or the economic well-being of the country, for the prevention of disorder or crime, for the protection of health or morals, or for the protection of the rights and freedoms of others.

The Act has similar implications to the Crime and Disorder Act in that local authorities have to be able to demonstrate in their decision-making that relevant aspects of the Human Rights Act were taken into account. Otherwise, it is more likely that a legal challenge to a particular decision could succeed.

National Planning Guidance

Circular 5/94: 'Planning out Crime' (DoE 1994) has been a key aspect of national planning guidance. It was cancelled in 2005 and government advice is now stated in 'Safer Places: The Planning System and Crime Prevention' (ODPM/Home Office 2004). Circular 5/94 particularly addressed the issue of design and stated that good planning alone cannot solve the problem of crime but, when co-ordinated with other measures, its contribution can be significant. An important point is that it recognized that crime prevention could be a material planning consideration. It stated that there should be a balanced approach to design which attempts to reconcile the visual quality of a development with the need for security and crime prevention. An example would be the need to strike a balance between tree and shrub screening of a building and the need for an open aspect to allow surveillance and remove the possibility of hiding places for criminals attempting to gain entry to the building. The circular referred to key factors such as:

- desolate, sterile and featureless surroundings can engender feelings of hostility, anonymity and alienation;

- attractive and well-managed environments help discourage anti-social behaviour;
- authorities should avoid the juxtaposition of land uses that could potentially give rise to conflict;
- local planning authorities are advised to consult police ALOs at an early stage in assessing new developments;
- crime prevention is one of the social considerations to which regard must be given in development plans.

(DoE 1994)

Local action was to fit into a crime prevention strategy for a wider area. This was a forerunner of the strategies required under the Crime and Disorder Act 1998. A 'neighbourhood' approach was suggested for housing developments, to encourage a sense of ownership for residents of the immediate area. The circular drew on the general principles of designing out crime theory and practice, suggesting that defensible territory, variety and open areas be applied to landscaping and roads, paths and subways.

'Safer Places: The Planning System and Crime Prevention' (ODPM/Home Office 2004) was intended to be a companion guide to the policy set out in 'Planning Policy Statement 1' (ODPM 2005). The guidance reflects the lack of certainty of success in applying standard crime prevention measures to differing environments and socio–economic circumstances. It puts forward examples of best practice in the UK but recognizes that there is no universal solution to every problem and what works in one place may not work in another. It states that the prevention of crime and enhancement of community safety are matters which a local authority should consider when exercising its functions under Town and Country Planning legislation. It therefore follows the requirements of section 17 of the Crime and Disorder Act 1998. A central message is that well-considered planning and collaboration between interested parties from the outset of a project can minimize conflict and reduce the need for compromise. The emphasis is therefore on people working together within an environment of guidelines rather than prescriptive intervention directly backed by statute. It recognizes that the relationship between design and crime is complex and that it is difficult to isolate the effects of design from those of social composition.

The guide is underpinned by reference to the framework set by Ekblom's 'Conjunction of Criminal Opportunity' (Ballantyne *et al.* 2000: 30). The essence of this is that the various causes of crime may be blocked, weakened or diverted by the intervention of crime prevention measures. Seven attributes of safer, sustainable communities are identified that are particularly relevant to crime prevention. These are:

1. access and movement;
2. structure;
3. surveillance;

4. ownership;
5. physical protection;
6. activity;
7. management and maintenance.

These attributes are to be used to prevent crime, based upon an understanding of the particular local circumstances. This understanding is
usually provided by the police ALO or CPDA. The local context may also
be established by reference to community strategies, crime and disorder
reduction strategies, Local Transport Plans and Housing Strategies. Area
regeneration programmes are also important and provide an opportunity
for investment and community involvement to reduce opportunities for
crime. A more detailed local picture may be provided by crime pattern
analysis and crime risk assessments.

'Safer Places: The Planning System and Crime Prevention' (ODPM/Home
Office 2004) is an important document which needs to be embraced by
planners and developers. It does not set policy or legal requirements and
has the status of guidance. It could therefore be easily diminished by both
groups as carrying little weight in the decision-making process. Its degree
of weight will be tested through the planning appeals process and case
law.

The statement in Circular 5/94 that crime prevention may be a material
planning consideration was important as this challenged the traditional
planning emphasis on land use rather than social considerations. Indeed,
an earlier government joint circular had stated that: 'The possible influence
of proposed land use development on crime will be unlikely to determine
whether planning permission is granted or refused' (DoE 1984: para. 12).
The perceived fear of crime may also be a material consideration, as established in the case of a proposed extension to a bail and probation hostel in
the West Midlands which was the subject of a High Court challenge.
The important point in decision-making is to examine the evidence for the
perceived fear and accord weight to that as a factor when balancing
the various issues in coming to a planning decision (West Midlands
Probation Committee 1996).

The government supplemented advice in circulars by Planning Policy
Guidance Notes (PPGs). These are now generally under review and are
being replaced by Planning Policy Statements (PPSs). They represent
national planning policy and are a material consideration in the determination of planning applications. The following references to crime and
disorder appear in current PPSs and PPGs:

PPS1: 'Delivering Sustainable Development' (ODPM 2005)

Paragraph 27 sets out specific objectives for delivering sustainable development. These include promoting communities which are inclusive, healthy,

safe and crime free, whilst respecting the diverse needs of communities, and the special needs of particular sectors of the community. Paragraph 36 indicates that design policies should encourage developments which, amongst other things, create safe and accessible environments where crime and disorder, or fear of crime does not undermine quality of life or community cohesion.

PPG3: 'Housing' (DTLR 2000)

Paragraph 56 states that local planning authorities should adopt policies which promote designs and layouts which are safe and take account of public health, crime prevention and community safety considerations. The encouragement of higher-density housing schemes through PPG3 has provided a particular challenge for designing out crime.

(ODPM 2005) PPS6: 'Planning for Town Centres'

This lists relevant government policy aims, such as promoting good design, improving the quality of public open spaces, protecting and enhancing the architectural and historic heritage of centres, and ensuring that town centres provide an attractive and safe environment for businesses, shoppers and residents. It extols positive planning and a plan-led approach, using tools such as town centre strategies, to address the transport, land assembly, crime prevention, planning and design issues associated with the growth and management of town centres. Local authorities are also urged to prepare planning policies to help manage the evening and night-time economy. In doing so they should consider the scale and quantity of leisure developments they wish to encourage and their likely impact, including the cumulative impact on the character of the centre, anti-social behaviour, crime, and the amenities of nearby residents.

PPS12: 'Local Development Frameworks' (ODPM 2004b)

This states that local development documents should include policies that set out strategic design and access objectives in line with PPS1 (ODPM 2005).

PPG13: 'Transport' (DETR 2001)

Paragraph 6 states that local authorities should consider how best to reduce crime and the fear of crime and seek by the design and layout of developments and areas to secure community safety and road safety. Authorities are encouraged to create more direct, safe and secure walking routes and ensure that the personal safety concerns of pedestrians are addressed. This has led to local authority initiatives such as creating safe routes to schools.

PPG17: 'Planning for Open Space, Sport and Recreation' (ODPM 2002)

Paragraph 18 indicates that local authorities should promote better use of open spaces and sports and recreational facilities, by the use of good design to reduce crime. Paragraph 20 mentions that in identifying where to locate new facilities local authorities should carefully consider security and personal safety, especially for children.

It is interesting to note that PPS7: 'Sustainable Development in Rural Areas' (ODPM 2004a) has little reference to crime and disorder, whereas it is clearly not just an urban problem.

Regional Planning Guidance

Regional Planning Guidance has been replaced by Regional Spatial Strategies in accordance with the Planning and Compensation Act 2004. These strategies are now part of the development plan and therefore fundamental to decision-making for planning applications. The recent referendum which led to a decision not to establish a regional assembly for north-east England has put a question mark against the importance of regional government and the role of these regional strategies for the future. In any event, their policies in relation to crime prevention will be at a broad level and the local development plan documents are likely to be of more direct relevance.

Local Development Plan Policies and Supplementary Planning Guidance

A number of local planning authorities have included specific references to crime prevention in their development plan policies and some have gone further by issuing supplementary planning guidance. An example is Fareham Borough in Hampshire. The development plan for the area is the Hampshire County Structure Plan Review 1996–2011 and the Fareham Borough Local Plan Review which was adopted in 2000. The Structure Plan concentrates on strategic initiatives and policies. The council adopted a Community Safety Strategy 1999–2002, with the aim of reducing crime, to raise awareness of crime and to work with others to make the borough a safer place for residents and visitors. The council has been involved in crime reduction initiatives including CCTV, seeking to reduce the number of young offenders and measures to reduce drug- and alcohol-related crimes. These initiatives are linked with planning policies and processes.

The Local Plan includes Policy DG5: 'Design' (Fareham Borough Council 2000a). This indicates that development will be permitted providing that it meets a number of criteria, including that where appropriate the council is satisfied that it has respect to crime prevention measures. Paragraph 3.34 refers to former Circular 5/94 'Planning out Crime' and the council's supplementary planning guidance on 'Crime Reduction through Design' (Fareham Borough Council 2000b). Such guidance can carry significant weight in planning decisions if it has been the subject of a full consultation process with interested parties. The local plan encourages developers to consider layouts and designs that promote safety and security measures. Attention should be paid to issues such as the location of lighting, fencing, landscaping, open space and footways. It also advises that the lighting of garages and car parking areas in an environmentally acceptable manner should be considered. However, it should be noted that the policy wording allows developers considerable room for manoeuvre and thus to avoid implementation. The lighting issue also shows another matter of balance in the planning process; i.e. balancing the security benefits of lighting against the problems of nuisance for neighbours and even light pollution for astronomers.

The supplementary planning guidance sets the following design principles for crime reduction and community safety:

- the number of people using the area should be maximized through a mix of uses and activities;
- building design should deter criminal and anti-social activity;
- public and private spaces should have clearly defined boundaries;
- opportunities for the observation of criminal and anti-social behaviour should be maximized;
- security measures should be an integral part of the design;
- footpaths and cycleways should be designed to maximize their use and prevent opportunities for concealment;
- landscape design should prevent opportunities for concealment and access to property;
- lighting should deter criminal and anti-social behaviour while minimising light pollution;
- buildings, signs and public spaces should be designed to minimize the opportunities for vandalism and graffiti.

(Fareham Borough Council 2000b)

These principles are backed up by detailed checklists for housing and other types of development. Again, these matters are advisory and the willingness of developers to comply and sometimes incur additional expenditure often depends upon the negotiation skills of the ALO and development control officer.

Planning decisions

Circular 5/94 was a significant attempt to integrate concerns about crime as a social issue into the traditionally land-use oriented field of town and country planning. It addressed some of the issues and modern types of crime which were emerging in our major towns and cities. In my view, planners were slow to respond and awareness of the circular was generally low. The move towards the 24-hour city, increase in binge drinking fuelled by the changes of use from retail and commercial premises to bars and clubs and associated late-night take-aways have raised the profile of planning control as one means of preventing the circumstances in which anti-social behaviour may flourish. Added to this, section 17 of the Crime and Disorder Act 1998 has made crime prevention a serious consideration for local authorities in the determination of planning applications. The work of police ALOs has risen in importance as a consequence and raises resource issues as many such advisers may be covering a geographical area which receives 2,000-plus planning applications per year.

Designing out crime as a topic for study has not featured highly in the education of town planners to date (Schneider and Kitchen 2002: xix). One positive aspect of the Crime and Disorder Act is that local authorities have taken steps to inform staff of councils' new corporate duty under section 17 of the Act and this leads to questions as to how planners can make a contribution. There is a key opportunity here for ALOs to hold seminars with planning staff to explain crime and disorder issues in their locality and explore ways of improving partnership working, for example:

- agreeing criteria for the type, size and location of planning applications on which ALOs should be consulted;
- adopting appropriate standard planning conditions;
- exploring situations where adverse crime and disorder implications could be a reason for refusing a development; and
- agreeing circumstances in which an ALO may wish to make verbal representations directly to a Planning Committee.

ALOs primarily rely on goodwill and persuasion to implement SBD. This is because of the limitations of planning powers and the Building Regulations. They mainly have to use planning guidance and advice at the national level in order to support their recommendations. At the local level, they may have more scope to require changes and improvements to schemes which are the subject of planning applications if there are relevant and robust development plan policies. Some measures can be achieved through the imposition of planning conditions, such as securing improved lighting. Even so, these conditions have to meet the requirements in paragraph 3 of government Circular 11/95: 'The Use of Conditions in Planning Permissions' (DoE 1995); i.e. be necessary and reasonable, and precise and relevant both to planning and to the development to be permitted. The lack of mandatory powers can be a serious weakness in approach and there is no guarantee that new housing schemes will have the most effective security measures. However, this may change for building security if proposed amendments to the Building Regulations are implemented. This could involve setting minimum security standards for the design and specification of locks, doors and windows in a similar way to which standards are already set for energy conservation measures in new housing. However, no matter what standards are imposed, crime prevention will always be a constant battle between the installation of the latest technology and the ingenuity of criminals in finding new ways of avoiding the various security measures which are in place.

In a situation where powers are lacking it is crucial that planners and ALOs have a good working relationship so that developers receive a consistent message. Planners are under particular pressures to meet government Best Value Performance Indicator Targets which require the majority of planning applications to be determined within an eight-week period from receipt. A 13-week target is set for major developments. Consultees are therefore often seen as a delaying factor and it is all the more important for developers to submit schemes which incorporate measures to design out crime at the outset or to make any necessary design changes early in the planning process. There has been particular success in West Yorkshire through a strategy of placing ALOs directly in planning development control teams to integrate the consultation process more fully (Moss and Seddon 2001: 28). This allows for greater awareness of the issues between planners and ALOs and may allow staff time to be more effectively directed to key developments and policy issues.

The Crime and Disorder Act and Human Rights Act are separate pieces of legislation compared with the Town and Country Planning Acts. All three strands of the law have to be taken into account when a local planning authority makes a decision. However, because the legislation is separate, it is not appropriate to use the provisions of the Crime and Disorder Act as a direct reason for the refusal of a planning application which might have implications detrimental to community safety. In such circumstances, the relevant basis for a decision would be a policy in an adopted development plan and any supplementary planning guidance. In addition, reference could be made to PPGs, PPSs and guidance in 'Safer Places: The Planning System and Crime Prevention' (ODPM/Home Office 2004).

The Planning Inspectorate has expressed the view that section 17 of the Crime and Disorder Act is not in itself a material planning consideration. This, and the fact that section 17 does not apply to the Inspectorate, has been challenged by Moss, as it puts local authorities in a position where they may refuse an application on crime and disorder grounds, only to find it dismissed on appeal (Moss 2001: 43). It is important that planners and ALOs make continuous reference to emerging case law on this issue. For example, an appeal for a change of use of a restaurant in Torbay to a nightclub was dismissed by an Inspector in 2004 on the ground that it would be likely to prejudice the regeneration of the harbourside. The Inspector stated that it was unsatisfactory for the appellant to argue that the issue of disorderly behaviour could be left to the licensing authority because the proposal would have land use implications (Royal Town Planning Institute 2004: 21).

Conclusion

The complexities of the interaction between the environment, social factors and crime and disorder mean that legislation to design out crime can only be applied in a restricted manner. There is no guarantee that a particular design feature will totally eliminate crime. Planning legislation and guidance provide a framework within which ALOs and planners must operate. Physical measures to help prevent burglary, such as ensuring high-quality doors, windows and locks in new construction, may be made mandatory through the Building Regulations. However, it is not possible to be so prescriptive and to require standards for other design aspects of the environment because of the differing site circumstances and social characteristics. This presents a dilemma for ALOs who can only recommend changes to schemes and not insist upon them. Planners and ALOs therefore need to respond to challenges by being creative in influencing and using planning policies and guidelines to achieve their objectives. The education of architects and planners in techniques for designing out crime and disorder is also an important issue. Although the issue has not figured strongly in the growth of planning legislation, crime and disorder and the fear of crime are clearly matters of significant public concern and a major influence on the quality of life which people perceive and experience as individuals. Practical measures to create safer places need to be backed up by evidence of subsequent crime reduction or changes in the nature of crime and disorder and carefully evaluated. This will add to our knowledge of what constitutes best practice in differing local circumstances.

The goal of 'sustainable communities' will require good planning if it is to be achieved and to realize one of its objectives, i.e. a reduction in crime and disorder. In some ways, the concept echoes the desire to set the right conditions for encouraging the general harmony of citizens which the early planning philanthropists had envisaged. Planners, the police, architects, developers and citizens need to work together and get to grips with shaping the future of our town and city centres in a positive way. City centre strategies or action plans under the new development plan regime could provide a way forward. This may mean more direct intervention to guide the private market away from problems such as the trend of creating more bars and hot food take-aways to serve a binge-drinking culture. The future policing of city centres, their day-to-day management, and the maintenance of the street environment are all factors which require early consideration in the process of development and regeneration. Whilst crime and disorder will always be a characteristic of human behaviour, the application of law and the positive management of places can help to create an environment which hinders, rather than helps, those with criminal intent.

The author gratefully acknowledges the help of Paul Hey, Architectural Liaison Officer in the West Yorkshire Police Force, for his useful comments on an earlier draft of this chapter.

Bibliography

Armitage, R. (2000) 'An Evaluation of Secured by Design Housing in West Yorkshire', Home Office Briefing Note 7/00, London: Home Office.

Ballantyne, S., Pease, K. and McLaren, V. (2000) *Secure Foundations – Key Issues in Crime Prevention, Crime Reduction and Community Safety*, London: Institute for Policy Research.

Chandran, P. (1999) *A Guide to the Human Rights Act 1998*, London: Butterworths.

Cherry, G. E. (1974) The Evolution of British Town Planning, Leighton Buzzard: Leonard Hill Books.

Colquhoun, I. (2003) *Design Out Crime, Creating Safe and Sustainable Communities*, London: Elsevier.

Connolly, P. (2002) 'The Human Deterrent', *Regeneration & Renewal*, 16–17, 4 October.

Crowe, T. (1991) *Crime Prevention through Environmental Design: Applications of Architectural Design and Space Management Concepts*, Stoneham, MA: Butterworth-Heinemann.

DETR (2001) Planning Policy Guidance Note 13: 'Transport', London: TSO.

DoE (1984) Circular 1/84: 'Crime Prevention', London: HMSO.

DoE (1994) Circular 5/94: 'Planning out Crime', London: HMSO.

DoE (1995) Circular 11/95: 'The Use of Conditions in Planning Permissions', London: HMSO.

DTLR (2000) Planning Policy Guidance Note 3: 'Housing', London: TSO.

Eaton, R. (2002) *Ideal Cities, Utopianism and the (Un) Built Environment*, London: Thomas Hudson.

Edwards, S. (2004) 'Making Wardens Work', *Regeneration and Renewal*, 22–3, 24 September.

Emsley, C. (1987) *Crime and Society in England 1750–1900*, London: Longman.

Fareham Borough Council (2000a), Local Plan Review, Fareham Borough Council.

Fareham Borough Council (2000b), Supplementary Planning Guidance: Crime Reduction through Design, Fareham Borough Council.

H.M. Government (1999) 'A Better Quality of Life – A Strategy for Sustainable Development in the UK', Cm 4345, London: TSO.

H.M. Government (2004) 'Building Communities, Beating Crime: A Better Police Service for the 21st Century', Norwich: HMSO.

Jacobs, J. (1961) *The Death and Life of Great American Cities*, London: Jonathan Cape.

Morgan Report (1991) 'Safer Communities: The Local Delivery of Crime Prevention through the Partnership Approach', London: Home Office.

Moss, K. (2001) 'Crime Prevention v Planning: Section 17 of the Crime and Disorder Act 1998. Is it a Material Planning Consideration?', *Crime Prevention and Community Safety: An International Journal*, 3(2), 43–8.

Moss, K. and Pease, K. (1999) 'Crime and Disorder Act 1998: Section 17, "A Wolf in Sheep's Clothing"?', *Crime Prevention and Community Safety: An International Journal*, 14, 15–19.

Moss, K. and Seddon, M.H. (2001) 'Crime Prevention and Planning: Searching for Common Sense in Disorder Legislation', *Crime Prevention and Community Safety: An International Journal*, 3(4), 28–30.

Newman, O. (1973) *Defensible Space: People and Design in the Violent City*, London: Architectural Press.

ODPM (2002) Planning Policy Guidance Note 17: 'Planning for Open Space, Sport and Recreation', London: TSO.

ODPM (2004a) Planning Policy Statement 7: 'Sustainable Development in Rural Areas', London: TSO.

ODPM (2004b) Planning Policy Statement 12: 'Local Development Frameworks', London: TSO.

ODPM (2005) Planning Policy Statement 1: 'Delivering Sustainable Development', London: TSO.

OPDM (2005) Planning Policy Statement 6: 'Planning for Town Centres', London: TSO.

ODPM/Home Office (2004) 'Safer Places: The Planning System and Crime Prevention', Tonbridge: Thomas Telford.

Royal Town Planning Institute (2004) 'Development Control Casebook in Planning', *Journal of the Royal Town Planning Institute*, 21, 3 December.

Scanlan, D. E. (1998) *The Crime & Disorder Act 1998: A Guide for Practitioners*, London: Callow Publishing.

Schneider, R.H. and Kitchen, T. (2002) *Planning for Crime Prevention: A TransAtlantic Perspective*, London: Routledge.

Watkin, D. (2000) *A History of Western Architecture* (3rd ed.), London: Laurence King Publishing.

West Midlands Probation Committee v. *SSE & Walsall MBC*, August (1996), (CO/157/96) Deputy Judge Purchas.

3 Local authorities, crime reduction and the law

Stephen Brookes

Introduction

It takes a minute for a government Minister to come up with a good idea; a day for one of his officials to work this up into a proposal and probably a month for the official's team to write a consultation paper. It takes longer to present and steer through a Bill and months or even years for local agencies to implement its enacted provisions. By the time they have, along comes another government and a new Minister who, within another minute, has thought of another good idea.

Central government makes policy, and lots of it. Local government and other organizations and agencies have to implement this policy and they do so in huge amounts. The need for policy is accepted but its proper implementation can lead to frustration because policies come from so many different directions. The Audit Commission (ODPM 2004c: 3) recently noted the fractured nature of the messages coming from central government and observed that policies appeared to 'go down separate silos to different local partners'. This is what the Commission, in providing guidance on the newly introduced policy of Local Area Agreements, described as the 'Humpty Dumpty effect'.

This chapter focuses on some of the ways in which local authorities not only provide local services but also have a key role in the delivery of crime reduction and the extent to which legislative provisions either help or hinder them in fulfilling this role. It begins with a brief history of local governance to contextualize its community safety role. It describes the case for partnership arrangements between local authorities, the police and other agencies in the task to improve community safety and discusses the strengths and weaknesses of current arrangements by giving a brief outline of existing legislative support. Specifically, this chapter asks three questions. First, to what extent has legislation effectively structured local authorities to play a meaningful role in crime reduction activity? Second, to what extent does legislation currently enable local authority executives to make decisions and choices based on locally determined needs whilst also satisfying national priorities? Third, how effective is the support provided by legislation to improve the safety of communities? Using examples of current schemes, the chapter illustrates how partnership working can support aims to improve community safety and to tackle youth crime, anti-social behaviour and alcohol-fuelled behaviour. In conclusion, the future of local government and the ongoing support being proposed in legislation are discussed.

Historical perspective

Local government has traditionally had a key responsibility in providing local services and support. This sort of provision has historically been within either a national or a regional framework but today it is central government that provides the framework nationally. It is interesting to note, at a time when a return to a regional agenda was recently rejected in the north-east of England, that the concept of regional governance actually dates back to medieval times when lords had rights over the local population (Triggle 2004: 4) and social control was implemented locally. From the early days of medieval serfdoms through to the creation of unitary authorities in the early 1990s, the ability to raise taxes locally to support the delivery of services within communities existed. Local communities and parish authorities also had responsibilities to deal with local crime problems. For example, in the days of Alfred the Great the responsibility for catching, convicting and indeed punishing people lay within the local community. Failure to bring these people to account resulted in severe financial penalties being imposed on the communities themselves. This chapter does not argue for a return to such sanctions but it does highlight the important role that communities, in addition to local authorities, have always had in relation to crime reduction.

Local government as it is understood in structural terms today was established by the 1835 Royal Commission on Municipal Corporations. The Commission established boroughs across the country, with directly elected councillors and mayors. Urban and district councils were created by the end of the century.

The role of local government, the community and the police

Traditionally, the police have always been viewed as the major crime prevention agents and only recently has it become more widely accepted that local authorities, other agencies and the community have a role to play in building safer communities. It is axiomatic to say that the definition of community safety refers to the overall safety of communities. However, the principle of this ideal is far more complex. The term has a very wide meaning and the elusiveness of definitions has led to considerable confusion about the importance of crime reduction in particular and of community safety in general. For a number of years, the Association of

Chief Police Officers (ACPO) struggled to accept the term 'community safety'. It was their opinion that this detracted from the key role of the police – that of controlling crime. Such a debate was no doubt located within a paradigm where 'policing' was viewed purely as a matter for the police; where the community was seen as the recipient of this policing, and where local authorities responded to the clarion call to support the police as and when required. This is what Fielding (1995: 198) describes as 'conventional policing' in contrast to 'community policing'. In the former, the police mandate is the control of crime with an emphasis on professional crime fighting and with the police alone managing the mandate. In the latter, the police mandate is community order with crime control as a means to this end. In this community model, there is a focus on preventative as well as reactive policing. The police are one of several agencies of order and the community plays an active role. The community is viewed as a 'client' in the community model as opposed to a 'recipient' of policing in the conventional model.

Similar views have been expressed within an American context. Bayley (1994) describes this notion of the police controlling crime as a myth. Peak and Glensor (1996) identify three key components of successful partnership working in relation to safer communities – these being the police, local agencies and the community. Further, they contend (Peak and Glensor 1996: 121) that it involves 'actively mobilising the efforts of the police, other agencies and the communities themselves in efforts to improve safety'.

For the purposes of this chapter and to help clarify the role of local authorities, the term 'community safety' can be defined as follows (Ekblom 2001: 5):

> an aspect of the quality of life ...

> a state of existence in which people, individually or collectively, are sufficiently free from a range of real and perceived hazards including crime and related misbehaviour; are able to cope with those which they do experience; and are sufficiently protected from their consequences if unable to cope alone and to enable them to pursue the necessities of their social and economic lives, exercise their skills and create and enjoy wealth in the widest sense.

Put simply, community safety is about individuals and groups in our communities being able to go about their lawful business untroubled and in relative safety. The definition helps us to understand the role that local authorities undertake in creating safer communities and how legislation can support or indeed hinder this. Before looking in more detail at the way in which legislation supports the structure of local government, it is important to highlight exactly what is meant by 'partnership working' in this context.

The case for partnership working

The importance of multi-agency crime reductive partnerships came to the fore with the publication of the Morgan Report (Home Office 1991). This report influenced the informal creation of community safety partnerships but its recommendations did not receive legislative support until the enactment of the Crime and Disorder Act 1998. This gave local authorities a legal obligation to engage in crime prevention activity for the first time (under section 17) and as such can be seen as a way of actively mobilizing communities to this end. It is important to note, however, that the idea of actively mobilizing the community has had a spasmodic history. Only recently has it become a key strand of government community safety programmes, and more needs to be done to make community engagement a reality. To date, it has been argued that the involvement of the community has been predominantly passive in terms of 'being consulted' or 'listened to' as opposed to more active involvement in terms of 'engagement' and 'influence' (Brookes 2004: 36). More recently, the role of the community has been made explicit by the government. For example, the then Home Secretary stated in 2001 that: 'Government depends upon active participation by citizens in order to achieve the goals pursued on their behalf' (Blunkett 2001: 1).

Partnership working is also important because it appears to be at the centre of the recent modernizing government agenda. In its introduction, the local government White Paper 'Modern Local Government – In Touch with the People' (1998a: 1) commented that: 'We want to see councils working in partnership with others, making their contribution to the achievement of our aims for improving people's quality of life.'

The chapter now reviews the extent to which current legislative provisions either help or hinder the local authority in working in partnership to create safer communities.

Legislation and the structure of local government

To what extent does legislation introduce structures for local governance that support community safety efforts? In 1972 the local government landscape began to change. The Local Government Act of that year set up six new metropolitan counties, with borough councils operating within each. Further reform followed in 1986 as the Conservative administration under Margaret Thatcher replaced the metropolitan counties with 36 metropolitan boroughs and 32 London boroughs. Elsewhere, county councils and district councils operated under a two-tier system. A further key opportunity to reform local government was presented in the early 1990s. The Local Government Act 1992 created the Boundaries Commission, whose responsibility to undertake structural reviews of local government – known as the Banham Report – introduced a further 47 unitary authorities. It has been contended that the Banham Report did not provide consistency. For example, Stewart (1995: 3031) argued that the review focused on the wrong priority, that of structural rather than strategic reform, saying that: 'The tragedy is that it was a reorganisation of boundaries and tiers, whereas the problems of local government relate to its role and responsibilities.'

Similarly, Morley (1995: 45) remarked on how the Local Government Commission surprised both central and local government with some of its decisions. Central government's preferred policy of a blanket of unitary authorities covering England has been transformed into an *art nouveau* patchwork quilt of unitaries and the two-tier system. The result is single-tier unitary authorities in many of our major cities and towns with the two-tier system of county and district councils operating in less urban areas. This makes partnership working within a community safety context more complex than it should be.

Legislation and local government priorities

To what extent does legislation enable local authority executives to make decisions and choices based on locally determined need whilst also satisfying national priorities? This chapter contends that in order to achieve any vision, local government must have a set of shared priorities at the outset. The Crime and Disorder Act 1998 (hereinafter referred to as 'CDA') (HMSO 1998b) had the potential to 'bridge the gap' between the specific constitutional accountability of the police and the more general accountability of local authorities to prevent crime and disorder. The statutory responsibility of local authorities to work in partnership with the police and a range of agencies was made explicit by sections 5 and 6 of the Act which stated that responsible authorities (defined as local councils, police forces acting in co-operation with police authorities, probation authorities and, by later amendment, primary care trusts and fire authorities) should formulate and implement, for each relevant period, a strategy for the reduction of crime and disorder in the area (HMSO 1998a).

In relation to a local authority, it is not the CDA that is the impetus for its executives in determining priorities. An organization does what it is measured on and, in the case of local authorities, this relates to legislation under various Local Government Acts beginning with Best Value (HMSO 1999), which seeks to secure continuous improvement through reviews and, more recently, the Comprehensive Performance Assessment (hereinafter referred to as 'CPA'). CPA was introduced to assist local councils in improving local services for their communities (HMSO 2003a). It aims to identify how well a local authority delivers its services; how well it is run and how this impacts on the services it delivers. Whilst community safety is now an integral feature of CPA, this has not always been the case. This has resulted in the CDA being very much the poor relation in comparison with local government legislation on the setting of priorities. Difficulties in relation to the implementation of the CDA are comprehensively reviewed in Chapter 1 by Moss. This includes an apparent reluctance to mainstream community safety activity in accordance with section 17 of the Act and to exchange information within the spirit of section 115.

A final point to consider before turning to operational examples of local authority delivery is that of Public Service Agreements (hereinafter referred to as PSAs). The government introduced PSAs following the 1998 Comprehensive Spending Review (a three-year review of government spending priorities) and linked these originally to the Best Value programme. The agreements introduced clear targets showing what departments aimed to achieve in terms of public service improvement for the first time. Progress against those targets has been reported every year in departmental reports (HMSO 2002a). To give one example, included within the basket of Best Value performance indicators for local authorities and the police were agreements between the Home Office and the Treasury to reduce burglary by 30 per cent over a four-year period. However, one of the difficulties associated with the Best Value targets was that there was a whole myriad of separate targets for local government and it was quite possible for the reduction of burglary target, for example, to be lost among the mass of others.

What are described as 'shared priorities' were introduced across local government through the creation of a single national public service agreement for local government. These priorities are intended to help authorities and central government focus their efforts in key areas where joint working is necessary to deliver improvements – thus supporting the case for partnership working. The shared priorities are described as fundamental to and linked with the CPA programme (ODPM 2003a).

The first shared priorities were about raising the standards across schools, transforming the local environment and meeting local transport needs more effectively (ODPM 2002). Shared priorities were later added to 'create safer and stronger communities by working with the police and other local agencies to reduce crime and anti-social behaviour, strengthen community cohesion and tackle drug abuse' (ODPM 2003a: 23). A much smaller number of better-focused performance indicators were included in the Best Value basket of indicators for local authorities. This was entirely consistent with targets set for policing which are illustrated in Figure 3.1.

Legislation and local authority intervention

Three examples of delivery within a local government perspective will now be discussed, with a view to illustrating how legislation can help local authorities to fulfil their statutory responsibilities to engage in community safety.

These examples have been chosen because each requires a strong partnership approach and, as the conclusion contends, local authorities have a clear leadership role in this (and other) areas. They include tackling youth crime, anti-social behaviour and alcohol-fuelled behaviour.

Youth crime

In relation to the offending behaviour of young people, the CDA introduced a range of measures to tackle youth crime. Youth Offending Teams (YOTs) were created by section 39 of the Act. Local authorities were given a central role in the work of the YOTs and they were given a statutory duty to act in co-operation with the police, probation and health authority to establish YOTs. The main role of a YOT is to work with offenders aged 10 to 17 years, delivering a range of community-based penalties with an emphasis on reparation and intervention to prevent re-offending. It does this by engaging with young people and case managing those who offend.

The impact of young offending should not be underestimated. A recent MORI Youth Survey (MORI 2004) estimates that over a quarter of young people of secondary school age stated that they have committed a criminal offence, with a peak age for offending of 14. The survey also underpinned the need for 'joined up' activities and policies across local government. For example, 60 per cent of excluded young people have offended. Numerous studies have made a significant link between exclusion and offending. Similar evidence can be adduced from the Social Exclusion Unit report 'Reducing Re-offending by Ex-prisoners' (HMSO 2002b), including the facts that almost a third of offenders have spent time as children in care and more than half did not have a single qualification.

A whole array of activity is therefore necessary in tackling youth crime and its causes. The role of local authorities in addition to those agencies that have direct responsibility for providing services to young people is critical. Education authorities, for example, have a responsibility to improve educational attainment (low attainment having been identified as a link with offending behaviour). In addition, they have a responsibility to prevent truancy and to minimize exclusions – which themselves are risk

---

Statement of Shared Priorities: Performance Targets
Reduce crime and the fear of crime; improve performance overall, including by:
  Reducing the gap between the highest Crime and Disorder Reduction
  Partnership areas and the best comparable areas; and reduce:
  • vehicle crime by 30% from 1998–99 to 2004;
  • domestic burglary by 25% from 1998–99 to 2005;
  • robbery in the ten Street Crime Initiative areas by 14% from
    1999–2000 to 2005; and maintain that level.

Figure 3.1 Statement of shared priorities.
        Source: ODPM 2003: 26

indicators of offending behaviour. The MORI survey also reported that 26 per cent of pupils truant for at least one day but this remained consistent among excluded young people.

The need for local authorities to engage in preventive activity is explicit within the Children's Bill that will significantly change the way in which local government works with young people. In the Green Paper 'Every Child Matters' (HMSO 2003a), the government's proposals build on existing measures to ensure that protection is given to children at risk of harm and neglect and that support is given to all children to develop their full potential. As is often the case, the background to the changes relates to a tragic incident – in this case the death of Victoria Climbié in which joint failings by the police, social services and the NHS were identified. There were striking similarities with other tragic cases. The common threads, which led in each case to a failure to intervene early enough, were poor co-ordination; a failure to share information; the absence of anyone with a strong sense of accountability; and frontline workers trying to cope with staff vacancies, poor management and a lack of effective training. These barriers could be applied to partnership working generally.

Anti-social behaviour

The second example of local authority engagement in community safety is in relation to tackling anti-social behaviour. Anti-social behaviour includes a range of problems – noisy neighbours, abandoned cars, vandalism, graffiti, litter and youth nuisance.

Anti-social behaviour orders (ASBOs) were introduced by the CDA in 1998 and have been available to the police and local authorities since April 1999. They are civil orders made by a court and are used to protect the public from behaviour that causes harassment, alarm and distress, in cases where criminal proceedings are not appropriate. Home Office guidance describes an ASBO as the last stage of a structured approach to tackling anti-social behaviour that includes warning letters, mediation or an Acceptable Behaviour Contract. Effective partnership arrangements are thus essential in securing these less intensive interventions as well as the orders. If the former interventions are not successful then it is open to both the police and local authorities to seek an ASBO. Initially, take-up was slow. The cumbersomeness of proceedings and indeed the cost of taking such proceedings discouraged many authorities from taking such action. Over the year to the end of March 2004 the number of ASBOs doubled. Home Office figures (Home Office 2004) state that 2,400 ASBOs were issued across England and Wales since they were introduced in 1999 with 1,323 taken out in the year to March 2004.

Further legislation followed. The Anti Social Behaviour Act received Royal Assent in November 2003. It enables local authorities and the police to close down and board up crack houses, control the sale and use of fireworks and airguns, prevent graffiti and litter and disperse intimidating gangs who may be out on the streets threatening local people. Further powers are also being given to tackle anti-social behaviour by tenants living in local authority or housing action trusts although there are still many difficulties in tackling anti-social behaviour by those classed as private sector tenants. Encouraging efforts are being made by some Registered Social Landlords but more statutory provisions would assist further in tackling the reluctant private landlords.

To illustrate, section 218A of the Housing Act 1996 (as amended) requires landlords that are local housing authorities, housing action trusts or registered social landlords to prepare and publish policies and procedures in relation to anti-social behaviour by the end of December 2004. These statements of policy and procedures should complement the priorities of the local authorities. The definition of 'anti-social behaviour' as determined by the Act is illustrated in Figure 3.2.

These new provisions offer strong potential for the local authority to be a major partner in tackling those issues that strike at the heart of local communities – often referred to in modern times as 'the neighbour from hell'. The legislation requires landlords to set out their commitment to eradicating anti-social behaviour, the obligations of tenants, how they intend to provide support for witnesses to anti-social behaviour, racial harassment, domestic violence, multi-agency partnerships and the use of available legal remedies. Some encouragement can be drawn from the efforts to tackle anti-social behaviour. British Crime Survey data (Dodd *et al.* 2004: 1) shows that 'the proportion of people estimated to perceive a high level of disorder in their local area fell from 21 per cent to 16 per cent between 2002/03 and 2003/04'.

Alcohol-fuelled behaviour

The final example concerns an issue that is very closely aligned to anti-social behaviour – that of alcohol-fuelled behaviour. This provides a good

---

For the purposes of this legislation anti-social behaviour is defined as conduct which:
- Is capable of causing nuisance or annoyance to any person (for example, anyone living or working in the neighbourhood);
- Directly or indirectly relates to or affects the housing management functions of a relevant landlord (for example, the landlord cannot fulfil his responsibilities). Direct activities are those that may affect, for example, maintenance and repairs, rent collection, neighbourhood management and dispute resolution. Indirect activities may include social care and housing support, environmental health and refuse collection.
- Consists of or involves using or threatening to use housing accommodation owned or managed by a relevant landlord for an unlawful purpose.

Figure 3.2 Housing Act 1996: Definition of Anti Social Behaviour.

illustration of how legislation both helps and hinders community safety efforts. Primarily, legislation such as this can help prevent the problems associated with alcohol consumption in public places. Local authorities can use this legislation to restrict alcohol consumption in designated areas. Specifically, the Criminal Justice and Police Act 2001 introduced new powers to reduce problems arising from under-age drinking, public drunkenness and alcohol-related violence. The legislation does help to provide consistency, as previously over 100 local authorities had introduced byelaws to restrict consumption in public places but only a very small number had powers to confiscate alcohol. Restricting alcohol consumption in this way is a very simple but effective measure to tackle issues such as young people gathering in public spaces and becoming inebriated through the purchase of cheap alcohol. In partnership with the police, local authorities can also have a key role to play in targeting retailers who sell such alcohol to young people.

Of particular significance currently is the impending transfer of licensing responsibility from the police to local authorities. The Licensing Act 2003 establishes a single integrated scheme for licensing premises, which are used either for the supply of alcohol, to provide regulated entertainment or to provide late-night refreshment. It will also allow for 24-hour drinking in certain circumstances. Although the sponsor government department (Department of Culture, Media and Sports) point to what it describes as the 'crime prevention aspects' of the Licensing Act, concerns have been raised that this may act to the detriment of community safety. For example, senior police officers have expressed concern that longer hours and more relaxed approaches to licensing legislation will lead to more alcohol-related violence and disorder. Sir John Stevens, the former Commissioner of the Metropolitan Police, stated that: 'The trend towards drunken, loutish behaviour is nationwide and all-hours drinking will stretch police resources' (*Daily Mail* 2005).

The legislative provisions in the Act doubtless work to modernize some of the existing offences in relation to licensed premises and also provide additional police powers in respect of the closure of particular premises for up to 24 hours, thus helping to target problem premises through a range of mechanisms (DCMS 2005). What it does not do is address the problems caused by alcohol in town and city centres. It also draws into question what could be viewed as potentially conflicting priorities for local authorities. On the one hand, many local authorities – predominantly unitary/metropolitan authorities – are keen to encourage inward investment to the authority area. This often includes the encouragement of a night-time economy. On the other hand is the local authority's responsibility to work in partnership with the police and other agencies in securing safer and stronger communities. A local authority as the 'licensing authority' may well therefore be in a difficult position when identifying 'need'. Thus, should the 'need' (for example for new premises' licenses) be based on an economic need or a social need (to reduce crime and anti-social behaviour)? There is also a current debate about 'who picks up the costs' of this legislation, namely the cost of both the licensing regimes and the alcohol-related violence. In relation to the former, there are strong concerns being expressed by local authorities. As Smulian (2005: 1) reports: 'Almost every council will be out of pocket – some by millions of pounds – unless the government increases the fees they can charge pubs, clubs and late-night food outlets for licenses.'

Senior police officers would also argue that the brewers should also pick up some of the costs of policing. This brings into question the contentious issue of 'does the polluter pay?' This concept is important in that it argues that manufacturers or managers can create opportunities in which crimes can occur and yet they bear no cost of these crimes to society (Roman and Farrell 2002). It is an interesting issue, and one that legislation has yet to address. The responsibility at present rests with the local authority who must resolve this. However, this dilemma is a clear example of where greater consideration of section 17 of the CDA should take place. This section states that it shall be the duty of each authority to exercise its various functions with due regard to the likely effect of the exercise of those functions on crime and disorder, and the need to do all it reasonably can to prevent crime and disorder in its area.

The practical effect of this section is that it requires councils to be mindful of community safety issues when planning and delivering their core services. It also requires the police, in addition to their core activities, to give due regard to actions within their communities that focus on the reduction and prevention of crime and disorder, anti-social behaviour and the fear of crime. Implementation of this provision has been patchy, as Moss, in Chapter 1 of this book, has already argued. In many cases, local authorities view this as simply the need to 'put a tick in the section 17 box'. The complex problems concerning the conflicting priorities of encouraging a night-time economy whilst needing to secure safer and stronger communities are the type of issues that section 17 is designed to support. In all of its decision-making the local authority should consider the crime and disorder implications. This should be done through the work of the Crime and Disorder Reduction Partnership (CDRP) and its links with the wider 'umbrella' group of the Local Strategic Partnership. Through these wider partnerships the opportunity is present to draw the principles of section 17 much closer to the leadership role envisaged for local authorities. It is this issue of wider partnerships and community leadership to which the chapter now turns.

Legislation and the future of local authorities

Earlier sections of this chapter referred to the role that local authorities have in relation to community leadership. This concept is integral to the debate about whether legislation works to help or hinder local authorities in their crime-reductive capacities. The reason for this is that whilst so many agencies are involved in the delivery of local services and the reduction of crime at the local level, the danger is that without clear leadership, the responsibility to reduce or prevent crime could so easily be passed from one agency to another, without substantive results. For this reason the notion of community leadership, in helping to make crime reduction through legislation a reality, is crucial. It is the importance of this ideal which is now discussed.

In its ten-year vision for local government, central government described community leadership as having a number of distinct strands. For example, the paper from the Office of the Deputy Prime Minister (ODPM) 'The Future of Local Government: Developing a 10-Year Vision' (ODPM 2004b: 9) identified that:

> There is leadership in decision-making and the accountability for what is delivered directly by the council. There is a role in leading local partnerships and bringing stakeholders together to help meet local needs and priorities, providing a focal point for local decisions. And there is a leadership role in enabling communities to lead themselves, developing social capital, fostering greater engagement in local decisions, and taking action to promote inclusion.

Enshrined within this concept of community leadership is a change of legal emphasis which has direct relevance to the role of legislation in shaping local government engagement in community safety. Recent legislation, namely the Local Government Act 2000, gives councils a new power to improve the quality of life of local people. A significant point is that this changes the age old doctrine of *ultra vires* in relation to local authorities. It is an accepted principle of public administration that the decision and actions of officials must never be *ultra vires* (or beyond their legal powers), or put another way, that local authorities 'can do only those things which they are specifically empowered by law to perform' (Greenwood and Wilson 1984: 9). This recent legislation has been described as a reversal of the previous prohibitive legal framework (Woolfe 2001).

The Local Government Act 2000, therefore, now allows authorities to do anything *not* prohibited by law in the name of promoting the economic, social and environmental well-being of communities. Specifically, section 5 of the Act sets out the statutory requirement for the promotion of well-being through the development of a community strategy based on consultation. In practice, the principal expression of this idea has been the emergence of what are known as Local Strategic Partnerships (LSPs). Although they have no legal status *per se*, LSPs are intended to bring together service deliverers, local communities, those who use local services, the voluntary sector, social enterprises and businesses, in seeking to develop a concerted approach to both problem solving and service delivery in relation to a number of themed areas. These include crime, employment, education, health and housing. Nearly all of the 367 local authorities have an LSP (ODPM 2003b). These partnerships were originally required to manage neighbourhood renewal funding in the 88 most deprived areas, although the concept has now been extended beyond these. There are some close similarities with CDRPs. These similarly have to develop a strategy based on consultation but the key difference relates to their statutory basis. CDRPs have a statutory basis under the CDA whereas LSPs do not. As the concluding section points out, this represents a clear opportunity to improve joined up activity in relation to community safety.

Reform programmes and the importance of localism

The creation of safer and stronger communities is a key feature in both Home Office (police) and ODPM (local authority) reform and shows an encouraging desire for the two Whitehall departments to work together. It should be viewed as a real opportunity to develop partnership efforts in improving community safety. A further aspect of local government reform that has such potential is the proposal to introduce what are called Local Area Agreements. Local Area Agreements are a new way of working to build a more flexible and responsive relationship between central government and a locality on the priority outcomes that need to be achieved at local level. Achieving this new relationship will require a significant shift in the way central and local government relate to each other and to other local partners.

The prospectus published by ODPM in August 2004 (ODPM 2004c) described the agreements as a set of measures to achieve a step change in the relationship between government, councils and local partners. It could be argued that the new arrangements place emphasis on achieving local solutions to local problems that meet local needs whilst also contributing to national priorities. The key elements of the proposals include a framework and a shared understanding of national and local priorities; improving performance by allowing more flexible use of resources between partners in achieving shared outcomes; enhancing efficiency by rationalizing funding programmes; providing support to an area; and reducing bureaucracy associated with the numerous small funding schemes and area based initiatives. The prospectus also points out the aim to help partners to join up at a local level and enhance the community leadership role for local authorities.

Of significance is the inclusion of a simplified funding scheme for Safer and Stronger Communities alongside similar streams for children and young people and healthier communities and older people. Police reform proposals have similar strong potential. As well as supporting the Safer and Stronger Communities fund the emphasis on localism is clear. With the creation of neighbourhood policing teams and the greater involvement of communities and citizens in determining how their communities are policed, the stage is set for raising the game of those involved in the creation of safer and stronger communities. It also recognizes the key role that local authorities undertake by acknowledging that keeping communities safe is not just a job for the police. The White Paper states that: 'Effective partnership work involving other criminal justice agencies, local government and health agencies, children's services and the voluntary and business sectors is vital' (HMSO 2004: 19).

The police reform White Paper also introduces a review of important provisions of the CDA as they apply to partnership working. This review will look at governance arrangements, effective structures and improved delivery, information sharing and accountability issues.

Conclusion and challenges

It could be argued that the scene is set to improve the opportunities for local authorities to engage more significantly in community safety programmes. There are, however, three key challenges for local authorities, the law and crime reduction and these are encompassed within the concept of leadership.

First, central government must continue its efforts to legislate and support local government. One key area could be to create a statutory responsibility for Local Strategic Partnerships to be responsible for delivering the local authority's community leadership role and to build on the encouraging approaches now being made to bring together 'joined up' policies such as the local area agreements. There is a need to co-ordinate policies and remove the fractured messages that often appear. At the broader level, the local government and police reform proposals hold strong potential – but only if they deliver real improvements on the ground. To what extent are structures fit for purpose? To what degree can executives make innovative choices and decisions and to what extent can local communities be truly engaged?

Second, central government has acknowledged that legislation is not the panacea for improving local government. In its ten-year vision it states that:

> the weight it [community leadership] carries within the community, amongst local people and with local partners, cannot simply be legislated for. This will depend on the effectiveness of individual councils and their leaders. It must be earned, not granted, but the space must also be made for local authorities to take on and demonstrate this capacity.
>
> (ODPM 2004b: 11)

The second challenge is thus for local authority leaders to accept their community leadership role. They should not be overly preoccupied with direct delivery of services but should be asking what they can do to improve local delivery and the well-being of communities through partnership working.

The third challenge is about leadership at local level. True community engagement will only come if real leadership is displayed at all levels and where local leaders are prepared to hold deliverers to account but without becoming over parochial. In turn, those charged with delivery should also be held to account by their managers and those services should be focussed in accordance with local need. The forthcoming Police Reform Act will require the creation of a neighbourhood policing model which will demand this local form of accountability. It will be important for senior police officers not to perceive this as a threat but to embrace it as a means of satisfying the challenge for leadership at the local level.

There has never been another time in history when there has been so much legislative change for both local government and the police. All of this comes under what is currently called the 'modernizing government' agenda. The rhetoric of this agenda and its supporting legislation gives room for optimism but the real challenge is to turn this rhetoric into reality. To do this will require strong leadership.

Bibliography

Alderson, J. (1984) *Law and Disorder*, London: Hamish Hamilton.

Audit Commission (2003) 'DC CPA: Self-Assessment Guidance for District Councils v F1.1', April 2003.

Bayley, D. H. (1994) *Police for the Future*, New York: Oxford University Press.

Blunkett, D. (2001) *Politics and Progress: Renewing Democracy and Civil Society*, London: Politicos Publishing.

Brookes, S. M. (2004) *A Question of Style: Identifying the Conditions that Help or Hinder the Development of Community Policing*, unpublished Ph.D. thesis, Nottingham Trent University.

Daily Mail (2005) 'Tories slam "binge-drinking" Government', 20 January.

DCMS (2005) *Alcohol and Entertainment: Crime and Disorder*, online: http://www.culture.gov.uk/alcohol_and_entertainment/licensing_act_2003/crime_and_disorder.htm (accessed 21 January 2005).

Dodd, T., Nicholas, S., Povey, D. and Walker, A. (2004) 'Crime in England and Wales 2003/2004: British Crime Survey', Home Office Statistical Bulletin.

Ekblom, P. (2001) *The Conjunction of Criminal Opportunity: a Framework for Crime Reduction*, London, Home Office, online: http://www.crimereduction.gov.uk/learningzone/cco.htm

Fielding, N. (1995) *Community Policing*, Clarendon Studies in Criminology, Oxford: Clarendon Press.

Greenwood, J. and Wilson, D. (1984) *Public Administration in Britain*, Boston MA: Allen and Unwin.

HMSO (1998a) White Paper: 'Modern Local Government – In Touch with the People'.

HMSO (1998b) Crime and Disorder Act 1998 (c. 37).

HMSO (1999) Local Government Act 1999 (c. 27).

HMSO (2000) Local Government Act 2000 (c. 22).

HMSO (2001) Criminal Justice and Police Act 2001 (c. 16).

HMSO (2002a) 'Public Service Agreements 2002'.

HMSO (2002b) Social Exclusion Unit Report: 'Reducing Re-offending by Ex-prisoners', July 2002.

HMSO (2003a) Green Paper: 'Every Child Matters'.

HMSO (2003b) Nottingham City Council Act 2003 (c. ii).

HMSO (2003c) Licensing Act 2003 (c. 17).

HMSO (2004) 'Building Communities, Beating Crime: A Better Police Service for the 21st Century', November 2004, Cm 6360.

Home Office (1991) 'Safer Communities: The Local Delivery of Crime Prevention through the Partnership Approach', Standing Conference on Crime Prevention.

Maguire, M. (1997) 'Crime Statistics, Patterns and Trends' in Maguire, M., Morgan. R. and Reiner. R. (eds) *The Oxford Handbook of Criminology* (2nd ed.), Oxford: Clarendon Press.

MORI (2004) Youth Survey 2004, July.

Morley, M. (1995) 'The Real Challenges facing Local Government', *Association of District Councils Review,* January/February, 5.

ODPM (2001) 'Strong Local Leadership – Quality Public Services', DTLR, December.

ODPM (2002) 'New Shared Priorities To Focus Improvements In Public Services', press release, online: http://www.lga.gov.uk/Documents/Press_Release/ODPM-033.pdf#search='shared%20priorities.

ODPM (2003a) Circular 03/2003: 'Local Government Act 1999: Part 1: Best Value And Performance Improvement'.

ODPM (2003b) 'Evaluating Local Strategic Partnerships: Report of a Survey of all English LSPs', ODPM and Department of Transport, February.

ODPM (2004a) 'The Future of Local Government', published by ODPM, June 2004.

ODPM (2004b) 'The Future of Local Government: Developing a 10-year Vision', published by ODPM, July 2004.

ODPM (2004c) 'Local Area Agreements: A Prospectus', August 2004.

Peak, K. and Glensor, R. (1996) *Community Oriented Policing and Problem Solving: Strategies and Practices*, New Jersey: Prentice Hall.

Roman, J. and Farrell, G. (2002) 'Cost–benefit Analysis for Crime Prevention: Opportunity Costs, Routine Savings, and Crime Externalities', in N. Tilley (ed.) *Evaluation for Crime Prevention, Crime Prevention Studies*, 14, 53–92.

Smulian, M. (2005) 'Late-night Binge proves an Expensive Round', *Local Government Chronicle*, 21 January, 1.

Stewart, J. (1995) 'The Wrong Approach to Local Government', *Parliamentary Brief*, February, 3(4), 3031.

Triggle, N. (2004) 'Land of Confusion', *Local Government Chronicle*, 18th June.

Wolfe, A. (2001) *Community Leadership: The Issue Explained*, online: http://www.SocietyGuardian.co.uk (accessed 21 March 2005).

4 No through road: closing pathways to crime

Ken Pease

the path of the just is as the shining light, that shineth more and more unto the perfect day.

Psalms 4:18

Life considered as a journey is a recurring metaphor in religion, literature and developmental psychology. Sometimes the destination matters, as in Dorothy's journey to the Emerald City in *The Wizard of Oz* (Baum 1995), or the Pilgrim in the most famous of human allegories *The Pilgrim's Progress* (Bunyan 1909). Sometimes only the journey itself is of consequence. Even when the destination matters, the route by which it is reached contributes to the value derived from the destination. As in *The Pilgrim's Progress*, it is the hardship of a pilgrimage as much as the shrine at its end which confers religious virtue. The mission of the starship *Enterprise* was primarily to go where no one has gone before, and only secondarily to seek out new civilisations. Dorothy and her companions had their lives and virtues validated not by reaching the end of the Yellow Brick Road, but by being told by the Wizard what the journey had revealed about them (see Baum 1995). Sometimes, retracing one's steps is difficult, and the range of practicable destinations is limited by what has gone before.

The pathway metaphor as applied to crime and criminality seems to be routinely accepted, and gives its title to at least two current major research enterprises. Perhaps the reason for this lies in the notion that early choices preclude certain later choices, so that choices made early in a path change the probability of later choices being available. This can be conceptualized in terms of Markov processes, notions of amplification of deviance or, more poetically, in Robert Frost's poem, *The Road Not Taken*:

> ... knowing how way leads on to way
> I doubted if I should ever come back
> I shall be telling this with a sigh
> Somewhere ages and ages hence
> Two roads diverged in a wood, and I –
> I took the one less travelled by,
> And that has made all the difference.

Prosaically, at each stage in human development, the interaction between the individual's agency and setting preferences, and the characteristics of their current activity field, are contended to have an important role in influencing their future development and change (Wikström 2005).

Individual path preferences

The besetting problem of criminological theory has been the connection of individual and ecological levels of explanation (Reiss 1986; Jensen and Akers 2003). To every choice point, the traveller brings a general path preference, shaped by the experience of having taken one or other of the presenting alternatives at different points in the path so far travelled. Path divisions also have different attributes favouring one or other of the presenting alternatives. There can now be no reasonable doubt that there are genetic factors predisposing people to make certain kinds of choice. In her admirable, unfashionable classic *The Nurture Assumption*, Judith Rich Harris (1998) contends that the substantial contributions which parents make to their children's development primarily consist of their genes and where they set up home, taking the local peer group to be the primary agent of socialization. Her perspective is interesting in that she had previously made her living writing textbooks on socialization, coming late and in chronic ill health to her 'Road to Damascus' realization of how much conventional interpretation could be ascribed to assumptions about 'true' causal factors. For example, she points out how in the socialization literature within psychology, the effects of parenting styles are confounded with those of shared genes. She reviews the literature on the relationship between parent characteristics and child characteristics and demonstrates that either the same characteristics must have different and largely unpredictable effects on children, or that those influences are largely illusory. The literature of developmental criminology, with its listing of risk factors and hygiene factors conducive to criminality, is vulnerable to reinterpretation insofar as it does not control for shared inheritance. Is poor parenting a risk factor in a child's development, or do parents tending to (for example) impulsivity transmit that attribute through the conventional genetic means, or set up home in places where the peer group gives free rein to the expression of impulsivity? Or take no notice of their children's behaviour, except in the light of interfering with their own comfort or pleasure, such that their children gain by both their nervous systems, and their conditioning? Familial inheritance is always both the result of genetic endowment and environment, but environments are made, and are often correlated with the dispositions of those who inhabit them (Scarr and McCarthy 1983). There are at least two kinds of relationship to be found here: passive and evocative correlation. In passive correlation the properties of the parents form a great backdrop – for example, musical parents give their children musical opportunities not afforded to others. In the case of evocative correlation, the child's disposition influences the behaviours of nearby adults. Genetic explanations always have the shadow of eugenics at their shoulder. No effort to explain their subtlety should be forgone, and the point is laboured here and elsewhere in this chapter.

Because the risk–hygiene factor approach is well accepted, and under-pins large government programmes on parenting skills and the like, the problem of disputed causality should be mentioned in somewhat more detail. It is better recognized by the scholars who carried out the research than by the politicians and practitioners who seek to apply it (see, for example, Coie 1996; Homel *et al.* 2005). This major shortcoming of the risk-hygiene factor approach has been repeatedly stressed by Farrington (2000 and 2003). It is difficult to know which of the measured factors are causes and which are merely correlates. Variables come in bundles and the limits on experimental interventions are thankfully severe. Farrington *et al.* (2002: 54) contend that 'the concept of cause fundamentally refers to the concept of change within individual units', and advocate the analytic strategy of focusing on 'comparing within-individual changes in risk factors over time with within-individual changes in delinquency over time'. Focusing on within-individual change (rather than between-individual variation) takes us somewhat further in distinguishing causes from corre-lates, but it does not overturn the Rich Harris contention that pre-existing differences permit or preclude changes in both risk factors and criminality. A risk factor's status as causal must await specification of a credible mech-anism detailing how the risk factor in question is translated into criminal action. In other words, if changes in an individual's risk factors are followed by changes in the same individual's crime involvement, this is an indication that the former may be a cause (or part cause) of the latter, or that both are consequences of a shared cause.

The implications of Rich Harris's work are profound, but should not be a surprise to those familiar with the earlier literature on criminality and adoption (see, for example, Mednick and Christiansen 1977), where crimi-nality in the biological parent is reflected in a higher prevalence of criminality in the child, whatever the criminal record status of the adoptive parent. The perspective is lent support by the recent work of Terrie Moffitt and her collaborators (Moffitt 1993, 1997 and 2003) whose distinction of adolescent-limited and life-course persistent offenders casts the latter as pre-disposed as a result of inherited and/or early acquired neuropsychological deficit. Of particular current interest is the gene variant MOAO which lowers the activity of the enzyme monoamine oxidase A and which seems implicated in violence. This relationship is stronger among maltreated children (Caspi *et al.* 2002). Of course, reflecting Rich Harris's insights, it is not necessarily the case that maltreat-ment activates the propensity to violence. Equally plausible is the notion that MOAO and other as yet to be identified violence-relevant genes drive both parental violence (in the form of maltreatment) and child aggression.

In path terms, the message is simply that one ignores at one's peril genetic or other early factors disposing to preferences.

Because of its fraught history and presumed eugenic subtext, it is important to stress that there can be no such things as genes for criminality. There seem to be genes for attributes such as violent behaviour (see above) and novelty-seeking (see Hamer and Copeland 1998), which may be associated with criminality. The danger lies in searching for a 'chopstick gene'. 'The gene for blue eyes is common in people who are bad at using chopsticks, but nobody would dream of suggesting that chopstick skill is genetically determined by the gene for eye colour' (Ridley 1999: 164). In the same way, the route whereby protein synthesis is manifest in behaviour will scarcely ever be obvious and never simple. The danger of searching for chopstick genes is evident in tabloid coverage in the days before writing this chapter. A gene which seemed to distinguish statistically between women unfaithful to their partners and others spawned headlines like 'Doomed to stray?', revealing both spectacular naivety about genetic determination and foreclosure on the nature of the relevant trait (could the distinguishing trait have something to do with honesty in answering intimate questions?).

Path preferences and human evolution

In the discussion above, attention was given to predispositions which vary among people according to genotype–environment interactions. However, the emergent discipline of evolutionary psychology is concerned with behaviours which can plausibly be regarded as adaptive, favouring the survival of one's own offspring (more relevantly one's own genes) over those of others. This has both obvious and more arcane forms of expression. Straightforwardly, it accounts for the much higher incidence of child abuse by carers who are not biologically related to the child victim, the ratio of 100:1 being mooted. Wilson and Daly (1997) confirm that considering intra-familial abuse without making this distinction yields a misleading picture. Daly and Wilson's (1998) book *The Truth about Cinderella* makes the point fully and disarmingly (one would say 'entertainingly' were the topic they treat not so painful).

The more subtle criminal pathway choices derive from the notion of discounting. Organisms discount the future when they value imminent goods over future goods. If you aren't going to be around tomorrow, you prefer even risky rewards today. Worker bees assume more dangerous foraging activities as their wings wear and in response to life-truncating infection (Woyciechowski and Kozlowski 1998). The notion that offenders find deferral of gratification difficult (don't we all – but beyond the norm) has a very long history (see, for example, Herrnstein's (1983) review). The phenomenon is now known as time discounting. Wilson and Daly (1997), noting that the poor, the young and the criminal discount the future steeply, contend that is what we should expect, being a rational response to information indicating a diminished probability of survival or other obstacles to reproductive success. Risk-taking is rational when the expected benefits of safer courses of action are negligible. Thus, early and aggressive sexual behaviour is linked with time discounting. This need not be conscious; in fact if it is an evolutionary stable strategy, then the chances are it is wired in.

The evolutionary psychological perspective is rich in heuristic implications, but remains contentious (see Brannigan 1998). For public policy generally, the consequences, were it to have general application, are profound. For example, we would expect epidemics such as HIV/AIDS to be associated with elevated levels of sexual activity. As for the development of criminality, the role of public policy would become the nurturance of the reality and perception of anticipated individual reproductive success. In an unpublished doctoral thesis Brown (2001) presents evidence suggesting that those items of which young offenders distinctively feel themselves in need are smart clothes, footwear and the like. Put crudely, these are items which are presentationally important in what one may quaintly term 'courtship'.

To rehearse the argument thus far, there are both individual path preferences (owing to genotype–early environment interactions) and those which are, speculatively general and driven by considerations of evolutionary 'fitness'. These general attributes are expressed differentially according to presenting circumstance. Acceptance of the existence of such attributes is in no way suggestive of genetic determinism.

Before leaving the notion of intrinsic path preferences, mention should be made of the work of Donohue and Levitt (2000 and 2003). They persuasively show rates of crime to be inversely related to earlier abortion rates, the time lag reflecting time to age of maximum criminality. The suggestion is thus that attributes (for example of impulsivity) which yield unwanted pregnancies, possibly genetically shared with the resulting foetus, combining with parental styles reflecting both the same impulsivity which led to the pregnancy and possible resentment felt towards the resulting child, results in a greater likelihood of criminal involvement. The Levitt and Donohue work does not disentangle the skein of causal routes. Still less does it argue for abortion rather than less troubling modes of fertility control. However, it does suggest that an unwanted pregnancy may be, for whatever reasons, a marker for future criminality. Any of the plausible causal routes would be closed off by the avoidance of such pregnancies.

Thus equipped, the path winds onward

Criminological research has detailed the routes which people take into, through and out of criminal activity. The study of 'criminal careers' (Blumstein *et al.* 1986), or 'developmental criminology' (Loeber and LeBlanc

1990; LeBlanc and Loeber 1998) or Farrington's (2003) 'development and life-course criminology' focus on how individual involvement in crime develops and changes over time (within-individual variation). The key concepts refer to individuals' involvement in crime (e.g. participation and frequency), stability and change in crime involvement (e.g. onset, persistence and desistance), the nature of involvement in crime (e.g. crime seriousness, specialisation and versatility), and changes in the nature of crime involvement (e.g. escalation and de-escalation) (Wikström 2005: 88). These routes are generally thought of as careers, comprising onset, frequency, type of activity (in criminal careers typically seriousness) and desistance. The path metaphor is usable when thinking about career choices generally, and has some advantages, notably that path choices leading to transitions between types of activity within the career are of interest. This invites the question of whether it is meaningful to speak of a criminal career, rather than a career as a robber, a burglar or whatever. The overwhelming evidence from criminal career research is that the degree of offence specialization is less remarkable than offender versatility (see, for example, Tarling 1993). It thus remains meaningful to speak of criminal careers. Research has documented a range of important non-random routes through an individual's offending career (Thornberry and Krohn 2003; Piquero *et al.* 2003). However, what is less well understood are the path choices which are the constituents of these patterns. The central argument is that criminal career patterns (e.g. onset, duration, escalation and desistance) can be explained with reference to patterns of development and change in individuals' perceived context of action, interpreted in the light of dispositions and accumulated experience. Wikström (2004) avers that crime propensity may be conceptualized as the individual tendency to see crime (the breaking of a moral rule) as an alternative and to choose that option. Individual-level studies in criminology have contributed much to an understanding of the relationship between individual characteristics and involvement in crime (for an overview, see Farrington 2002). The early part of this chapter has suggested that such understanding will imminently be extended by advances in genetics and evolutionary psychology. However, most individual propensity theory fails to specify in any detail the situational mechanisms by which individual characteristics and experiences are translated into criminal acts. General reference is made to the importance of choice of path, guided by some kind of personal calculus of costs and benefits (which is likely to be a genetic/environment correlated factor), which will vary according to propensity and its linked time-discounting. Van Dijk (1992) and Farrell *et al.* (2000) propose formal economic models consistent with known facts about the distribution of criminality and victimization which offer a way forward in thinking about issues of path attractiveness.

For Gottfredson and Hirschi (2003: 11) the role of settings appears to be restricted to influencing the expression of propensity. They talk about, 'the interaction of varying individual predispositions for delinquency and logically possible opportunities', and give the following example of the role of opportunity: 'the 12-year-old who cannot steal a car may well steal a bicycle; the 30-year-old who cannot be truant from school may well be truant from work and family obligation' (2003: 10). On the other hand, Felson (2003) appears to assign a significant motivational role to the setting. He claims, for example, that 'temptation helps to produce criminal acts that might not otherwise occur' (2003:17) and goes on to state that the saying '"Opportunity makes the thief"; reflects this insight' (2003: 17) (Wikström 2005: 88). Felson's view seems more persuasive, and it is his theoretical contribution which will be discussed next.

The theoretical approach in criminology that has most strongly advo-cated the importance in crime causation of the intersection of individual and setting is the routine activity approach (Cohen and Felson 1979; Felson 2003). In this approach, the coincidence of three elements results in a crime. These elements are a motivated offender, a suitable victim and (the absence of) a capable guardian. Recourse is not had to an account of how the offender got to be motivated, any variation in degree of motiva-tion, and how that motivation intersects with presenting features of a situation. Cornish and Clarke (1986) go some way to acknowledging the complexity of the situation by presenting flow charts which respectively address the acquisition of a standing decision to commit crime, and the cues in the immediate situation which favour its commission.

Routine Activity Theory, supplemented by related perspectives (e.g. Brantingham and Brantingham 1993), has done a lot to advance our understanding of the role of settings in crime causation. It contends that crime rates may best be regarded as an unwanted consequence of the routines of everyday life. Burglary, for example, varies with the value and portability of objects in homes. Felson also addresses issues such as the widening gap between sexual maturity and economic independence as a factor inclining to crime (an insight consistent with the perspective from evolutionary psychology noted above). However, Felson's approach has concentrated (very helpfully) on the supply of criminal opportunities and general social factors determining the supply of motivated offenders. The approach addresses itself less to individual differences amongst offenders and others. Neither has the routine activity approach sought the mecha-nisms through which at the intersection of individual and setting, individuals are moved to commit illegal acts of acquisition and aggression.

Attempts to link Routine Activity Theory (Ecological Theory), Self-Control Theory (Individual Propensity Theory) and Rational Choice Theory (Action Theory) are acknowledged (e.g. Clarke and Felson, 1993; Felson, 2003; Hirschi, 1986; Hirschi and Gottfredson, 1988; Gottfredson and Hirschi, 1989; Gottfredson and Hirschi, 1990: 22–5; Nagin and Paternoster, 1993; Wikström, 1998; Gottfredson and Hirschi, 2003). However, this has so far mostly been a question of saying it is a good idea and possible to link these types of theory, or that they are complementary, rather than actually suggesting that they should (or how they can) be integrated (Wikström 2005: 88).

Let us draw back for the moment from talk of integration and discuss 'affordances'. The word is preferred to 'opportunity' for two reasons. First, an opportunity implicitly exists outside people. Floating Google on the stock market constitutes an investment opportunity for everyone. By contrast, affordance is a perception of what actions come to mind in a particular setting. Second, affordance is a concept familiar to designers, in a way in which opportunity is not.

Design seeks to maximize good, generally recognized, affordances. When access to a room is to be gained by turning some device, a knob is to be preferred. A plate on a door implies pushing, a recessed handle implies pulling. The designer/psychologist Donald Norman (1998) regards affordances as the beginning of a psychology of materials, and illustrates his point by vandalism of railway property:

> The term affordance refers to the perceived and actual properties of the thing, primarily those fundamental properties that determine just how the thing could possibly be used … A chair affords ('is for') support and therefore affords sitting. A chair can also be carried. Glass is for seeing through, and for breaking. Wood is normally used for solidity, opacity, support or carving. Flat, porous, smooth surfaces are for writing on. So wood is also for writing on. Hence the problem for (railways): when the shelters had glass, vandals smashed it; when they had plywood, vandals wrote on and carved it. The planners were trapped by the affordances of their materials.
>
> (Norman 1998: 9)

Although Donald Norman does not develop the argument, affordances will vary across people and must be acquired and refined by personal or vicarious experience. An open window may afford an invitation to a burglar or assessment of household taste in curtains to an interior designer. A trapped head in a rugby scrum may afford eye-gouging as a course of action. In the Norman example, is wood really seen as something to write on before one has seen writing on wood? The broken windows hypothesis is based upon the notion that a damaged building affords damage in a way that an undamaged building does not (Kelling and Coles 1997). Likewise, Zimbardo's (1973) study of 'auto-shaping' suggests that initial offending against a target accelerates repetition, so the perception of the vehicle with a missing wheel affords opportunities which a complete vehicle denies. In other psychological traditions, this is known as behavioural contagion. Whatever it is called, it invites consideration of whether and how propensity translates into the proliferation of criminal affordances: whether porcelain figures behind a net curtain on a window ledge are seen as something quaintly old fashioned, or a clue to a probably elderly house-holder vulnerable to confrontational burglary; whether the sight of a mobile phone at someone's ear is a pleasant reminder that he or she has friends, or constitutes an invitation to robbery. In short, does propensity translate to crime via the perception of affordances? In a preliminary, as yet unpublished study, Jeanette Garwood (2004) asked a student sample about its criminality, and administered to the same group a Uses of Objects test (see Getzels and Jackson 1962; Hudson 1966) in which people were shown everyday objects and asked to think of their possible uses. Some of the uses were criminal. There was an association between an individual's self-reported criminality and the percentage of criminal uses identified. While Garwood would be the first to recognize that her conclusions must be provisional, the approach seems highly promising. Affordance is the perception which makes tool use possible. A tool is only a tool when affordance is perceived. There is much extant research to consider in relation to affordance, such as Richard Wortley's elaboration of opportunity makers and opportunity takers (Wortley 2001), and studies of cues used by offenders in seeking or recognizing opportunity (Nee and Taylor 1988). Affordance is, one may speculate, the psychology which links predisposition to setting.

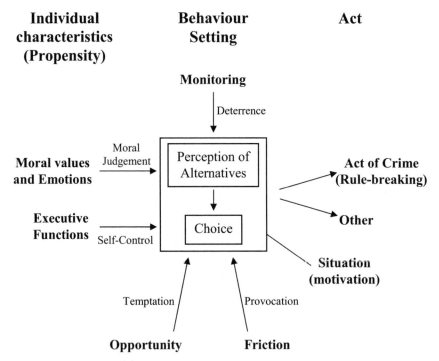

Figure 4.1 An overview of key factors and mechanisms of the Situational Action Theory of Crime Causation. Modified from Wikström (2005).

Neglected here is the stage of transforming affordance into action.

Individuals not only react differently to their environment (see different action alternatives), they also differ in their capacity to regulate their reactions (emotions and behaviour) depending on their executive functions (see, for example, Shonkoff and Phillips 2000: 93–123; Barkley 1977: 51–58; Ishikawa and Rain 2003) (Wikström 2005: 88).

Even if the concept of affordance does not find favour, the role of perception in successful crime reduction is difficult to overestimate. Generally, the way in which perceptions seem to drive rates of crime was illustrated by Smith *et al.* (2002). They took all the published evaluations of crime reductions they could find, and selected those for which the time course of the reduction was presented in detail. It was found that in some 40 per cent of cases where crime had declined, it had done so before the initiative in question started. Thus, the active ingredient in crime reduction is very frequently some change which anticipates implementation. Work in progress suggests that publicity expenditure is a major factor in perception change and crime reduction.

The story so far

To rehearse the argument to this point, there are dispositional and adaptive factors leading to differential path selection. These are structured by the development of perceptions of objects and people in terms of the kinds of behaviour one can exhibit towards them (their affordances). If we could understand the processes whereby dispositions and affordance perceptions interact, we would be closer to understanding the dynamics of the trajectory of the criminal career. So what? Each of these elements has policy implications and can reasonably lead to a range of plausible interventions. Effective fertility control and taking steps to reduce time discounting in adolescence address predisposition. In the same way, the design and presentation of objects can go some way to limiting their criminal use (see, for example, Press *et al.* 2001; Dewberry 2003).

Although couched in somewhat different terms, in his proposed Situational Action Theory of Crime Causation (Wikström 2004), the key suggested characteristics of the setting, influencing whether an individual perceives crime as an action alternative and whether they chose to act upon it, is conceptualized as opportunity and friction (promoting) and monitoring (inhibiting). This conceptualization is pleasing in that it seems equally applicable to the rules and regulations laid down to control members of the professions.

Wikström argued that:

> the key promoting mechanisms linking the characteristics of the setting (opportunity and friction) and individual action (acts of crime) are temptation, defined as a perceived option to satisfy a particular

desire (need, want) in an unlawful way, and provocation, defined as a perceived attack on the person's (or his or her significant others) property, security or self-respect encouraging an unlawful response. Temptation occurs in response to opportunity, while provocation occurs in response to frictions. An individual's morals influence (through the moral judgements made) what opportunities he or she finds tempting, and what frictions he or she finds provoking. The key suggested inhibiting mechanism is conceptualized as deterrence, defined as the perceived risk of intervention, and associated risk of sanction if acting unlawfully in pursuing a temptation or responding to a provocation. Deterrence occurs in response to monitoring. The potentially deterrent effect of monitoring is influenced by the individual's executive functions, through the self-control exercised.

(Wikström 2005: 88).

The Wikström approach suggests a research agenda. However, the present book is about crime reduction and the law. For some practical purposes, we may not need to wait for research. The practically important question concerns whether we urgently need to understand disposition–affordance interactions. By analogy, measles injections are given to all children, whether they already have natural immunity or not. If they already have immunity, the injection will do them no harm. If they do not, it will protect. There are three simple possibilities, or alternatives, for the relationship between the perception of criminal affordance and disposition to crime:

1   disposition and criminal affordance are independent, so that those dispositionally prone to crime are no more or less likely to see objects and people affording scope for criminal acts;
2   disposition and criminal affordance co-vary positively, so that those disposed see more opportunities for crime;
3   disposition and criminal affordance co-vary negatively, so that those disposed see fewer opportunities for crime.

Jeanette Garwood's work cited earlier (and everything we know about skilled performance generally) suggests that the second alternative is the one to bet on. Wikström and Loeber (2000) demonstrated that individual propensity (as indexed by risk and hygiene factors) interacts with area characteristics such that late-onset adolescent offenders were greatly influenced by area of residence. If area characteristics can be regarded as a proxy for training in criminal affordances, the Wikström and Loeber evidence inclines one towards Alternative 2. Alternative 1 cannot be rejected. Alternative 3 is implausible in the extreme. Is it really possible that robbers see baseball bats as more useful for games in the park and less useful for assault than other people? If we can reject Alternative 3, then a dual track approach to crime reduction is justified without further research. This is not to say that Alternatives 1 and 2 are identical in their implications, merely that both are consistent only with a dual track approach of some sort. Speculatively, the difference will be that under Alternative 2 a wider range of products and services will have to be crime-proofed than under Alternative 1, since those most criminally inclined will see more marginal objects as presenting criminal opportunities.

Where and how may law promote crime reduction?

If the arguments in this chapter are well founded, the purposes to which legislation should aim are the following. Detailed legislative suggestions have been avoided, so as not to provide specific hostages to fortune when alternative routes to the same end are possible.

- Effective control on fertility, with the aim of reducing the number of children born of impulsive liaisons.
- Designing education and social policy so that adolescents (adolescent boys in particular) can reasonably anticipate reproductive success in the middle term. The components of such policy would include reducing their perceived likelihood of death by disease or misadventure and their reasonable anticipation of financial viability by legitimate means in the short and middle term.
- Incentivizing central government, designers and the private sector to embrace crime-reductive design. Section 17 of the Crime and Disorder Act 1998 places a statutory responsibility on local Crime and Disorder Reduction Partnerships to take into account the consequences of all decisions upon crime. Moss's Chapter 1 in this book discusses section 17 at length. Perversely, but unsurprisingly, central government exempted itself from section 17 responsibility. Some legislative means, whether by extending the reach of section 17 or some other device, should be found to extend to central government and the private sector the responsibility for crime proofing products and services. Pease (1998) details a range of specific suggestions whereby central government could incentivize crime reduction, few of which require primary legislation.
- Target prolific and persistent offenders, for whom dispositions and affordances have combined to yield high frequencies of crime, while introducing safeguards to ensure that such targeting takes place accurately (Townsley and Pease 2002b).

Conspicuously omitted from this list are three policy thrusts conventionally thought to be central. These are:

- the manipulation of risk and hygiene factors in early childhood;
- the rehabilitation of convicted offenders;
- drugs as causal of crime.

The reason for exclusion differs in the three cases. For the first, early intervention programmes may impact upon a range of measures of quality of life, and to consider them alongside affordance reduction measures of crime reduction is unfair to both. It is unfair to early intervention programmes because it seeks to narrow their compass to crime reduction. It is unfair to affordance reduction because by setting this alongside an enterprise which is palpably worthy in seeking to realize human potential, it makes affordance reduction seem mechanistic and amoral. Early intervention programmes do not need to be justified in terms of crime reduction. In recent years a process has been under way known as the criminalization of social policy, whereby measures of crime are taken to be central in judging the efficacy of social policy. Making crime reduction central over the realization of human potential generally is one means by which this pernicious process is advanced.

The reason for not stressing intervention in the lives of those already embarked upon a criminal career is that it seems to be less profitable in reducing levels of crime, at least within the range of intensities of intervention which are routinely practicable (see, for example, Goldblatt and Lewis 1998).

The reason for not stressing drug use as a driver of crime is that to do so would confer upon it a special status as causal which it does not merit. Many crime types are symbiotic (for example, pimping, prostitution and drug supply; see Felson and Clarke 1998). Drugs are better seen as an element of a lifestyle in which crime also features rather than the threshold to a criminal career (see Cohen 2000 as a remedy against simplistic conclusions about cause).

If there is a simple conclusion to the role of law in shaping life-course pathways to avoid those which are self-destructive by dint of crime, it may be that the intervention points are not necessarily those which feature most in policy debates. They centre on fertility control, and shaping the reality and perceptions of likely mid-term success for those tempted to prefer risky short-term rewards. They centre on the design of objects and perceptions so as to minimize criminal affordances. The more traditional emphasis on nurturance and education may have some impact on developing criminality, but is surely better justified by more basic concerns about the fulfilment of human potential. All paths lead to the tomb, and to arrive there having centred upon crime reduction as one's primary policy aim would not make for a peaceful death or a satisfactory obituary.

Acknowledgement

I am hugely indebted to Per-Olof Wikström and Jeanette Garwood, the first for showing me a pre-publication version of a book chapter which inspired me to write this paper (Wikström 2005), and the second for introducing me to the notion of affordance, together with its implications.

Thanks also to Ross Homel of Griffith University, Brisbane, for his comments on a late draft.

Bibliography

Barkley, R. A. (1997) *ADHD and the Nature of Self-Control*, New York: The Guilford Press.

Baum, L. F. (1995) *The Wonderful Wizard of Oz*, Harmondsworth: Penguin.

Blumstein, A., Cohen, J., Roth, J. A. and Visher, C. A. (1986) *Criminal Careers and Career Criminals*, Vol. 1, Washington, DC: National Academy Press.

Brannigan, A. (1998) 'Criminology and the Holocaust: Xenophobia, Evolution and Genocide', *Crime and Delinquency*, 44, 257–76.

Brantingham, P. J. and Brantingham, P. L. (1993) 'Environment, Routine and Situation. Toward a Pattern Theory of Crime', in R. V. Clarke and M. Felson (eds) *Routine Activity and Rational Choice*, New Brunswick: Transaction Publications.

Brown, R. (2001) 'Adolescent Needs, Social Theory and Crime', unpublished Ph.D. thesis, London School of Economics.

Bunyan, J. (1909) *The Pilgrim's Progress*, New York: Collier.

Caspi, A., McClay, J., Moffitt, T. E., Mill, J., Martin, J., Craig, I., Taylor, A. and Poulton, R. (2002) 'Evidence that the Cycle of Violence in Maltreated Children Depends on Genotype', *Science*, 297, 851–4.

Clarke, R. V. and Felson, M. (eds) (1993) *Advances in Criminology Theory 5*, New Brunswick, NJ: Transaction.

Cohen J. (2000) 'Distinguishing between Effects of Criminality and Drug Use on Violent Offending', Final Report to the National Institute of Justice, Grant 92-IJ-CX-0010.

Cohen, L. E., and Felson, M. (1979) 'Social-Change and Crime Rate Trends – Routine Activity Approach', *American Sociological Review*, 44(4), 588–608.

Coie, J.D. (1996) 'Prevention of Violence and Antisocial Behavior', in R. De V. Peters and R. J. McMahon (eds), *Preventing Childhood Disorders, Substance Abuse, and Delinquency*, London: Sage.

Cornish, D. and Clarke, R. (1986) *The Reasoning Criminal*, New York: Springer-Verlag.

Daly, M. and Wilson, M. (1998) *The Truth about Cinderella: a Darwinian View of Parental Love*, London: Weidenfeld and Nicolson.

Dewberry, E. (2003) 'Designing out Crime: Insights from Ecodesign', *Security Journal*, 16, 39–49.

Donohue, J. J. and Levitt, S. D. (2000) 'The Impact of Legalised Abortion on Crime', NBER Working Paper 8004, Cambridge, MA: National Bureau of Economic Research.

Donohue, J. J. and Levitt, S. D. (2003) 'Further Evidence that Legalised Abortion Lowered Crime: A Reply to Joyce', NBER Working Paper 9532, Cambridge, MA: National Bureau of Economic Research.

Farrell, G., Chamard, S., Clark, K. and Pease, K. (2000) 'Towards an Economic Approach to Crime and Prevention', in N.G. Fielding, A. C. Clarke and R. Witt (eds) *The Economic Dimensions of Crime*, London: Macmillan.

Farrington, D. P. (2000) 'Explaining and Preventing Crime: The Globalization of Knowledge – The American Society of Criminology 1999 Presidential Address', *Criminology*, 38, 1–24.

Farrington, D. P. (2002) 'Human Development and Criminal Careers', in M. Maguire, R. Morgan and R. Rainer (eds), *The Oxford Handbook of Criminology*, Oxford: Clarendon Press.

Farrington D. P. (2003) 'Developmental and Life-Course Criminology: Key Theoretical and Empirical Issues' , *Criminology*, 41, 201–35.

Felson M. (2003) *Crime and Everyday Life* (3rd ed.), New York: Sage.

Felson, M. and Clarke, R. (1998) 'Opportunity Makes the Thief', Police Research Series 98, London: Home Office.

Garwood, J. (2004) 'Does Self-reported Offending Behaviour in Post 18 Year Olds Predict the Perception of Criminal Opportunity? A Correlation Study', unpublished manuscript, Leeds Metropolitan University.

Getzels, J. W and Jackson, P. W. (1962) *Creativity and Intelligence: Explorations with gifted Students*, Oxford: Wiley.

Goldblatt, P. and Lewis, C. (eds) (1998) 'Reducing Offending: An Assessment of Research Evidence on Ways of Dealing with Offending Behaviour', Home Office Research Study 187, London: HMSO.

Gottfredson, D. C. and Hirschi, T. (1990) *A General Theory of Crime*, Stanford, CA: Stanford University Press.

Gottfredson, M. R. and Hirschi, T. (2003), 'Self-Control and Opportunity', in C. L. Britt and M. Gottfredson (eds), *Control Theories of Crime and Delinquency: Advances in Criminological Theory*, 12, New Brunswick: Transaction Publications.

Hamer, D. and Copeland, P. (1998) *Living with our Genes*, New York: Doubleday.

Herrnstein, R. J. (1983) 'Some Criminogenic Traits of Offenders', in J. Q. Wilson (ed.), *Crime and Public Policy*, San Francisco: Institute for Contemporary Studies.

Hirschi T. (1986) 'On the Compability of Rational Choice and Control Theories of Crime', in D. B. Cornish and R. V. Clarke (eds), *The Reasoning Criminal*, New York: Springer-Verlag.

Hirschi, T. and Gottfredson, M. (1986) 'The Distinction Between Crime and Criminality' in T. F. Hartnagel and.R. A. Silverman (eds), *Critique and Explanation: Essays in Honor of Gwynne Nettler*, New Brunswick: Transaction Publications.

Hirschi,T. and Gottfredson, M. (1988) 'Towards a General Theory of Crime', in W. Buikhuisen and S. A. Mednick (eds), *Explaining Criminal Behaviour*, Leiden: E. J. Brill.

Homel, R., Freiberg, K., Batchelor, S., Carr, A., Lamb, C., Hay, I., Elias, G. and Teague, R. (2005) 'Pathways to Participation: A Community-based Developmental Prevention Project in Australia', *Children and Society*, in press.

Hudson, L. (1966) *Contrary Imaginations: A Psychological Study of the English Schoolboy*, London: Methuen.

Ishikawa, S. S. and Raine, A. (2003) 'Prefrontal Deficits and Antisocial Behavior: A Causal Model', in B. B. Lahey, T. E. Moffitt and A. Caspi, *Causes of Conduct Disorder and Juvenile Delinquency*, New York: The Guilford Press.

Jensen, G. F. and Akers, R. L. (2003) '"Taking Social Learning Theory Global": Micro–Macro Transitions in Criminological Theory', in R. L. Akers and G. F. Jensen (eds), *Social Learning Theory and the Explanation of Crime: Advances in Criminological Theory*, 11, New Brunswick: Transaction Publications.

Kelling, G. L. and Coles, C. M. (1997) *Fixing Broken Windows*, New York: Touchstone.

LeBlanc, M. and Loeber, R. (1998) 'Developmental Criminology Upgraded', in M. Tonry (ed.), *Crime and Justice*, 18, Chicago: University of Chicago Press.

Loeber, R. and Leblanc, M. (1990) 'Toward a Developmental Criminology', *Crime and Justice*, 12, Chicago: University of Chicago Press.

Mednick, S. A. and Christiansen, K. O. (1977) *Biosocial Bases of Criminal Behaviour*, New York: Gardner Press.

Moffitt, T. E. (1993) 'Adolescence-Limited and Life-Course-Persistent Antisocial-Behavior – a Developmental Taxonomy', *Psychological Review*, 100, 674–701.

Moffitt T. E. (1997) 'Adolescent-Limited and Life-Course Persistent Offending: A Complementary Pair of Developmental Theories', in T. Thornberry (ed.), *Developmental Theories of Crime and Delinquency: Advances in Criminological Theory*, New Brunswick: Transaction Publications.

Moffitt, T. E. (2003) 'Life-Course-Persistent and Adolescent-Limited Antisocial Behavior', in B. B. Lahey, T. E. Moffitt and A. Caspi (eds), *Causes of Conduct Disorder and Juvenile Delinquency*, New York: The Guilford Press.

Nagin, D. S. and Paternoster, R. (1993) 'Enduring Individual Differences and Rational Choice Theories of Crime', *Law and Society Review*, 27, 467–96.

Nee, C. and Taylor, M. (1988) 'The role of cues in simulated residential burglary', *British Journal of Criminology*, 28, 396–403.

Norman, D. (1998) *The Design of Everyday Things*, London: MIT Press.

Pease, K. (1998) 'Crime, Labour and the Wisdom of Solomon.' Policy Studies, 19, 255–65.

Piquero, A. R., Farrington, D. P and Blumstein, A. (2003) 'The Criminal Career Paradigm', *Crime and Justice*, 30, Chicago: University of Chicago Press.

Press, M., Erol, R. and Cooper, R. (2001) *Off the Shelf: Design and Retail Crime*, London: Design Council.

Reiss, A. J. (1986) 'Why Are Communities Important in Understanding Crime?', in A. J. Reiss and M. Tonry (eds), *Communities and Crime*, Chicago: University of Chicago Press.

Rich Harris, J. (1998) *The Nurture Assumption*, London: Bloomsbury.

Ridley, M. (1999) *Genome*, London: Fourth Estate.

Scarr, S. and McCartney, K. (1983) 'How Children Make their Own Environments', *Child Development*, 54, 424–35.

Shonkoff, J. P. and Phillips, D. A. E. (2000) *From Neurons to Neighborhoods: The Science of Early Childhood Development*, Washington, DC: National Academy Press.

Smith, M., Clarke, R. V. and Pease, K. (2002) 'Anticipatory Benefits in Crime Prevention', in N. Tilley (ed.), *Analysis for Crime Prevention*, Monsey, NY: Criminal Justice Press.

Tarling, R. (1993) *Analysing Offending: Data, Models and Interpretations*, London: HMSO.

Thornberry, T. P. and Krohn, M. D. (2003) *Taking Stock of Delinquency: An Overview of Findings from Contemporary Longitudinal Studies*, New York: Kluwer Academic/ Plenum Press.

Townsley, M. and Pease, K. (2002a) 'How Efficiently can we Target Prolific Offenders?', *International Journal of Police Science and Management*, 4, 323–31.

Townsley, M. and Pease, K. (2002b) 'Hot Spots and Cold Comfort', in N. Tilley (ed.) *Analysis for Crime Prevention*, Monsey, NY: Criminal Justice Press.

Van Dijk, J. (1992) 'Understanding Crime Rates: On the Interaction Between Rational Choices of Victims and Offenders', *British Journal of Criminology*, 34, 105–21.

Wikström, P.-O. H. (1998) 'Communities and Crime', in M. Tonry (ed.) *The Handbook of Crime and Punishment*, New York: Oxford University Press, pp. 269–301.

Wikström, P.-O. H. (2004) 'Crime as Alternative: Towards a Cross-level Situational Action Theory of Crime Causation', in J. McCord (ed.), *Beyond Empiricism: Institutions and Intentions in the Study of Crime: Advances in Criminological Theory*, Vol. 13, New Brunswick: Transaction Publications.

Wikström, P.-O. H. (2005) 'The Social Origins of Pathways in Crime: Towards a Developmental Ecological Action Theory of Crime Involvement and its Changes', in D. P. Farrington (ed.), *Integrated Developmental and Life Course Theories of Offending: Advances in Criminological Theory*, Vol. 14, New Brunswick: Transaction Publications.

Wikström, P.-O. and Loeber, R. (2000) 'Do Disadvantaged Neighborhoods Cause Well-Adjusted Children to Become Adolescent Delinquents?', *Criminology*, 38, 1109–42.

Wilson, M. and Daly, M. (1997) 'Life Expectancy, Economic Inequality, Homicide, and Reproductive Timing in Chicago Neighbourhoods', *British Medical Journal*, 314, 1271.

Wortley, R. (2001) 'A Classification of Techniques for Controlling Situational Precipitators of Crime', *Security Journal*, 14, 63–82.

Woyciechowski, M. and Kozlowski, J. (1998) 'Division of Labour by Division of Risk according to Worker Life Expectancy in the Honeybee (Apis mellifera L)', *Apidologie*, 29, 191–205.

Zimbardo, P. G. (1973) 'A Field Experiment in Auto-shaping', in C. Ward (ed.), *Vandalism*, London: Architectural Press.

5 Police performance targets, repeat victimization and crime reduction

Steve Everson

Introduction

This chapter highlights a number of changes that have taken place over the past two or three decades that have impaired the ability of the police to respond to calls on their service. Over that time period we have seen a substantial increase in the number of such calls accompanied by an effective reduction in the number of personnel available to service them. The changes described are an illustrative sample and in no way intended as an exhaustive list.

This unwelcome impact upon both the demand and supply of policing resources has consequently led to a focusing of those resources upon a narrow band of activities. Such focus is determined by the Home Office and implemented and monitored by way of police performance targets or Key Performance Indicators (KPIs). That process has been successful in addressing those issues upon which the resources have been focused. Commenting upon crime trends in the British Crime Surveys (BCSs) up to 2003–4, Dodd *et al.* (2004: 7) state: 'Since 1995 BCS crime has fallen by 39 per cent, with vehicle crime and burglary falling by roughly half and violent crime falling by over a third during this time.' However, there remains a swathe of activity that was formerly a fundamental feature of policing in the United Kingdom that has now been marginalized. All required close police/public interaction and co-operation and are typified by victim support, crime prevention advice, school liaison and the work of community constables. It is contended in this chapter that these and other similar policing activities were key elements in the provision of 'policing by consent'.

Demand, supply and the thin blue line

Despite the much-vaunted recent increases in police manpower in England and Wales, the rise in crime has been much steeper, over the past 30 years, than the rise in the number of police officers. Figure 5.1 illustrates this point (Home Office 2004a).

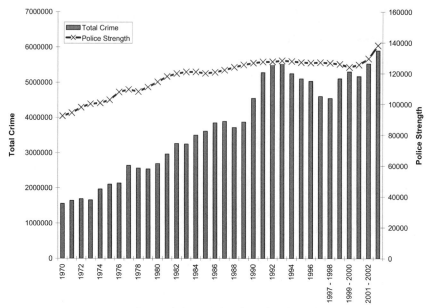

Figure 5.1 Comparison of recorded crime levels and police officer numbers in England and Wales.

Calls for service are a more appropriate index of work pressure, and Figure 5.2 shows the level of crime recorded by the police against the numbers of emergency '999' calls received by one of the larger metropolitan police forces in England and Wales between 1981 and 2002 (West Yorkshire Police 1981–2002) – local statistics are used here because comparable national statistics for '999' calls are unavailable. It can be seen that, whilst recorded crime has doubled over that period, the number of '999' calls has increased by almost a factor of five. The figures shown have been adjusted to eradicate duplicate calls relating to the same incident.

Lost in cyberspace

In 1970, 35 per cent of households in the UK had a telephone; by 2001–2 this had risen to 94 per cent (National Statistics 2003a). In recent years mobile phones have effectively given a significant majority of the population a communication facility wherever they may be and at whatever time of day. Between 1996 and 2002 the percentage of households owning a mobile phone increased from 16 per cent to 65 per cent (National Statistics 2003a). Ignoring, for a moment, the impact upon the crime figures that accompanied this rise in mobile telephone ownership through thefts and robberies, the ability to communicate readily with the police and report incidents has necessitated major changes in the way that calls

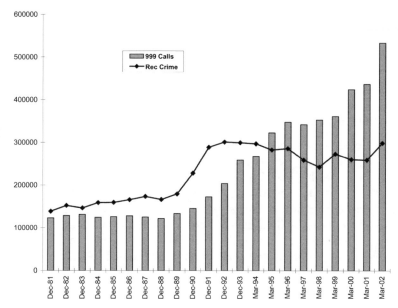

Figure 5.2 Comparison of number of '999' calls to recorded crime levels in England and Wales.

are handled by the police. Despite the increased use of advanced technology, it has also required that much greater numbers of staff are utilized merely to process those incoming calls, many of which relate to the same incidents. Chris Fox, the current President of the Association of Chief Police Officers (ACPO) and former chief constable of Northamptonshire Police wrote that his former headquarters' control room, 'which covers our motorways, was swamped with more than 80,000 mobile phone calls to 999 last year ... coming in from well meaning people' (Fox 2002). Whilst in some ways this is beneficial to the police in that, potentially, additional witnesses to incidents become known to them, if their personal details are provided, it does create a logistical problem in dealing with the increased communication traffic.

Internet crime, whether fraud- or sex-related, is a growing phenomenon that was not a feature of policing in the 1980s or even most of the 1990s. One notable example of this would be 'Operation Ore', the massive policing operation against internet paedophiles which resulted in 1300 arrests and threatened to dislocate the whole criminal justice system (BBC News, 13 January 2003). The National Hi-Tech Crime Unit was set up, following a statement by the Home Secretary in November 2000, to combat national and transnational serious and organized hi-tech crime impacting upon the United Kingdom. Resources have had to be found to police such crime. It is often argued that insufficient resources are devoted to such work but the reality is that, like all other demands upon resources, personnel can only be utilized in new ventures or in an expanded sector of policing if they are diverted from duties that were previously performed in other fields of activity – unless there is a substantial net increase in such resources. In addition to the increased demands made upon policing resources, the growth of crime in cyberspace also calls into question the territorial organisation of policing. Cyberspace has no border posts.

New toys, new crimes

The increased sophistication of consumer products has resulted in an increase in their attractiveness to criminals. 'Criminals are interested in high value, portable items that are easy to dispose of and difficult to identify' (Kock *et al.* 1996: 11). Clarke (1999: 23) describes the six characteristics of 'hot products' – those 'consumer items that are most attractive to thieves' – by using the acronym 'CRAVED'. These characteristics are concealable, removable, available, valuable, enjoyable and disposable. The more a consumer item displays such characteristics, the more likely it is to be stolen. Modern electronic goods, in particular, tend to display all six characteristics. Felson and Clarke (1998: 22) describe four stages in the life-cycle of mass-produced consumer goods. These are innovation, growth, mass market and saturation.

Products in the innovation stage are usually attractive only to a small group of consumers and are likely to be subject to radical improvements before the later stages of the life-cycle are reached. Products in this stage are not sought by thieves as they are generally very difficult to dispose of. During the growth stage the product becomes subject to changes that make it easier to use, usually more compact to carry and cheaper to buy. This makes them attractive to a much larger section of the public and therefore the number of thefts increases. In the mass market stage the product is even more attractive and therefore thefts of the product become more common. In the saturation stage, however, most people who want such products have already obtained one, the cost has been minimized and therefore their appeal to a thief reduces significantly.

Unfortunately, for those in the business of crime reduction, the rate of change in technology is such that there is no shortage of new or significantly altered products coming into the marketplace to maintain the momentum of crime unless something radical takes place to make the individual product less appealing to the criminal. Technology can provide that radical solution. However, it is important to guard against complacency. The use of security codes in car radios had a marked effect upon the rate of theft of those products when they were first introduced, rendering the radios useless in other vehicles. In time the procedure was defeated by the thieves and so the process repeats. It is important that manufacturers seeking to bring new technology to the marketplace consider both the attractiveness of their products to thieves and ways in which they could be made more secure for the legitimate purchasers. This rarely happens, certainly at the early stages of the life-cycle of the product. Any security enhancements that are introduced are usually woefully late. A cynic might suggest that it is not in the economic interest of a manufacturer to minimize the risk of theft until the saturation stage of the life-cycle has been reached.

Economic imperatives

It would be difficult to argue against the proposition that the 'average' citizen in the UK has become more prosperous over the past three decades. On most indices, such as vehicle ownership, number of holidays taken, types and value of personal goods owned, home ownership and so on, the trend is definitely upward. For example, between 1971 and 2002 home ownership increased from 49 per cent to 69 per cent, according to government figures (National Statistics 2004a).

Figure 5.3 shows the trend of car ownership in the UK since 1972 (National Statistics 2004b). Whilst the percentage of households owning one vehicle has remained consistent, the percentage of households without a vehicle has dropped significantly. The percentage of households owning two vehicles has significantly increased and there has been a steady increase in the percentage of households owning three or more vehicles. This in turn has led to a significant increase in the number of vehicles available as potential crime targets.

However, the spread of wealth across the population is far from even. Figure 5.4 shows that the wealthiest 1 per cent of the UK population owns 23 per cent of its marketable wealth and that the wealthiest half of the population owns 95 per cent of its wealth (National Statistics 2003b). These figures include the value of buildings owned. When housing is excluded the figures become even more skewed, giving figures of 33 per cent and 97 per cent respectively. This situation of inequality has steadily worsened over the past three decades. In a situation of increasing national prosperity, coupled with increasing inequality of distribution of that prosperity, it might be argued that this constitutes a catalyst for crime levels to increase. Taylor (1997: 272) commented that:

> There is a ... distinct body of ... literature which has been more interested in thinking about inequalities in the distribution of economic return or economic well-being, and the broad social effects of such inequalities, e.g. in respect of crime.

Demography, victim vulnerability and other assorted burdens of recent prominence

In 1971, according to the Office for National Statistics, 18 per cent of households were single-occupancy dwellings of which two-thirds were

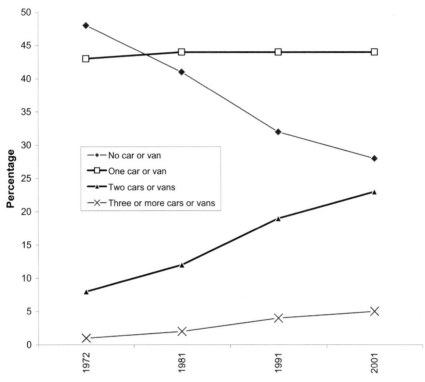

Figure 5.3 Car Ownership Changes in the UK.

occupied by those of pensionable age. By 1999, 29 per cent of dwellings were single occupancy of which approximately half were occupied by those of pensionable age. These figures reflect the decline in marriage, an increase in the average age at marriage and the increasing proportion of marriages that result in separation and divorce. Over the same period of time the percentage of households with a single parent and dependent children has more than doubled. The percentage of households occupied by couples with no children has slightly increased whilst there has been a reduction from 35 per cent of households occupied by couples with dependent children in 1971 to 23 per cent of such households in 1999. Such statistics reflect the changing trends in family and partnership formation and also the increased availability of suitable housing for single parent families. But we know that single parent households, particularly those on low income, are far more likely to become victims of burglary than those occupied by couples and persons of pensionable age (Dodd *et al.* 2004).

The number of crimes recorded in England and Wales in which firearms have been used has almost doubled between 1992 and 2002–3 (Povey 2004: 43), with a similar increase in the number of crimes recorded in which firearms were reported to have caused injury (Povey 2004: 48). For

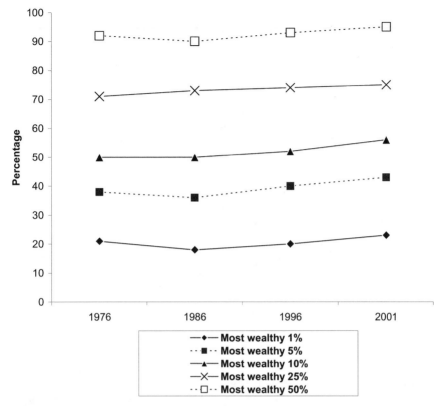

Figure 5.4 Distribution of wealth across the UK.

reasons of safety, both for members of the public and the police officers involved, and to assuage public concern, offences involving the use of firearms generally utilize far more police resources than similar non-firearm offences. A recent thematic inspection report by Her Majesty's Inspectorate of Constabulary (HMIC) commented that 'whilst representing only half of one percent of reported crime, gun crime is still increasing albeit at a slower rate than in recent years' (HMIC 2004: 5). The report went on to say that there 'is evidence of the increasing use of guns on the street by criminals, frequently such incidents are related to drugs' (HMIC 2004: 6).

In the decade from 1990 the number of seizures of controlled drugs more than doubled, as did the quantity of drugs seized. Over the same period, the number of individuals dealt with for drug-related offences rose by over 130 per cent (Corkery 2002: 48). Even more alarming than the rise in numbers of drug seizures made over that period is the fact that the percentage of those seizures involving Class A drugs has risen from 12 to 27 per cent. Whilst the number of seizures has increased for all three drug classes, there has been an almost four-fold increase in the number of Class

A drug seizures between 1990 and 2000 (Corkery 2002: 50). Again, the investigation of drug offences tends to be more officer intensive compared to most other crime categories. However, the linkage of drugs to other criminal activity, such as theft, burglary and assault, has also had a major impact upon policing resources and strategies. Drug users commit crime to obtain cash to buy drugs and the influence of drugs can make their behaviour unpredictable and violent.

Arguably, an even greater problem for policing, certainly in terms of scale if not in perception of seriousness by the general public, is alcohol abuse and alcohol-related offending. A recent Home Office study into the links between alcohol and crime commented that:

> Dealing with anti-social behaviour as a result of drunkenness is perhaps one of the greatest burdens on police resources. Urinating in the street, throwing missiles, minor public disorder conduct and minor criminal damage may seem insignificant, but, if left unchecked, can lead to fear of crime in the local community and a gradual acceleration of public disorder in an area. Manning (1996) states that a highly visible police presence is required to deter such behaviour. This is resource intensive.
>
> (Deehan 1999: 16)

The true scale of the problem is difficult to measure. Drunkenness offences *per se* are not notifiable to the Home Office and therefore not readily accessible. Figures that are available give the impression that drunkenness is a diminishing problem. On the Home Office's Crime Reduction website, reference is made to a Home Office report (Home Office 1997). This report showed a 43 per cent drop in offences of drunkenness between 1985 and 1995. However, this could be the result of marked changes in the way in which police forces and the courts dealt with simple drunkenness offences.

In a recent study which examined over 1,500 custody records in the Metropolitan Police area, it was found that in almost a third of those records alcohol was a factor in the arrest. It was also found that those arrested for alcohol-related offences were detained significantly longer than those being dealt with for alcohol-specific offences. Many of the latter were merely being detained in a supervised environment to sober up and then released without any charges being brought. They also found that detainees arrested for alcohol-related or alcohol-specific offences 'were more likely to be noisy, disruptive, agitated, abusive, aggressive and violent whilst in custody' (Man *et al.* 2002: 1). Deehan's study noted that:

> The care of drunken detainees must address issues of fitness to be detained/interviewed, alcohol withdrawal, general well being and safety. How important these issues are in individual cases will depend

on how much the detainee has drunk and if they are dependent on alcohol. Drunken detainees are a major problem for the police and are one of the main groups to die in custody.

(Deehan 1999: 18)

There are other recent studies that indicate that alcohol-related offences are a significant problem. In her analysis of the 1996, 1998 and 2000 sweeps of the British Crime Surveys, Budd estimates that there were approximately 1.2 million alcohol-related violent incidents in 1999. She further commented that:

Just over a third of incidents were between strangers and a further third between acquaintances. A quarter of the incidents were domestic assaults between partners, relatives or household members. Only five per cent were muggings (robbery and snatch thefts).

(Budd 2003: iv)

Even more perturbing is her additional comment that:

Incidents were by no means trivial. More than half of incidents resulted in some form of injury. In a fifth of incidents, the perpetrator had a weapon which they threatened to use, most often a glass or drinking bottle.

(Budd 2003: v)

In an examination of the crime and disorder audits published by the 376 Crime and Disorder Partnerships in England and Wales between September and November 2002, it was reported that almost 'all (97%) of [the] audit documents mentioned alcohol as an issue in some form' (Home Office 2004b: 2).

In recent years there has been increased reporting of 'binge drinking' by young people in the towns and cities of the UK, the definition of a 'binge drinker' in those reports being 'someone who gets very drunk at least once a month'. An examination of the 1998–9 Youth Lifestyles Survey, in which almost 5,000 young persons were interviewed, found that 39 per cent of 18- to 24-year-olds were classified as 'binge drinkers' (Richardson *et al.* 2003: 1). They concluded that 'binge drinking is strongly associated with offending behaviour, particularly violent incidents, even when other factors are taken into account' (Richardson *et al.* 2003: 4).

Two further issues that have had a significant effect upon policing and utilization of police resources, particularly over the past two decades, are domestic violence and racially motivated incidents. That is not to say that the issues did not exist before then but they were policed, if at all, in a very low-key manner. Such incidents were treated on the perceived merits of each individual event whether as an alleged assault, act of criminal damage or whatever. It is certainly the case that the experience of victims of such attacks, of the police and the criminal justice system generally, did not encourage the reporting of such incidents. One recent Home Office report (Walby and Myhill 2000: 1) commented that the 'analysis and extent and nature of domestic violence, and of programmes to reduce it, has developed rapidly over the last two decades, but is still at an early stage compared with the analysis of many other crimes'.

The strategies implemented by individual police forces to deal with domestic violence were of variable rigour and effectiveness. In 1990 the Home Office asked police forces to develop proactive policies and operational interventions to combat domestic violence and incorporate arrest, investigation and recording of such incidents. A subsequent Home Office inter-agency circular in 1995 'encouraged statutory and voluntary agencies, including the police, to work together to respond effectively to domestic violence' (Hanmer and Griffiths 2000: 1). This inter-agency circular was subsequently updated (Home Office 2000).

In the NACRO briefing guide to partnership agencies dealing with domestic violence issues, the authors note that despite all the encouragement from government sources and the recognition and emphasis now placed upon the issue by major agencies, there remain 'high levels of under-reporting by survivors to agencies and significant under-recording of incidents by agencies and that domestic violence accounts for one quarter of all violent crime' (Hall and Wright 2003: 2). Drawing on evidence from the British Crime Surveys and other sources, they observe that it 'is estimated that only 25 per cent of survivors will report to the police ... and that survivors will suffer an average of 35–37 assaults for an average period of seven years before informing any agency' (Hall and Wright 2003: 3).

Similarly, a Home Office Research Study remarked that:

> Racially motivated crime was a largely uncharted phenomenon until the 1980s. In the 1990s a series of high-profile cases of racist murders resulted in a much wider recognition that racially motivated crime needed to be tackled more effectively. It was significantly highlighted in the Stephen Lawrence Inquiry Report (Macpherson, 1999).
>
> (Clancy *et al.* 2001: 21).

The same study notes that the recorded crime figures for racist incidents show a sharp increase between 1997–8 and 1999–2000 which is not reflected in the British Crime Survey figures. This increase is attributed to a 'mixture of increased reporting by victims and improved recording practice by the police' rather than a real increase in number of incidents. The discrepancy between the 48,000 incidents recorded by the police in 1999–2000 and the 150,000 estimated in the 1999 British Crime Survey implies that there is 'further "headroom"; for an increase in police recorded racial incidents' (Clancy *et al.* 2001: 40).

Both of these issues have had a significant impact upon policing and police resource utilization and both, due to the high levels of under-reporting, are likely to have an increasing impact. The British Crime Surveys provide differing expectations for future trends. In relation to racially motivated incidents the 'BCS provides no support for the view that there has been a real increase in the number of incidents' (Clancy *et al.* 2001: 40). An analysis of the trend in relation to domestic violence, however, shows an increase in total incidents between 1981 and 1995 of 242 per cent (Mirrlees-Black 1999: 67).

Not more law!

Over the past three decades there have been dozens of new pieces of legislation introduced which have impacted upon the operation of criminal justice in general and policing in particular. The author will concentrate upon three that have brought about major changes to the way in which policing operates in England and Wales, particularly in terms of investigation and the compilation and presentation of evidence in court.

The Police and Criminal Evidence Act 1984 (PACE) had a radical impact upon the way in which the police service dealt with arrested persons. It was enacted in the light of a number of high profile miscarriages of justice and gave a clear framework within which the police should operate whilst giving protection to the individual. The principles of the Act are codified to enable police officers to interpret the provisions of the Act on a day-to-day basis. The Act and its Codes of Practice have recently undergone a major review instigated by the Home Secretary and are in the process of being updated and reorganized to reflect societal changes over the past 20 years. There is little doubt that the Act has standardized police practices in relation to the arrest, detention and interview of arrested persons in particular. It has, however, made the whole process far more bureaucratic and time consuming, albeit more professional.

The Prosecution of Offenders Act 1985 introduced the concept of an independent prosecution facility, the Crown Prosecution Service (CPS), to examine and present criminal cases rather than utilizing lawyers employed or retained by the police or senior police officers to present such cases at Magistrates' Courts. Whilst, on the face of it, this might appear a measure that, at worst, had a neutral effect upon policing resources, in reality it again added to the bureaucratic burden placed upon police officers. Whilst, ultimately, prosecution files would become far more professional they took far longer to prepare. Solicitors employed by the CPS work to the Code for Crown Prosecutors which is established in the Act. According to the Code, a case must first pass 'the evidential test', a standard of evidence that would give a 'reasonable prospect of conviction', that is to say that a jury or bench of magistrates would be more likely than not to convict the defendant on the alleged charge (Crown Prosecution Service

2000: 5). Additionally, the decision whether or not to prosecute a particular case must also pass the 'public interest test'. The Code states that a 'prosecution will usually take place unless there are public interest factors tending against prosecution which clearly outweigh those tending in favour' (Crown Prosecution Service 2000: 8). These two tests were not in force prior to the inception of the Crown Prosecution Service and it is fair to say that there are many cases that fail to reach the prosecution stage that would have done prior to the Act. This is particularly true of cases heard in the Magistrates' Courts. The comment is made not as a criticism of the CPS but as a statement of fact. The system of court file preparation conducted both by the police and the CPS is far more bureaucratic and time consuming.

The Criminal Procedure and Investigations Act 1996 introduced the 'disclosure' procedure and incorporated details of a code of practice in relation to the duties of the police officer who should be appointed as 'disclosure officer'; namely, to record details of materials gathered in the course of the investigation and deal with that information in accordance with the Act. Again the system of file preparation has become even more time-consuming and bureaucratic albeit more professional and much less liable to unfair bias against the defendant. All of this echoes the comments of one eminent criminologist that 'the last 15 years have seen less police "out there". More rigorous legal accountability ... has reduced patrolling time' (Hough 2001).

Not more government directives!

An article in *The Economist* (4 September 1993), as reported in a recent research paper (Drake and Simper 2001: 7), postulated that the 1980s introduced 'managerialism' into the police service, with increasing numbers of civilian staff undertaking roles previously performed by police officers and other such tasks being undertaken by the private security industry.

The catalyst to this process was, arguably, Home Office Circular 114/1983 (Home Office 1983). This was issued against a backdrop of year-on-year growth in funding for the police over the previous three years and crime figures that had increased considerably over the same period. The circular informed chief officers of police that further increases in manpower and funding would only be sanctioned by the Home Secretary if certain criteria were satisfied. One criterion was that it must be shown that existing resources were being used efficiently. This linked into the annual reports made by HMIC which in turn led to the introduction of performance targets (Walker 2004).

The process of civilianization that also ensued has had mixed results. Whilst it has undoubtedly enabled a greater percentage of police officers to operate in non-support roles than would otherwise have been the case, and has opened up the 'police culture' to some extent at least, there have also been perceived disadvantages to the process. Members of the public can no longer expect to deal with a police officer as their first point of contact on most mundane policing issues. This lack of contact between members of the public and police officers, other than those suspected of committing offences, may well have impacted upon the way in which the police service is perceived by individuals and reflected in public surveys.

The setting of policing performance targets was subsequently undertaken by the Home Office, the Audit Commission, HMIC and ACPO. The Audit Commission are required, under the Local Government Act 1992, to determine a set of indicators for local authority services, including the police. HMIC, initially established by the County and Borough Police Act 1856, are now empowered by section 54 of the Police Act 1996. In June 1993 Home Office Circular 17/1993 (Home Office 1993) sought to consolidate the various requirements for performance information into one 'streamlined package'.

The Police and Magistrates' Courts Act 1994 empowered the Home Secretary to set key objectives for the police service and chief officers, and police authorities were required to have regard for them from 1995–6 onwards. From 1997, the objectives became Ministerial Priorities and they have become much more strategic rather than tactical in nature. Since the introduction of the Crime and Disorder Act 1998 there has also been a distinct strategic movement towards partnerships. In the National Policing Plan 2003 – 2006, the Home Secretary stated that the primary objective for the police service over that three year period was to:

> deliver improved police performance, which will in turn contribute to the overall reduction of crime, the fear of crime and anti-social behaviour. To achieve these goals, the police service will need to work in partnership with other national and local agencies in support of crime reduction; to develop better relations with minority ethnic groups; and to engage all sections of the community in the fight against crime.
>
> (Home Office 2002: 35)

However, throughout this process the performance indicators that have been utilized have been, in relation to crime management, hard statistical returns on recorded crime and detection rates. Such outcomes have been measured on an annual basis for the purposes of the reports back to the Home Office and internally by police forces on at least a monthly if not far more frequent basis. This would be understandable if the measures were all-embracing to the work of police officers and gave a true reflection of what the public wanted to see from its police service. It is the contention of the author that this is not the case. Vital areas of policing, some that reach to the core of what the British police service is all about and for which it gained a justifiable international reputation, are missing from the equation.

Some of those features, such as public reassurance and long-term projects to reduce crime, are not measured. The old management saw 'what gets measured gets done', usually attributed to Tom Peters, is pertinent here. Since the introduction of performance indicators, there has been a skewing of resources towards activities that lead to addressing those indicators. An H.M. Treasury document on police performance measurement commented that 'some police work might have only an indirect link to outcomes – crime preventative work and foot patrols might be examples' (Spottiswoode 2000: 11). A recent online Home Office report addressed this point:

> Performance indicators and targets appear to impact on the ability of partnerships and police forces to implement effective crime reduction projects. The problem is caused because local managers allocate resources to meeting performance indicators and targets. If the aim of a crime reduction project is to reduce a different type of crime or problem, there is less incentive to focus resources in that area.
>
> (Bullock *et al.* 2002: 37)

A Home Office report on the evaluation of policing activity found that 'police officers are frequently "results driven", with priorities commonly determined by short term considerations or by centrally imposed targets ...' (Stockdale *et al.* 1999: 42). The Deputy Commissioner of the Metropolitan Police, in a recent lecture, spoke of the three facets of policing, the first being the 'traditional staples of policing, dealing with allegations of assault, robbery, burglary, auto crime: answering calls for service: dealing with football matches and marches, traffic accidents and pub fights' (Blair 2004: 1). These were areas in which successive governments have lavished the attention of a performance regime and were generally well served by the police service. The second facet was the threat of serious violence such as terrorism, homicide and rape. He argued that the public were concerned about such issues but, generally, due to the relative scarcity of such incidents, felt that they happened to 'other people'. The main public concerns were with the growing levels of unchecked 'incivilities' (Wilson and Kelling 1982), such as broken bus shelters and abandoned vehicles, 'those aspects of modern life that make people feel insecure ... it is these aspects of local community safety with which the public wish the police to engage' (Blair 2004: 1). Commenting upon the work of Bill Bratton, who famously reduced these problems as police chief in New York City, Blair said that he was:

> policing a city with the same population but half the geographic area as London, with only one political head and only one objective, with a budget of £1 billion (or 13,000 cops) more and with the FBI, the DEA and the US Secret Service to assist in those parts of the mission which are represented by Scotland Yard's national and international responsibilities.
>
> (Blair 2004: 2)

In a comparative study of policing in London and New York for the Institute for the Study of Civil Society (Civitas), it is argued that there has been a failure of government to meet increasing crime levels with corresponding increases in police numbers. This has caused the crime situation to deteriorate so that 'crime has overwhelmed police forces' (Dennis *et al.* 2003: 18). They contrast the ratio of crimes to the number of police officers in both cities. Comparing the 1993 figures, there were 296 robberies per officer in New York whilst in London the figure was 105. Both of these ratios showed a massive increase over the previous 30 or 40 years despite a gradual increase in police manpower in both cities. Between 1993 and 2002 there was a continued gradual increase in police strength in London but a substantial increase in police numbers in New York. The corresponding ratios of robberies per police officer in 2002 were 68 for New York and 170 for London. In the same study and referring to an earlier report (Kelling and Sousa 2001) they attribute the relative success in New York and failure in London to the

> NYPD's return to the principles of law enforcement enunciated by Sir Robert Peel as the basis of effective policing that 'the basic mission for which the police exist is to prevent crime and disorder' ... and that the proper test of police efficiency is 'the absence of crime and disorder, not the visible evidence of police dealing with them'.
>
> (Dennis *et al.* 2003: 46)

Accepting that there were policy differences in the policing strategies for London and New York, and in this matter London was no different to the rest of England and Wales, why should there have occurred such dramatic and opposite effects in both areas? The answer may lie in 'Tipping Point' theory:

> The best way to understand the emergence of fashion trends, the ebb and flow of crime waves ... or any number of the other mysterious changes that mark everyday life is to think of them as epidemics. Ideas and products and messages and behaviours spread just like viruses do.
>
> (Gladwell 2001: 7)

'[The] possibility of sudden change is at the centre of the idea of the Tipping Point' (Gladwell 2001: 12). Epidemics are examples of geometric progressions where the numbers double and then double again, repeatedly. The term was first used to describe the phenomenon experienced in the older cities of the north-east of the USA during the 1970s; when the percentage of African Americans reached a certain percentage in neighbourhoods the community was said to 'tip' and 'most of the remaining whites would leave almost immediately ... The Tipping Point is the moment of critical mass' (Gladwell 2001: 12).

In the crime context, it is the author's contention that once the ability of a police force to be seen to deal with these 'incivilities' is seriously challenged, then the situation begins to deteriorate rapidly, in epidemic proportions. Conversely, once it is perceived that an area suffering high crime and disorder is being addressed in a long-term and consistent manner then the return to 'normality' will occur in an equally rapid process.

Crime reduction and repeat victimization: a muted blast from the recent past

The increasing focus of policing activity towards intelligence-led proactive initiatives has, in reality, been concentrated upon detecting crime and targeting known criminals. Such activity can be readily measured but has led to the almost total exclusion of other crime reduction activity with one major exception, repeat victimization ('rv'). From the late 1980s Ken Pease and various associated researchers have doggedly demonstrated and reinforced the message that one of the key features of any effective crime reduction programme must be the reduction of repeat victimization. By the mid-1990s this had been recognized to the extent that repeat victimization was incorporated into the Home Secretary's police performance indicators. In 1995–96 every police force had to 'demonstrate their capability of identifying repeat victims' – something that the majority, up to that time, were incapable of carrying out. In the following year, police forces had to develop a strategy to 'reduce repeat victimization for any locally relevant offence' – this allowed the local police Basic Command Units (BCUs) to address those issues of concern to them rather than have imposed upon them a centrally chosen specified offence. In 1997/98 the police forces had to implement their strategy and in the following year set targets for the reduction of the incidence of repeat victimization. In the Home Office evaluation of the process it was commented that: 'Probably ... [the] most significant action in encouraging rv onto the police agenda ... was in ... its adoption as one of the Home Secretary's police performance indicators for the prevention of crime (Farrell *et al.* 2000: 2). The same study concluded that:

> Forces are clearly trying to respond to the requirement that they address repeat victimisation, but it seems likely from many of their responses that not only are the tactics not obviously targeted to the protection of victims, but many have a weak preventative mechanism ... Although the notion of preventing repeat victimisation has penetrated police strategic thinking, the associated tactics have not been successful. This is a challenge for researchers.
>
> (Farrell *et al.* 2000: 15)

Notwithstanding the relatively poor implementation of repeat victimization strategies found in the study, it is apparent that the Home Office is keen to continue their encouragement and promotion. The benefits of an effective repeat victimization programme are emphasized in the government White Paper on police reform which urges that 'concentrating police resources on repeat victims is one of the most effective ways to reduce overall crime' (Home Office 2001: para. 3.80). The White Paper continues:

> ... the Home Office will therefore work closely with the police to find the best way of ensuring that police resources are focused on repeat victimisation. This will simultaneously reduce the further risks to victims and substantially increase the chances of persistent offenders being caught.
>
> (Home Office 2001: para. 3.86)

Having established the link between prolific offenders and repeat victimization, effective strategies to reduce repeat victimization have two important built-in bonuses. They provide:

> an opportunity for a much needed quality of service to those members of the community that are most in need of that service and they also curtail the activities of those offenders who are committing the most crime within that community. They are also bonuses that accrue without the penalty of civil libertarian objection.
>
> (Everson 2003: 193)

Never mind the width ... never mind the quality either

It is the quality of service issues that, arguably, have been the hardest hit by the increase in demand upon policing resources and the skewing of resource allocation towards that narrow band of issues that have been measured in the performance indicators, until very recently at least. In a recent study of policing in London it was noted that:

> Many police officers felt very frustrated at their inability to respond to people's needs and, in particular, to deliver the quality of service the public expect. They felt that victims frequently had to wait too long for the police; and they were not able to spend enough time with them when they did arrive ... They often blamed this on the pressure to meet targets for a narrow range of crimes, which represented a minority of the calls they had to answer. They also cited the demands of paperwork, including management information in relation to targets, and inadequate IT systems.
>
> (FitzGerald and Hough 2002: 5–6)

This has its effect across a wide range of police/public interfaces, two of which I will address.

Dealing with 'incivilities', which are given a low priority for police response, invariably means that when, or if, a police officer is sent it is invariably so long after the event that the perpetrator(s) has long disappeared. Delayed responses also signal a lack of police resolve to deal with such issues which, in turn, is likely to discourage any enthusiasm from witnesses to co-operate with the police in addressing the problems. This is in effect a pincer attack on the effectiveness of crime reduction: the failure to deal with 'incivilities' leads to more serious crime being committed (Wilson and Kelling 1982), and the dissociation of the public from the criminal justice system makes it increasingly difficult to convict offenders in those cases that are proceeded with.

Crime reduction activity that is not directly linked to the short-term crime performance targets has been significantly curtailed. Even activity that has been extensively researched and shown to be effective is not encouraged. Designing out crime has been shown to have an important influence upon crime and disorder (Pascoe 1999; Armitage 2000), yet police activity to encourage this has only received token support from senior police officers and no active encouragement from the Home Office. The lessons of the past, when poor design in residential and industrial development has encouraged rather than militated against the rise in crime, have not, apparently, been learned. There is now a golden opportunity to promote such work by encouraging the implementation of the guidance contained in the document recently published jointly by the Office of the Deputy Prime Minister (ODPM) and the Home Office (ODPM and Home Office 2004). This is true partnership activity with the principal players being the police, in the form of police Architectural Liaison Officers (ALOs) or Crime Prevention Design Advisors (CPDAs), and the local authorities, in the form of development control officers in planning departments. This is a crime reduction activity that is, arguably, tailor-made for local Crime and Disorder Reduction Partnerships (CDRPs) to champion and for the ODPM and the Home Office to encourage. It has minimal resource implications yet the potential to dramatically alter the scale and attributes of crime and disorder for generations to come. It is also an activity that would be welcomed by house purchasers who have been shown to desire a safe environment in which to live above all other features utilized by estate agents in house sales (Armitage and Everson 2003: 24).

Assuming that there is both intention and commitment to retain, or indeed regain, the traditional British concept of 'policing by consent' then a major effort is required to repair the damage inflicted upon the system over the past two or three decades. The police/public dynamic requires effective and professional contact to underpin 'policing by consent' – that is to say, a requirement for meaningful contact with victims, witnesses and members of the public in their everyday demands for reassurance, support and advice. It may require a radical re-think about the role of the police and may even challenge some traditional concepts. Whatever that outcome may be, it should be one that is considered and planned rather than a consequence of a series of random events and interventions, however well-intentioned each may have been, which is leading inexorably to a potentially irreversible change in the style of policing of the United Kingdom.

Bibliography

Armitage, R. (2000) 'An Evaluation of Secured by Design Housing in West Yorkshire', Home Office Briefing Note 7/00, London: Home Office.

Armitage, R. and Everson, S. (2003) 'Building for Burglars?', *Crime Prevention and Community Safety: An International Journal*, 5(4), 15–25.

BBC News (2003) 'Operation Ore: Can the UK Cope?', online: http://news.bbc.co.uk/1/hi/uk/2652465.stm (accessed 6 December 2004).

Blair, I. (2004) 'Police, Lawyers and Public Service Reform', Lecture to Civitas, 2 February 2004, online: http://www.civitas.org.uk/pdf/SirIanBlair_Feb04.pdf (accessed 25 August 2004).

Budd, T. (2003) 'Alcohol-related Assault: Findings from the British Crime Survey', Home Office Online Report 35/03: http://www.homeoffice.gov.uk/rds/pdfs2/rdsolr3503.pdf (accessed 19 August 2004).

Bullock, K., Farrell, G. and Tilley, N. (2002) 'Funding and Implementing Crime Reduction Initiatives', RDS On-line Report 10/02: http://www.homeoffice.gov.uk/rds/pdfs2/rdsolr1002.pdf (accessed 24 August 2004).

Clancy, A., Hough, M., Aust, R. and Kershaw, C. (2001) 'Crime, Policing and Justice: the Experience of Ethnic Minorities Findings from the 2000 British Crime Survey', Home Office Research Study 223, London: Home Office.

Clarke, R. V. (1999) 'Hot Products: Understanding, Anticipating and Reducing Demand for Stolen Goods', Police Research Series Paper 112, London: Home Office.

Condon, J. and Smith, N. (2003) 'Prevalence of Drug Use: Key Findings from the 2002/2003 British Crime Survey', Home Office Research Findings 229, London: Home Office.

Corkery, J. M. (2002) 'Drug Seizure and Offender Statistics, United Kingdom, 2000', Home Office Statistical Bulletin 04/02, London: Home Office.

Crown Prosecution Service (2000) *The Code for Crown Prosecutors*, London: Crown Prosecution Service.

Deehan, A. (1999) 'Alcohol and Crime: Taking Stock', Policing and Reducing Crime Unit, Crime Reduction Research Series No. 3, London: Home Office.

Dennis, N., Erdos, G. and Robinson, D. (2003) *The Failure of Britain's Police: London and New York Compared*, London: Civitas.

Dodd, T., Povey, D. and Walker, A. (2004) 'Crime in England and Wales 2003/2004', Home Office Statistical Bulletin 10/04, London: Home Office.

Drake, L. and Simper, R. (2001) 'The Economic Modelling of Policing and the Measurement of Efficiency', Economic Research Paper No. 01/04, Department of Economics, University of Loughborough, February.

Everson, S. (2003) 'Repeat Victimisation and Prolific Offending: Chance or Choice?', *International Journal of Police Science and Management*, 5(3), 180–94.

Farrell, G., Edmunds, A; Hobbs, L. and Laycock, G. (2000) 'RV Snapshot 2000: UK Policing and Repeat Victimisation', Crime Reduction Research Series Paper 5, Policing and Reducing Crime Unit, London: Home Office.

Felson, M. and Clarke, R.V. (1998) 'Opportunity Makes the Thief', Crime Detection and Prevention Series, Paper 98, Police Research Group, London: Home Office.

FitzGerald, M. and Hough, M. (2002) 'Policing for London: key findings', online: http://www.kcl.ac.uk/depsta/law/research/icpr/publications/findings.pdf (accessed 3 September 2004).

Fox, C. (2002) 'Let us be crime-fighters, not box-tickers', *The Guardian*, 1 October 2002, online: http://society.guardian.co.uk/publicvoices/police/story/0,12473,802058,00.html (accessed 10 August 2004).

Gladwell, M. (2001) *The Tipping Point: How Little Things Can Make A Big Difference*, London: Abacus.

Hall, T. and Wright, S. (2003) 'Making it Count: A Practical Guide to Collecting and Managing Domestic Violence Data', Community Safety Practice Briefing, London: NACRO.

Hanmer, J. and Griffiths, S. (2000) 'Reducing Domestic Violence … What Works? Policing Domestic Violence', Policing and Reducing Crime Briefing Note, January 2000, Crime Reduction Research Series, London: Home Office.

HMIC (2004) 'Guns, Community and Police: HMIC Thematic Inspection into The Criminal Use of Firearms', London: HMIC.

Home Office (1983) 'Manpower, Effectiveness and Efficiency in the Police Service', Home Office Circular 114, London: Home Office.

Home Office (1993) 'Performance Indicators for the Police', Home Office Circular 17, London: Home Office.

Home Office (1997) 'Aspects of Crime: Drunkenness 1995. Development and Statistics Directorate', London: Home Office.

Home Office (2000) 'Multi-agency Guidance for Addressing Domestic Violence', Home Office Circular 19/2000 London: Home Office.

Home Office (2001) 'Policing a New Century: A Blueprint for Reform', Cm 5326, White Paper presented to Parliament, December 2001.

Home Office (2002) 'The National Policing Plan 2003–2006', London: Home Office.

Home Office (2004a) 'Recorded Crime Statistics 1898–2002/03' online: http://www.homeoffice.gov.uk/rds/pdfs/100years.xls and http://www.police999.com/ukinfo/figures01.html (accessed 18 August 2004).

Home Office (2004b) 'Alcohol Audits, Strategies and Initiatives: Lessons from Crime and Disorder Reduction Partnerships', Home Office Development and Practice Report 20, London: Home Office.

Hough, M. (2001) 'How Politics can Tip the Scales of Justice', *The Guardian*, 5 June 2001, online: http://society.guardian.co.uk/crimeandpunishment/story/0,8150,501820,00.html (accessed 26 August 2004).

Kelling, G. L. and Sousa, W. H. Jr (2001) 'Do Police Matter?: An Analysis of the Impact of New York City's Police Reforms', Civic Report No. 22, New York: Center for Civic Innovation, Manhattan Institute, December 2001.

Kock, E.; Kemp, T. and Rix, B. (1996) 'Disrupting the Distribution of Stolen Electrical Goods', Crime Detection and Prevention Series, Paper 69, Police Research Group, London: Home Office.

Macpherson, M. (1999) 'The Stephen Lawrence Inquiry', Cm 4261–1, London: The Stationery Office.

Man, L.-H., Best, D., Marshall, J., Godfrey, C. and Budd, T. (2002) 'Dealing with Alcohol-related Detainees in the Custody Suite', Home Office Research Findings 178, London: Home Office.

Manning, H. (1996) 'Alcohol and the Work of the Police', *Alcoholism*, The Medical Council on Alcoholism, 15(6), 1–2.

Mirrlees-Black, C. (1999) 'Domestic Violence: Findings from a New British Crime Survey Self-completion Questionnaire', Home Office Research Study 191, London: Home Office.

National Statistics (2003a) 'Percentage of Households with Durable Goods 1970 to 2001–2', online: www.statistics.gov.uk/STATBASE/Expodata/Spreadsheets/D6711.xls (accessed 6 December 2004).

National Statistics (2003b) 'Share of the Wealth: 1% of Population Owns 23% of Wealth', online: http://www.statistics.gov.uk/cci/nugget.asp?id=2 (accessed 18 August 2004).

National Statistics (2004a) 'A Summary of Changes Over Time: Housing Tenure' online: http://www.statistics.gov.uk/cci/nugget.asp?id=821 (accessed 18 August 2004).

National Statistics (2004b) 'Living in Britain 2002: Datasets: 4.17 Cars or vans: 1972 to 2002', online: http://www.statistics.gov.uk/STATBASE/Expodata/Spreadsheets/D8066.xls (accessed 18 August 2004).

ODPM and Home Office (2004) 'Safer Places: The Planning System and Crime Prevention', London: The Stationery Office.

Pascoe, T. (1999) *Evaluation of Secured by Design in Public Sector Housing*, Watford: Building Research Establishment.

Povey, D. (2004) 'Crime in England and Wales 2002/2003: Supplementary Volume 1: Homicide and Gun Crime', Home Office Statistical Bulletin 01/04, London: Home Office.

Richardson, A., Budd, T., Engineer, R., Phillips, A., Thompson, J. and Nicholls, J. (2003) 'Drinking, Crime and Disorder', Home Office Research Findings 185, London: Home Office.

Spottiswoode, C. (2000), *Improving Police Performance*, Public Services Productivity Panel, London: H.M. Treasury.

Stockdale, J. E., Whitehead, C. M. E. and Gresham, P. J. (1999) 'Applying Economic Evaluation to Policing Activity', Police Research Series Paper No. 103, Policing and Reducing Crime Unit, London: Home Office.

Taylor, I. (1997) 'The Political Economy of Crime', in M. Maguire, R. Morgan, and R. Reiner (eds), *The Oxford Handbook of Criminology* (2nd ed.) Oxford: Oxford University Press.

Walby, S. and Myhill, A. (2000) 'Reducing Domestic Violence … What Works? Assessing and Managing the Risk of Domestic Violence', Policing and Reducing Crime Briefing Note January 2000, Crime Reduction Research Series, London: Home Office.

Walker, C. (2004) 'The Concern for "Value for Money"', online: http://www.leeds.ac.uk/law/teaching/law6cw/police/pol-ho2.htm (accessed 24 August 2004).

West Yorkshire Police (1981–2002) Annual Reports, Wakefield: West Yorkshire Police.

Wilson, J. Q. and Kelling, G. (1982) 'Broken Windows', *The Atlantic Monthly*, March, 29–38.

6 The law and mental disorder: an uneasy relationship

Herschel Prins

Introduction

Understanding the law relating to mental health (or rather ill-health) in general, and mental disorder in offenders or potential offenders, is a complex and difficult task, often beset by ethical and definitional problems. This chapter provides a modest overview of some of these, and comments on the extent to which the law has a part to play in reducing the extent of known mental disorder in offenders. The chapter can be likened to a large-scale map in which broad outlines have to be supplemented by those provided by the more detailed scale of a map such as the Ordnance Survey. Detailed information concerning many of the issues explored in this chapter can be found in the references and, in particular, Prins (2005). The chapter is divided, somewhat arbitrarily, into the following sections. First, a brief account of recent mental health and allied legislation and, in particular, the provisions for offenders. Second, very brief reference is made to mental disorders and their somewhat equivocal relationship to crime, particularly violent crime. Third, a short account of the manner in which mental states may be put forward in total or partial exculpation of responsibility (capacity). Finally, some account is given of the provisions available for the diversion of mentally disordered offenders from the criminal justice and penal systems. It is true to say that the manner in which the 'law' deals with mentally disordered offenders is to be found in a mixture of statute, case law and administrative 'devices', for example as in the provision of diversion. My use of the term mental disorder also requires a comment; the use of the term has advantages and disadvantages. In legal terms it covers concisely those disorders identified in current mental health legislation (mainly through the provisions of the Mental Health Act 1983, as amended from time to time). These are identified as follows: mental illness, usually taken to mean severe, disabling illnesses such as the schizophrenias and the affective disorders (depressive illness and hypomania); mental impairment; severe mental impairment; and psychopathic disorder. However, experience suggests that there are a number of mental conditions that would not necessarily fulfil the criteria

for compulsory admission under the 1983 Act. Because of t
ably more satisfactory to use the term 'mental disturbance'.

A brief historical context

Fashions, both in mental health and in penal and criminal justice practice,
'come and go'. For example, Allderidge suggested some years ago that
there are cycles in the care of the insane (Allderidge 1979). Similar 'cycles'
occur in criminal justice and penal policy. In respect of the latter, it is salu-
tary to consider the vast amount of legislation that has been introduced in
the field of criminal justice in the last 15 years. As is well known, the main
thrust of this has been in the area of public protection fuelled by media
'hype' and the resulting somewhat 'knee-jerk' responses to this by politicians, most notably successive Home Secretaries. So prolific and complex
has been much of this legislation that even the most experienced sentencers
have been frequently perplexed when having to implement some of the
provisions. Without wishing to under-estimate the legitimacy of public
concern about the past and likely future behaviour of certain individuals
thought to be dangerous, it would appear that a degree of 'moral panic'
(Cohen 1972) has provided a source for political concern and subsequent
frenetic and ill-considered legislative activity that has been described as
'controlism'. Soothill and Walby (2001) have demonstrated the extent to
which newspaper reporting significantly affects public perception of, and
attitudes towards, deviant conduct. Politicians might do well to borrow
from the aphorism about marriage, and remember that if you legislate in
haste you may repent at leisure. In this context it would also be wise for
them to remember that recourse to the law is not always the best means of
alleviating or curing social ill (Prins 1995 and 1996). In the past 20 years
or so, such ills have been subjected to a plethora of inquiries, particularly
in the mental health field; see, for example, Peay (1996) and more recently
Stanley and Manthorpe (2004).

Recent mental health legislation

The manner in which social and criminal justice policy have been shaped
in the post-Second World War years is described critically by Fitzgibbon
(2004: 19). One of her key arguments is that 'society has lost sight of the
importance of justice and that vengeance and risk management have
subsumed such principles [and] are gaining momentum'. For additional
insights into the limitations of the law as it touches upon mental disorder
(disturbance) see Eastman and Peay (1999), notably Chapter 13.

The Mental Health Act 1959 swept away nearly one hundred years of
legislation which had been based upon an over-riding emphasis on
'legalism'. One of the most significant changes brought about by the 1959
Act was the introduction of Mental Health Review Tribunals (MHRTs) as

.e arbiters of the need, or otherwise, for continuing compulsory detention of certain defined classes of mentally disordered patients and offender-patients. Other major revisions were incorporated into the 1983 Act. These provided for the further protection of patients' rights through the mechanism of an enhanced and more speedy review of detention and the introduction of the Mental Health Act Commission (MHAC) – a quasi-inspectorial body charged with the investigation of patients' complaints and their need for, and consent to, certain forms of invasive treatment such as ECT (Electro-Convulsive Therapy), hormonal treatment and certain forms of brain surgery. From a forensic-psychiatric point of view, the 1983 Act also gave MHRTs wider powers to deal with offender-patients, notably powers to discharge such patients, either absolutely or condition-ally. Under the 1959 Act, tribunals could only recommend discharge to the Home Secretary. In the years following the 1983 Act, changes in emphasis concerning psychiatric care, largely a devolving of care from hospital to community, led a number of observers to suggest that the legislation was in need of yet further revision. (See, for example, Blom-Cooper *et al.* 1995.) In addition, the deviant, disturbed and very occasional homicidal behaviour of a small number of mentally ill patients aroused further polit-ical apprehensions and led to the setting up of a number of inquiries.

There exists a common misunderstanding that there has been a marked increase in the number of homicides committed by mentally ill individuals. In the UK, Taylor and Gunn (1999) have provided convincing evidence that this is not the case and more recent work by some researchers in New Zealand supports the UK evidence. The New Zealand researchers also examined homicide rates in other jurisdictions and found comparable statistics. The notion that deinstitutionalization has led to increased violent activity by mentally ill individuals is not proven (see Simpson *et al.* 2004). Coupled with these concerns were the activities of a very small number of individuals adjudged to be suffering from serious disorders of personality such as the recently coined disorder known as Dangerous Severe Personality Disorder – a name coined by politicians and not by clinicians. In view of all these concerns, the government also set up a number of bodies to review mental health provision more generally (that is, in addi-tion to the more specific inquiries into individual cases already referred to). The first of these was an Expert Committee given the task of undertaking a 'scoping review', chaired by a distinguished professor of law, Genevra Richardson. Sadly, the committee's remit and time-scale were rigorously and unhelpfully prescribed by ministerial directive so that their task was made very difficult. The committee presented its report in July 1999 (Department of Health 1999a). The government soon followed this with its own Consultation Document which, interestingly, departed quite signif-icantly from the Richardson review (Department of Health 1999b and Department of Health and Home Office 2000; for summaries, see also Prins 2001a and 2001b). One lawyer member of the Richardson review committee made clear her own dissatisfaction with the government's response, describing it as a 'squandered opportunity'. She stated:

> It remains a mystery as to whether the Green Paper misrepresents the Richardson Report, fails to understand it, or is rejecting it in the politest of civil service fashions. But despite the laudatory language, reject it it most certainly has.
>
> (Peay 2000: 15)

In July 1999 the government also launched its consultation document on its proposals for managing people with Dangerous Severe Personality Disorder (DSPD) (Home Office and Department of Health 1999). The launch of this somewhat controversial document took the form of a very large conference attended briefly by the secretaries of State for Health and the Home Office. (For some criticisms of the government's proposals, see Prins 1999). Subsequently, the Department of Health and the Home Office issued further consultation documents and in 2002 published its first Draft Mental Health Bill. Seldom can a proposed piece of legislation have had such extensive and detailed consultative antecedents; a veritable avalanche of paper! When the first Draft Bill appeared, it was met with almost universal criticism on the basis that it contained unworkable and, more importantly, unethical provisions. In a very comprehensive analysis of the Bill, Eldergill includes a statement that summarizes its worst elements:

> The draft legislation seems designed to sweep from the streets, or to supervise and control, anyone whose behaviour causes the public significant concern, but whose behaviour does not allow the police or the courts to place them in custody in the absence of any proof of serious offending. In many respects, it does not comply with the European Convention on Human Rights, or with the minimum international standards agreed by nations as being the baseline for countries that wish to be considered civilized in this respect.
>
> (Eldergill 2002: 359)

(See also Gunn and Holland 2002; Law Society 2002; and Zigmond 2002.)

Perhaps because of the initial highly critical and adverse reactions to the first Draft Bill – from lawyers, mental health professionals, user and civil liberties groups and others, progress on the Bill from 2000 onwards appeared to falter and its anticipated appearance in the Queen's Speeches of that year and 2003 did not materialize. However, in June 2004, the Secretary of State For Health announced that the first Draft Bill would be contained as an item in the Queen's Speech in November 2004 (*The Independent*, 16 June 2004: 2). A second Draft Bill has now appeared and its proposals are currently being scrutinized by a joint Parliamentary Committee of MPs and Peers. (For a summary of the revised proposals, see Department of Health 2004.)

Brief clinical aspects

It is the very error of the moon;
She comes more near the earth than she was wont,
And makes men mad

(Othello, V.ii).

O let me not be mad, not that sweet heaven;
Keep me in temper; I would not be mad!

(King Lear, I.iv).

Canst thou not minister to a mind diseas'd?

(Macbeth, V.iii)

The above quotations illustrate three important points. The first reminds us of the many myths that surround mental disorders; the second suggests the fear that such disorders engender, and the third is indicative of our endeavours to replace them with sanity in offenders and offender-patients. The myths and fears surrounding 'madness' (especially if madness is linked to 'badness') account for the many problems involved in dealing with offender-patients, whether they be in hospitals of varying degrees of security, in hostels (now called 'approved accommodation') or in the 'open' community. These are the individuals that the public regard as 'mad, bad and dangerous to know' (as Caroline Lamb wrote of Lord Byron in 1812). Limitations of space preclude any detailed discussion of the aetiology, classification and management of mental disorders (disturbances). (For a fuller discussion, see Prins 2005 and Taylor 2004.) However, it is important to provide a very short commentary on the relationship between mental disorders (disturbances) and crime.

We are faced with the difficult task of trying to establish any clear causal connections, or even associations, between mental disturbance and criminality. This is because we are trying to make connections between two very complex and different phenomena; and these phenomena are the subject of much continuing debate concerning both definition and substance. It is as though the 'goalposts' for the 'game' are constantly being shifted. Mental illness is an example of this phenomenon.

There are those who have suggested that some forms of mental illness do not even exist. A well-known proponent of this view is Professor Szasz who argues that persons are often diagnosed as mentally ill on the grounds that they merely have problems in living and that these problems may affront society. Society then turns to psychiatrists to remove them from public view and conscience (see, for example, Szasz 1987). The foregoing is a bald and simplistic view of Szasz's work, and, to be fair, he provides substantial rebuttals of his critics (see, for example, Szasz 1993). His arguments do have a kernel of truth in that he alerts us to the manner in which psychiatry may be abused. They have a certain attractive seductiveness, but they also contain a quality of rhetoric which has been criticized by both psychiatrists and non-psychiatrists (see, for example, Roth and Kroll 1986; Sedgwick 1982).

In the 1960s, there existed a popular view that much mental illness had its origins in 'conspiracies' and 'mixed messages' within families. This view is exemplified in the work of the late doctor Ronald Laing and his colleagues (see, for example, Laing and Esterston 1964). At the other end of the 'spectrum', we have the more biologically orientated view that found expression in some of the earlier textbooks of psychiatry. Gunn (1977: 317) once put the position into perspective very ably when he stated that:

> somewhere in the confusion there is a biological reality of mental disorder ... this reality is a complex mixture of diverse conditions, some organic, some functional, some inherited, some learned, some acquired, some curable, others unremitting.

It is difficult to provide precise figures for the numbers of people suffering from mental disorders. In the government publication 'Modernising Mental Health Services' (Department of Health 1998), it is suggested that depression in one form or another will affect nearly half of all women and a quarter of all men in the UK before the age of 70. It quotes from a major survey published in 1995 which showed that

> one in six adults aged 16–64 had suffered from some type of mental health problem in the week prior to being interviewed, the most common being "neurotic" conditions like anxiety and depression; and a very small proportion of the population – less than 1 per cent – had a more severe and complex psychotic mental illness, such as schizophrenia.
>
> (Department of Health 1998: paras 1.2–1.4)

However, such statistics can provide only a very rough indicator of the mental health of a nation. This is because there are likely to be not inconsiderable numbers of individuals suffering from a degree of mental disturbance/distress who do not present for treatment at either their general practitioner (the most likely 'first port of call') or at a hospital (unless acutely mentally unwell, suicidal, etc.). We do know that the cost of mental disorders, both in terms of distress to the sufferers and their families, is very considerable. These predicaments are well described by Jeremy Laurance, Health Editor of *The Independent*, in his recent book on the mental health system (Laurance 2003). Many such disorders are 'hidden' from view and the available figures only represent the 'tip' of the 'iceberg'.

When we come to consider criminal behaviour we are faced with problems similar to those outlined above. At its simplest, crime is merely that form of behaviour defined by society as illegal and punishable by the criminal law. At various times in our history, acts once judged as criminal have been re-defined, or even removed from the statute books – as, for example, in the case of attempted suicide and adult (now near adult) male consenting homosexual acts committed in private. New offences are also created, particularly in time of war or civil commotion. Moreover, our increasingly complex technological society has required the introduction of a wide range of laws and regulations governing many aspects of our conduct. Since much criminal behaviour is somewhat arbitrarily defined, and there are arguments about the existence and definitions of mental disturbances, it is hardly surprising that we find difficulty in trying to establish the connections between these two somewhat ill-defined and complex behaviours. Be this as it may, there are occasions when some mental disturbances do seem to be closely associated with criminal conduct (particularly violent conduct), and aspects of this connection are now considered briefly.

Mental disturbances (disorders) have been classified in a variety of ways. The two most widely acknowledged classification systems – particularly for purposes of cross-cultural research – are the *Diagnostic and Statistical Manual of Mental Disorders*, published by the American Psychiatric Association (APA 2000) and the *ICD-10-International Classification of Mental and Behavioural Disorders*, published by the World Health Organisation (WHO 1992). These substantial texts cover every aspect of diagnosis and classification. Readers should also consult one or other of the standard textbooks of psychiatry, such as *The New Oxford Textbook of Psychiatry* (Gelder *et al.* 2000). A much-simplified classification of mental disorders includes the following: functional psychoses such as affective disorders and schizophrenic illnesses; neuroses including mild depression, anxiety, hysteria and obsessive–compulsive states; mental disturbance caused by ageing, such as the dementias; abnormalities of personality such as psychopathic disorders; substance abuse; and mental impairment (learning disability. It is important to note that some of these disorders may overlap – necessitating a dual diagnosis – as, for example, in the case of someone with a psychopathic disorder who may also suffer from depression.

Generally speaking, mental disorders are not associated with criminality to any great degree (see Prins 2005 for a full discussion). But there is some evidence to suggest that early intervention by general psychiatric services may help to avert breakdown resulting in offence behaviour (see Hodgins and Muller-Isberner 2004). The most significant association is that between severe personality disorder (in legal terms, psychopathic disorder in England and Wales) and crime. For over 200 years debates have continued over its aetiology, terminology and management. Suffice to say that those showing the disorder create well-nigh intractable problems of management. The recent government proposals for those at the more severe end of the spectrum (notably DSPD – see above) seem to be based upon a degree of treatment optimism not espoused with much enthusiasm by those charged with providing it (see also Prins 1999).

By way of general illustrations, I now describe briefly two major mental illnesses that exemplify the manner in which these can sometimes be associated with crime. The first is schizophrenic illness. (It is best to consider the term 'schizophrenia' as covering a group of illnesses rather than a single illness entity.) The key features of such illnesses are characterized to varying degree by a breakdown in personal and social functioning, sometimes accompanied by motor dysfunction and delusions and hallucinations. In recent years, evidence has been accumulating from a wide range of studies which suggests a real if somewhat small relationship between serious violence and some forms of schizophrenic illness, notably of the paranoid variety. In forensic-psychiatric terms, active delusions seem to be powerful factors in relation to violence when the individual perceives some threat, where there is a lessening of mechanisms of self-control and dominance of the individual's mind by perceived forces that seem to be beyond their control. It is important to emphasize that such disorders of thinking and behaviour are exacerbated by recent and current abuse of alcohol and other drugs; and by social disadvantage such as homelessness. It has also been noted that such patients, on first-time admissions to psychiatric hospitals and units, have sometimes engaged in personal violence during the period leading up to admission (see Hodgins and Isberner 2004, and Simpson *et al.* 2004).

Paranoid disorders and 'dangerous obsessions'

As already stated, one of the key characteristics of those suffering from one or other of the various types of paranoid illness is their systematized delusional beliefs (and sometimes hallucinatory experiences). These may, for example, take the form of an irrational and unshakeable belief that they are being persecuted by others, or that they need to be the persecutor. There are two cardinal points of importance that should be noted by all who have to deal with such individuals. First, they may begin to develop certain oddnesses of behaviour for some time before the disorder emerges in an acute or very obvious form. Sensitive and perceptive observation and possible intervention may, in some cases, help to prevent a tragedy. Second, persons developing paranoid beliefs may do so in a tightly contained form. Thus, a seriously paranoid person can appear perfectly sane and in command of him/herself in all other respects. The illness may be so well encapsulated that an unwary or less than skilled observer may be very easily misled. It is only when the matters which the delusional system has fastened on are broached that the severity of the disorder is revealed. The phenomenon may also be seen in so-called 'stalking' situations. (For a full discussion, see Prins 2005.)

Affective disorders and serious crime

Affective disorders are characterized by mood changes, in some cases, either abnormally low or abnormally high; these consist of serious depression on the one hand and mania or hypomania on the other.

Depression

From time to time, cases occur in which an individual charged with a serious crime, such as homicide, is found to have been suffering from a major depressive disorder at the time of the offence. West, in his classic study of cases of murder followed by suicide, sums up the picture as follows:

> [sufferers may] become so convinced of the helplessness of their misery that death becomes a happy escape. Sometimes, before committing suicide, they first kill their children and other members of the family … Under the delusion of a future without hope and the inevitability of catastrophe overtaking their nearest and dearest as well as themselves, they decide to kill in order to spare their loved ones suffering.
>
> (West 1965: 6)

Manic disorder

The cardinal features of mania (or hypomania) are the very opposite of those seen in depressive illness. Activities are speeded up, the sufferer becomes over-excited, demonstrates a euphoric mood, has grandiose but wholly unrealistic plans for the future, is irritable and disinhibited, does not eat or sleep (because they are too 'busy' to do so) and will brook no interference in their activities. It is the combination of disinhibition and inability to brook interference with their complete lack of insight that makes such individuals potentially highly dangerous. They require compulsory admission to hospital.

Responsibility before the law

Disputes between the disciplines of law, psychiatry and psychology are not uncommon in cases where there is a 'mental defence' to a criminal act. When we speak or write about responsibility for crime we mean the capacity to form a criminal intention and to have a guilty mind (*mens rea*, in legal terms). The word 'responsibility' has somewhat pejorative overtones so that, in my view, capacity is a better word to use. In general, men and women are held to be 'responsible' (i.e. have the capacity to be accountable) for their criminal acts. However, one legal pathway to erosion of capacity is the age of the offender. In England and Wales, children under the age of ten are not held to be responsible for their criminal acts. In many other jurisdictions – for example in the rest of Europe,

Scandinavia and the North Americas – the age is set considerably higher; in some instances as high as 15 or 16. Apart from the issue of the age of the offender, there are three other ways in which capacity for crime can be eroded, either totally or partially. The first of these is a finding of 'not guilty by reason of insanity' (NGRI). The criteria for establishing an insanity defence are very narrow and were founded at a time (in the 1800s) when the disciplines of psychiatry and psychology were in their infancy. The introduction of the Homicide Act 1957 and the later abolition of the death penalty have reduced its use considerably. (For a detailed discussion of *Hadfield's* and *McNaghten's cases*, on which NGRI was founded, see Reznek 1997; Mackay 1995; and Prins 2005.)

The second means by which total exemption from responsibility may be claimed is by a finding of what used to be called 'unfitness to plead', but now known as being 'under disability in relation to the trial'. In brief, this defence involves acceptance by the court of the following criteria: (1) the defendant is so mentally unwell at the time of the trial as not to be able to understand the trial process; (2) is unable to instruct counsel for their defence; (3) is unable to exercise their right to challenge a juror. The acceptance of these criteria will rely on expert medical testimony and, if accepted by the court, the accused will be entitled to what is called the 'special verdict' (as in the case of the insanity defence). Prior to the implementation of the Criminal Procedure (Insanity and Unfitness to Plead) Act 1991, such a finding would usually involve indefinite detention under the Mental Health Act, normally in a high-security hospital. With the introduction of the 1991 Act, the disposal is now more flexible and may involve hospitalization under the Mental Health Act (with or without restrictions on discharge); placement under a guardianship order; placement under supervision by a social worker or probation officer for a maximum period of two years (with or without psychiatric supervision); or being discharged absolutely.

Third is the defence of 'diminished responsibility'. Following the Report of the Royal Commission on Capital Punishment (1953), the concept of diminished responsibility in relation to a charge of murder was introduced in England and Wales by the Homicide Act 1957. A defence of diminished responsibility can only be put forward in murder cases. Basically, if the defence is successful, the charge of murder will be reduced to that of manslaughter, allowing judicial discretion in sentencing. However, establishing a defence of diminished responsibility is not always easy and often demonstrates the problematic relationship between psychiatry and the law. In the first place, the terms used in section 2 of the Act have caused endless debate. Partial exculpation of responsibility rests upon the court accepting that an 'abnormality of mind' (as defined in section 2 of the Act) exists to such a degree as 'substantially impairs' the defendant's responsibility for their acts. What constitutes a significant degree of abnormality of mind and the meaning of substantial have been hotly debated. A classic example is the case of Peter Sutcliffe – the so-called 'Yorkshire Ripper'. The jury did not consider that Sutcliffe's particular form of paranoid schizophrenia (as unanimously diagnosed by several very experienced forensic psychiatrists) constituted a sufficient degree of abnormality of mind within the meaning of the Act. He was therefore convicted of murder and given 13 mandatory sentences of life imprisonment, with a recommendation from Mr Justice Boreham that he serve a minimum of 30 years. However, subsequent events appear to have vindicated the views of the psychiatrists at his trial; his mental state deteriorated in prison. Some two years after being sentenced, the Home Secretary, acting on further psychiatric assessment, ordered his transfer to Broadmoor High Security Hospital under the terms of the Mental Health Act 1983. Sutcliffe's case and a number of others (for example that of Denis Nilsen – see Prins 2005) demonstrate the problems when law and psychiatry confront each other in courts of law. Law requires 'black and white' answers; psychiatry and psychology deal in grey areas of human conduct. In the light of these problems, it is agreed by all those involved in the system (judges, prosecution and defence lawyers, psychiatrists and others) that most of these problems would be avoided if we abandoned the mandatory sentence of life imprisonment for murder and allowed the judge discretion in sentencing; a discretion that would depend upon the circumstances in each case. To date, no Home Secretary has been willing to act on such a proposal.

Summary of disposals

Mental health and allied legislation currently provides powers for courts to remand to prison, hospital or on bail for reports to be prepared into an accused's mental state. A recent development has been the requirement to provide a psychiatric report when a longer than commensurate (extended) sentence or discretionary life sentence are being considered. (See O'Grady 2004 for discussion of some of the ethical implications involved for psychiatrists.) Upon conviction (or in some cases without proceeding to conviction) courts may make hospital or guardianship orders under the Mental Health Act 1983. If a crown court decides that there would be a risk of serious harm to others, it may add a restriction order to a hospital order. Such an order places considerable restrictions upon the medical authorities' powers to transfer or discharge the patient. Such offender-patients may apply for discharge to a Mental Health Review Tribunal if the Home Secretary (who has central government control over patients subject to restriction orders) refuses discharge. Rates of Tribunal and Home Office discharges are very low, reflecting the cautionary approaches taken by these bodies when dealing with high-risk cases (Prins 2005). Finally, it should be noted that a number of current provisions are likely to be subjected to major modifications if the powers proposed in the second Draft Mental Health Bill become law (Department of Health 2004: Chapter 6).

Earlier in this chapter I tried to demonstrate the manner in which, within certain clearly defined statutory frameworks, offenders may be deflected from the criminal justice and penal systems. I now complete the picture by considering some other means available to keep offenders out of the system altogether – namely the practice of diversion as a function of executive discretion as distinct from provision in statute.

Mentally disturbed offenders in the prison population

As long ago as 1991, the Home Office and Department of Health stated that in the UK:

> Although the actual number of prisoners requiring psychiatric services is not known, research has shown that the prison population has a high psychiatric morbidity ... It is estimated that 2–3 per cent of sentenced prisoners at any one time are likely to be suffering from a psychotic illness, and it is likely that the proportion is even higher in the remand population. Histories of alcohol and drug misuse are very common, as is neurotic illness.
>
> (Home Office and Department of Health 1991: Annex C)

Although the above extract provides an overall picture, more detailed recent studies of penal populations add to our knowledge. It would appear that about one third of the prison population requires some kind of psychiatric intervention, and that in remand populations this number is likely to be higher. Numerous studies have been made of both remand and sentenced prisoners. For example, Gunn *et al.* (1991) examined a series of sentenced prisoners in England and Wales. They contended, by extrapolation from their sample, that: 'The sentenced population included over 700 men with psychosis and [that] around 1,100 would warrant transfer to hospital for psychiatric treatment' (Gunn *et al.* 1991: 338).

Studies of remand prisoners tend to give even higher rates of psychiatric morbidity. More worrying is the evidence that suggests that psychiatric morbidity may be missed because of poor prison screening devices. Gavin et al. (2003) suggest that some 75 per cent of major mental illnesses in men and 66 per cent in women may be missed in this way. These authors reviewed screening processes in a local north of England prison taking male sentenced and remand prisoners, and they concluded that the numbers of new receptions screening positive for mental illness, and those in fact suffering from serious mental illnesses, were both in the range predicted from their earlier research, and in line with prevalence rates described in large scale remand prison surveys (see, for example, Singleton *et al.* 1998). Based on an admittedly small sample (616 new receptions over a 15-week period), Gavin *et al.* (2003: 253) suggest that 'it does not appear that large demands will be placed upon psychiatric resources if the proposed new reception health screening processes were in place, although a reorganization of the way in which services are delivered will almost certainly be required'. (See also Duffy *et al.* 2003; and Birmingham 2004.)

This question of reorganization is of vital importance. As things stand at present, prisoners cannot be afforded the application of compulsory powers for treatment under current mental health legislation because prison hospitals are not deemed to be hospitals within the terms of the 1983 Mental Health Act; the only exceptions being the need for urgent treatment without consent under the common law. However, the consultation document issued with the first draft Mental Health Bill proposed the possibility of compulsory treatment powers being available to prisoners who might have merited compulsory treatment in the community. There are some who consider that designating such health-care facilities as hospitals within the meaning of the Act would solve a number of problems, particularly in relation to suicidal behaviour (see, for example, Tumim 1990; and Towl *et al.* 2000). This may seem an attractive solution, but perhaps some caution should be espoused. If prison hospitals were to be designated as hospitals within the meaning of the Mental Health Act 1983, it might mean that unless rigorous safeguards were introduced they could become the 'dumping grounds' of the 'not nice' patients the NHS seems reluctant to take. A recent satisfactory answer has been the 'policy shift towards formal partnership between the NHS and the Prison Service for the provision of health care as a whole. This partnership is now set to evolve into the wholesale transfer of prison health care into the NHS over the next five years' (Kinton 2002: 305). Additionally, the provision of 'in-reach teams' in prisons by about 2006 should also help to alleviate problems caused by inappropriate detention (Kinton, 2002).

Some further words of caution are also necessary concerning the tendency to accept too readily the notion that those mentally disturbed offenders detained in prison are there because if they were not, they would be in hospital. For many years the view put forward by the distinguished geneticist, the late Sir Lionel Penrose (1939), that there was an inverse relationship between prison and mental hospital populations had held considerable sway. In 1939 he published his well-known study which became known in criminological circles as 'Penrose's law', namely that, as the prison population rose, mental hospital populations declined and *vice versa*. Bowden (1993), in a critical study of this so-called 'law', stated that:

> The suggestion appears to have been that there was a relatively stable mass of individuals who were in one form of environment, asylums, rather than another, prison. The two were used interchangeably. The benefit of the asylum was its effect on reducing crime.
>
> (Bowden 1993: 81)

Careful examination of remand and sentenced penal populations has revealed that such a state of affairs is not as clear-cut as Penrose and some later writers have suggested. Further support for such criticism comes from Fowles, who made a meticulous study of prison and mental hospital populations over a 25-year period. He suggested that:

> The mental hospitals have been run down but the full-blooded closure programme is still in its relatively early stages and its effects will not be felt for some time to come. Those remaining in the mental hospitals are unlikely to be of the age and sex normally associated with crime. [Moreover,] it is not possible to obtain comparable age distributions for prison populations and hospital residents.
>
> (Fowles 1993: 71–2)

Fowles goes on to suggest another complicating factor, namely:

> that former patients who are discharged from long-stay mental hospitals may be defined officially as living in the community but that may only mean that they are in the wards of a privately owned nursing home. The 'community' means any hospital/home not owned by the NHS.
>
> (Fowles 1993: 71–2)

Such criticisms of hypotheses that may have been all too readily accepted in the past indicate that the relationship between criminality and mental disturbance is much more complicated than would appear at first sight. The somewhat simplistic thinking of the kind briefly alluded to above has very important implications for the provision of both prison and health care services and the best use of the law and resources for their maintenance. Unless the proposed 'takeover' by the NHS of prison health care is well resourced, prisoners will receive no better service than they are receiving already.

Even if we adopt a somewhat cautious approach to the estimates of the numbers of mentally disturbed persons held in penal establishments at various stages of their careers, and accept the caveats entered by Fowles and Bowden, we are still compelled to acknowledge that a sizeable proportion of them should not be there. Moreover, we are also forced to conclude that not only should they not be in prison, but that perhaps they should not have entered the criminal justice system in the first place. As long ago as 1975, the Butler Committee recommended that mentally disturbed offenders might be dealt with other than through the courts:

> Where any apparent offender is clearly in need of psychiatric treatment and there is no risk to members of the public the question should always be asked whether any useful purpose would be served by

prosecution ... these remarks apply in cases of homicide or attempted homicide or grave bodily harm as in less serious cases.

(Home Office and DHSS 1975: 266)

Some 15 years later, the Home Office, in its now well-known circular No. 66/90 (Home Office MNP/90/1/55/8: para. 2), reiterated this view as follows:

> *It is government policy* that, wherever possible, mentally disordered persons should receive care and treatment from the health and social services. Where there is sufficient evidence, in accordance with the principles of the *Code for Crown Prosecutors*, to show that a mentally disordered person has committed an offence, careful consideration should be given to whether prosecution is required by the public interest. [emphasis added.]

The circular went on to provide very detailed advice to all those agencies likely to be involved in dealing with mentally disturbed offenders (for example, the police, Crown Prosecution Service, probation, social services, courts, health authorities and prison health care service). The emphasis on inter-agency co-operation has continued to be a central theme in all mental health policy making. Concern about the most appropriate action to be taken in respect of mentally disturbed offenders is, of course, not new. (See Prins 2005 for some early examples.)

The practice of diversion involves the exercise of discretion at various stages of the criminal justice process; discretion has a long, if somewhat obscure, history. Hetherington (1989) traces its origins to the reign of Henry VIII. However, it was not until the latter part of the nineteenth century that the office of Director of Public Prosecutions was introduced. Currently, the decision to prosecute rests with the Crown Prosecution Service, which is guided by a *Code for Crown Prosecutors* within which the prosecutor has to have regard for the need for prosecution in 'the public interest'. A number of factors govern this latter consideration, such as likely penalty, staleness (that is, the offence was committed so long ago that its prosecution would be of questionable merit), youth, old age and infirmity, complainant's attitude, and mental illness or stress. On this last aspect the Code states:

> Whenever the Crown prosecutor is provided with a medical report to the effect that an accused or a person under investigation is suffering from some form of psychiatric illness ... and the strain of criminal proceedings may lead to a considerable worsening of his condition, such a report should receive anxious consideration. This is a difficult field because, in some instances, the accused may have become mentally disturbed or depressed by the mere fact that his misconduct has been discovered and the crown prosecutor may be dubious about

a prognosis that criminal proceedings will adversely affect his condition to a significant extent. Where, however, the Crown prosecutor is satisfied that the probable effect upon the defendant's mental health outweighs the interests of justice in that particular case, he should not hesitate to discontinue proceedings. An independent medical examination may be sought, but should generally be reserved for cases of such gravity as plainly require prosecution but for clear evidence that such a course would be likely to result in a permanent worsening of the accused's condition.

(Crown Prosecution Service undated: 4)

A number of questions arise from this statement.

What variations are there in practice in making decisions whether not to prosecute, or to discontinue prosecution once it is underway within the terms of the general power to withdraw or to offer no evidence through section 23 of the Prosecution of Offences Act 1985? In 1991, Grounds (1991: 40) indicated that: 'There is a large gap in research knowledge in this area. Little is known about what happens to mentally disordered offenders *who do not enter criminal proceedings* and these gaps need to be filled if a complete picture is to be obtained' [emphasis added]. He continued: 'Such research might also indicate whether more mentally disordered offenders could, or should, be diverted away from criminal proceedings' (Grounds 1991: 40). Since the time Grounds called for such research, some headway has been made. For example, Rowlands *et al.* (1996) indicated in a follow-up study that a number of individuals subjected to the diversionary process and, in particular, those with substance abuse problems were lost to the psychiatric services; and on a follow-up after one year, 17 per cent had re-offended. They called for further long-term research. Shaw *et al.* (2001) reported that on a two-year follow-up period one third of those diverted to in-patient services had lost contact at twelve months; for those diverted to out-patient and community services about one third had also lost contact. They recommended better 'out-reach' assertive services.

Geelan *et al.* (2001) report more positive results. They suggest that 'if *appropriately* assessed in court, and *appropriate* hospital placements are arranged, successful outcome can be achieved for the majority of people diverted from custody to hospital in terms of improved mental states and a planned discharge' (Geelan *et al.* 2001: 127 [emphasis added]). From examination of these and earlier studies (for example, James and Hamilton 1991; Joseph 1992; and Joseph and Potter 1993), it would appear that success is heavily dependent upon detailed professional assessment and good communication within the system (that is, between the various professionals involved, magistrates, police, psychiatric, social and probation services. (See also Exworthy and Parrott 1993 and 1997; and Vaughan 2004.) Most studies have concentrated on male offenders and reports on diversion for females are somewhat sparse. However, Parsons *et al.* (2001) carried out a major survey of the prevalence of mental disorder in female remand prisons and found high rates of psychiatric morbidity, and that existing screening on reception (in prison) did not identify the majority of cases of mental disorder.

A statutory diversionary measure was originally contained in section 136 of the Mental Health Act 1959 and re-enacted with the same section number in the Act of 1983. This provides a constable with a power to remove to a place of safety a person found in a place to which the public have access, who appears to be suffering from mental disorder within the meaning of the Act and appears to be in immediate need of care, protection or control. (It should be noted that the Act specifies 'to which the public have access'. The provision is frequently misquoted, describing it as 'a public place'; the correct definition allows a much wider interpretation of the location.) The person may be detained for a maximum of 72 hours for the purposes of being examined by authorized mental health professionals. Such examination may or may not lead to admission to hospital, either informally, or under the compulsory powers of the Act. The section has certain merits, but it also has some accompanying disadvantages. All too often, a police station is used as a place of safety and police stations are clearly not the best places for detaining the mentally distressed. Although the police are not always certain of their powers, research seems to indicate that they are reasonably competent at recognizing a florid psychosis when they see one. However, there are often delays in the arrival of the relevant professionals (for example approved doctor and approved social worker) and communication between the parties is not always good.

Past research has indicated that the implementation of the provision afforded by section 136 is not uniform country-wide (NACRO 1993; more recent research is summarized in some detail by Laing 1999, notably Chapter 3). Diversion may also take place at the point of arrest. Riordan *et al.* (2000: 683) showed that intervention at the point of arrest had been successful in preventing some mentally disordered individuals being 'inappropriately taken into custody *and had fostered lasting and productive links between psychiatric services, the police and other agencies*' [emphasis added]. (See also Riordan *et al.* 2003.)

How much notice should be taken of an accused's view of his or her right to prosecution? Would some mentally disordered offenders prefer to be prosecuted in the normal way? This is of vital importance since the iatrogenic consequences of psychiatric disposal may be considerable. As already noted, until the introduction of the Criminal Procedure (Insanity and Unfitness to Plead) Act 1991, a successful defence of insanity or unfitness to plead would involve immediate hospitalization – sometimes with a restriction order and a comparatively rare chance of the facts of the case being explored and determined. Sometimes hospitalization under the Mental Health Act 1983 for offences may well result in a much longer spell of incarceration than if the defendant had been dealt with by way of imprisonment.

Given the current state of psychiatric services (and in particular general psychiatric services), is it certain that a psychiatric disposal will necessarily offer the best solution? This applies with considerable force to the personality disordered and (in legal terms) to 'psychopathic offenders'. Hospitals and psychiatrists seem increasingly reluctant to accept such persons and in particular to accept those categorized as suffering from dangerous severe personality disorder (DSPD). (See Prins 2002 and 2005; and Birmingham 2004.)

I have already noted how prisoners, particularly those on remand, may have varying degrees of mental disturbance which are not spotted by prison staff. For example, the depressed prisoner may be difficult to pick out in an already overcrowded remand prison; moreover, depression is an illness often unrecognized by the unwary and often contributes to suicides and suicidal gestures (see Towl *et al.* 2000). Some prisoners may conceal the fact that they have a serious mental health problem as, for example, in the case of the highly encapsulated delusional system of the morbidly jealous or psychotically deluded individual. Coid, in a study published in 1991, found a small number of inmates whose psychotic delusions appeared to be quite unknown to the prison staff.

An important jurisprudential question requires consideration. To what extent should offenders, even though mentally disturbed, be held responsible for their actions? We might exclude the floridly psychotic at the time of the offence and perhaps some of the seriously mentally impaired. How far down the line of what some have termed the 'psychiatrisation' of delinquency should we go? Such a practice tends to make the prison system the dumping ground for 'badness'; it also enables professionals to use prisons for the projection of their own 'badness', and it continues to negate rehabilitative measures within them. The disadvantages of non-prosecution have also been alluded to by some forensic psychiatrists. For example, Smith and Donovan suggest that:

> Excusing offending may not always be in the patient's interests. The formal legal process can be a valuable exercise in reality testing. The patient [in this instance they are writing about offences committed by psychiatric in-patients] ... can measure his or her own perceptions of his or her own behaviour against those of society. This can be a useful preparation for life outside hospital. The knowledge that prosecution is routine rather than exceptional, may deter further assaults and help aggressive patients to accept responsibility for their behaviour. Sometimes encouraging such patients to accept responsibility can be clinically beneficial and help to instil a sense of justice in other patients on a ward.
>
> (Smith and Donovan 1990: 380)

They also state that non-prosecution 'can reinforce the patient's belief that he or she need not control his or her behaviour. It may also leave staff feeling unsupported and there may be similar consequences if the court imposes a minimal penalty' (Smith and Donovan 1990: 381). For example, it is possible that had Christopher Clunis's offence behaviour been dealt with by a hospital order with restrictions, it would have been possible to exert more adequate control over his whereabouts and to have avoided the situation where he was able to disappear from view with, as we now know, lethal results (Ritchie *et al.* 1994).

In deciding upon diversion or discontinuance, how much consideration should be given to the views of victims? This is a delicate and difficult matter with considerable ethical implications. It needs to be seen against the climate of increasing attempts to allow victims more 'say' in what should happen to offenders and the establishment of opportunities for some offenders and victims to enter into 'dialogue'. It is an aspect of 'restorative' justice in which offenders witness at first hand the damage they have caused (*The Independent*, 23 July 2003: 9). In the past, such schemes have been limited to younger offenders, but they are now being extended to adults. Such participation has much to commend it, but the role of victims and the extent to which they actually participate in criminal justice and forensic-psychiatric decision-making processes requires very careful consideration. There is a fine dividing line between what may be quite appropriate involvement and undue influence being exerted by those who have been the victims, or who are a victim's family members. It should be remembered that our long established system of law-making and the delivery of justice have their roots in the avoidance of possible personal vengeance.

Can we identify more clearly those aspects of law and practice that tend to militate against the effective use of diversion? There is anecdotal evidence to suggest that agencies tend to disclaim responsibility (notably financial) for the individual. For example, the sad saga of patchy development of medium and low secure accommodation attests to the importance of trying to ensure that funds are 'ring-fenced' (Department of Health and Home Office 1992). At a more personal level, professionals are often reluctant to see a problem from a colleague's point of view. This is not necessarily deliberate obfuscation or intransigence on their part, but is a product of differences in role perceptions amongst professionals trained in different ways. Far more needs to be done to address relationship problems of this kind and forensic-psychiatric or criminology centres could play a significant role in this (see Riordan *et al.* 2003). In the midst of inter-professional squabbles, the offender/patient suffers and the more inadequate of them continue to play their 'stage army' parts in the criminal justice and health care arenas; parts so well described by Rollin as long ago as 1969 (Rollin 1969). The homeless, ethnic minority groups, particularly African–Caribbean populations, fare particularly badly in this respect. The mentally handicapped are another sad illustration – a truly vulnerable group whom nobody really wishes to own. As a result, they may find themselves with increasing frequency back within the criminal justice system – a phenomenon that the Mental Deficiency Act 1913 was designed specifically to prevent.

In an excellent review of ten years' published and unpublished contributions on diversion, James concluded that:

> Court diversion can be highly effective in the identification and acceleration into a hospital of mentally disordered offenders ... However, most court diversion services are currently inadequately planned, organized or resourced and are therefore of limited effect ... a central strategy is required, and properly designed and adequately supported court services should be incorporated into, and understood to be a core part of mainstream psychiatric provision. [He goes on to suggest that] without such action, the future of court diversion lies in doubt.
>
> (James 1999: 507)

(See also Birmingham 2004.)

Two further specific problems can be identified; a reluctance on the part of courts to grant bail in some suitable cases (Hucklesby 1997) and a problem in obtaining reports from increasingly busy general psychiatrists. Vaughan *et al.* (2003) suggest that more use could be made of a wider range of mental health professionals in the penal and community systems for obtaining information that would assist the courts in making mental health disposals (see also Vaughan 2004).

In summary, diversionary practice may be set out somewhat crudely in the following five stages:

Stage 1   Informal diversion by the police.
Stage 2   By statute; implementation of section 136 of the Mental
          Health Act 1983.
Stage 3   Referral for psychiatric examination before court hearing
          and discontinuance of prosecution at any stage thereafter.
Stage 4   Disposal through mental health services at court or after
          sentence.
Stage 5   Disposal through these services at a later stage in sentence
          – for example, transfer under the Mental Health Act from
          prison to hospital.

Note: These stages have been set out in a somewhat over-simplified fashion; they may, of course, overlap.
Finally, the effectiveness of diversion will be limited unless the following factors are taken into account:

- Placing current interest and activity concerning diversionary activities within the historical context of the development of services for mentally disordered offenders.
- Recognizing that collaboration, co-operation and effective team-work are much harder to achieve than has been thought to be the case hitherto.
- Recognizing that these fundamental difficulties may make their appearance in disguised form, for example through the guise of financial constraints and limitations.
- Recognizing the possibility that for a few offenders, diversion to the health care system in an under-funded and under-resourced state may be in some cases a less satisfactory option than entry into the criminal justice system.
- Recognizing that, despite some current useful research, we still lack adequate information about the long-term effectiveness of diversion on those diverted.
- Recognizing that it is all too easy to assume that offenders wish to be diverted and that, for some, diversion may reduce their sense of personal responsibility to adverse effect.
- Recognizing that diversion may deflect attention from the lack of medical and psychiatric facilities within penal establishments. However, the changes being implemented in prison health provision may help to remedy this.

Concluding comments

The relationship between mental disorders, criminality and the law is complex. In addition, both mental disorders and serious criminality tend to arouse powerful emotions, particularly those of fear. Such fear is exacerbated by the media, and 'moral panics' (Cohen 1972) are common and unhelpful phenomena. To all of this we must add political sensitivities; these often result in over-speedy recourse to inadequately thought through legislation. Such legislation produces difficulties for all those who have to implement it; and this in turn may lead to their best efforts being disparaged by the general public. Both mental disorders and crime require calm approaches; today, sad to relate, these are not always in evidence. There is, therefore, a very real need for all involved to confront their own 'demons'. Only by confronting them will some of the problems involved in the inter face between mental disorders and the criminal justice and penal systems become capable of resolution.

Bibliography

Alderidge, P. (1979) 'Hospitals, Madhouses and Asylums: Cycles in the Care of the Insane', *British Journal of Psychiatry*, 134, 321–4.
American Psychiatric Association (APA) (2000) *Diagnostic and Statistical Manual of Mental Disorders*, DSMIV(R) Text Revision (4th ed.), Washington DC: APA.

Birmingham, L. (2004) 'Mental Disorder and Prisons', *Psychiatric Bulletin*, 28, 39–7.

Blom-Cooper, Q.C., Sir L., Hally, H. and Murphy, E. (1995) *The Falling shadow: One Patient's Mental Health Care, 1978–1993*, London: Duckworth.

Bowden, P. (1993) 'New Directions in Service Provision', in W. Watson and A. Grounds (eds), *The Mentally Disordered Offender in an Era of Community Care*, Cambridge: Cambridge University Press.

Cohen, S. (1972) *Folk Devils and Moral Panics*, London: McGibbon and Key.

Coid, J. (1991) 'Psychiatric Profiles of Difficult Disruptive Prisoners', in K. Bottomley and W. Hay (eds), *Special Units For Difficult Prisoners*, Hull: Centre For Criminology and Criminal Justice, University of Hull.

Crown Prosecution Service (undated) *Code For Crown Prosecutors*, London: Crown Prosecution Service.

Department of Health (1998) 'Modernising Mental Health Services', Section 1, December, London.

Department of Health (1999a) Report of the Expert Committee: Review of the Mental Health Act 1983 ('Richardson Report'), London: TSO.

Department of Health (1999b) 'Reform of the Mental Health Act, 1983: Proposals for Consultation', Cm 4480, London: TSO.

Department of Health (2004) 'Improving Mental Health Law: Towards a New Mental Health Act', London: Department of Health

Department of Health and Home Office (2000) 'Reforming the Mental Health Act, Parts I and II', Cm 5016 I and II, London, TSO.

Department of Health and Home Office (1992) 'Review of Health and Social Services for Mentally Disordered Offenders and Others Requiring Similar Services' (Chairman Dr John Reed, C.B.) Final Summary Report, Cm 2088, London: HMSO.

Duffy, D., Lenihan, S. and Kennedy, H. (2003) 'Screening Prisoners For Mental Disorders', *Psychiatric Bulletin*, 27, 241–2.

Eastman, N. and Peay J. (1999) *Law Without Enforcement: Integrating Mental Health and Justice*, Oxford: Hart Publishing.

Eldergill, A. (2002) 'Is Anyone Safe? Civil Compulsion Under the Draft Mental Health Bill', *Journal of Mental Health Law*, 8, 331–59.

Exworthy, T. and Parrott, J. (1993) 'Evaluation of a Diversion Scheme From Custody at Magistrates' Courts', *Journal of Forensic Psychiatry*, 4, 497–505.

Exworthy, T. and Parrott, J. (1997) 'Comparative Evaluation of a Diversion From Custody Scheme', *Journal of Forensic Psychiatry*, 8, 406–16.

Fitzgibbon, D. W. (2004) *Pre-Emptive Criminalisation: Risk Control and Alternative Futures*, Issues in Community and Criminal Justice, Monograph No. 4.

Fowles, A. J. (1993) 'The Mentally Disordered in an Era of Community Care', in W. Watson and A. Grounds (eds), *The Mentally Disordered Offender in an Era of Community Care*, Cambridge: Cambridge University Press.

Gavin, N., Parsons, S. and Grubin, D. (2003) 'Reception Screening and Mental Health Needs Assessment in a Male Remand Prison', *Psychiatric Bulletin*, 27, 251–3.

Geelan, S. D., Campbell, M. J., and Bartlett, A. (2001) 'What Happens Afterwards? A Follow-Up Study of Those Diverted From Custody to Hospital in the First 2.5 years of a Metropolitan Diversion Scheme, *Medicine, Science and the Law*, 41, 122–8.

Gelder, M. G., Lopez-Ibor Jnr, J. J. and Andreason, N. C. (2000) (eds), *New Oxford Textbook of Psychiatry* (2 vols), Oxford: Oxford University Press.

Grounds, A. T. (1991) 'The Mentally Disordered Offender in the Criminal Process: Some Research and Policy Question', in K. Herbst and J. Gunn (eds), *The Mentally Disordered Offender*, London: Butterworth-Heinemann in association with The Mental Health Foundation.

Gunn, J. (1977) 'Criminal Behaviour and Mental Disorders', *British Journal of Psychiatry*, 130, 317–29.

Gunn, J., Maden A. and Swinton, M. (1991) *Mentally Disordered Prisoners*, London: Home Office.

Gunn, M. and Holland, T. (2002) 'Some Thoughts on the Proposed Mental Health Act', *Journal of Mental Health Law*, 8, 360–72.

Hetherington, T. (1989) *Prosecution in the Public Interest*, London: Waterlow.

Home Office and Department of Health (1991) 'Review of Health and Social Services for Mentally Disordered Offenders and Others Requiring Similar Services' (Chairman Dr John Reed, C.B.), London: HMSO.

Home Office and Department of Health (1999) 'Managing Dangerous People With Severe Personality Disorders: Proposals for Policy Development', London: Home Office and Department of Health.

Home Office and Department of Health and Social Security (1975) Report of the Committee on Mentally Abnormal Offenders ('Butler Committee'), Cmnd 6244, London: HMSO.

Hodgins, S. and Muller-Isberner, R. (2004) 'Preventing Crime by People with Schizphrenic Disorders: The Role of the Psychiatric Services', *British Journal of Psychiatry*, 185, 245–50.

Hucklesby, A. (1997) 'Court Culture: An Explanation of Varieties in the Use of Bail By Magistrates' Courts', *Howard Journal of Criminal Justice*, 36, 129–45.

James, D. (1999) 'Court Diversion at 10 Years: Can it Work, Does it Work and Has it a Future?', *Journal of Forensic Psychiatry*, 10, 507–24.

James, D. V. and Hamilton, L. W. (1991) 'The Clerkenwell Scheme – Assessing Efficacy and Cost of A Psychiatric Liaison Service to a Magistrates' Court', *British Medical Journal*, 303, 282–5.

Joseph, P. (1992) *Psychiatric Assessment at the Magistrates' Courts*, London: Home Office.

Joseph, P. and Potter, M. (1993) I 'Diversion From Custody – Psychiatric Assessment at the Magistrates' Court' and II 'Effect on Hospital and Prison Resources', *British Journal of Psychiatry*, 162, 325–30 and 330–4.

Kinton, M. (2002) 'Should We Allow Compulsory Mental Health Treatment in Prisons?', *Journal of Mental Health Law*, 8, 304–7.

Laing, J. (1999) *Care or Custody? Mentally Disordered Offenders in the Criminal Justice System*, Oxford: Oxford University Press.

Laing, R. D. and Esterson, A. (1964) *Sanity, Madness and the Family: Families of Schizophrenics*, Harmondsworth: Penguin Books.

Laurance, J. (2003) *Pure Madness: How Fear Drives The Mental Health System*, London: Routledge.

Law Society (2002) 'Law Society's Response to the Draft Mental Health Bill', *Journal of Mental Health Law*, 8, 373–5.

Mackay, R. (1995) *Mental Condition Defences in the Criminal Law*, Oxford: Clarendon Press.

NACRO (National Association For the Care and Resettlement of Offenders) (1993) 'Community Care and Mentally Disordered Offenders' (Policy Paper No. 1), Mental Health Advisory Committee (Chairman H. Prins), London: NACRO.

O'Grady, J. (2004) 'The Psychiatrist, Courts and Sentencing', Forum: Newsletter of the Forensic Faculty, Issue No. 8, September, Royal College of Psychiatrists, London: Royal College of Psychiatrists.

Parsons, S., Walker, L. and Grubin, D. (2001) 'Prevalence of Mental Disorder in Female Remand Prisons', *Journal of Forensic Psychiatry*, 12, 194–202.

Peay, J. (1996) (ed.), *Inquiries After Homicide*, London: Duckworth.

Peay, J. (2000) 'Reform of the Mental Health Act: 1983: Squandering A Lost Opportunity', *Journal of Mental Health Law*, 3, 5–15.

Penrose, Sir L. (1939) 'Mental Disease and Crime: Outline For A Study of European Statistics', *British Journal of Medical Psychology*, 18, 1–15.

Prins, H. (1995) '"I've Got a Little List" (Koko: Mikado). But is it Any Use? Comments on the Forensic Aspects of Supervision Registers for the Mentally Ill', *Medicine, Science and the Law*, 35, 218–24.

Prins, H. (1996) 'Can the Law Serve as the Solution to Social Ills? – The Mental Health (Patients in the Community Act) 1995', *Medicine, Science and the Law*, 36, 217–20.

Prins, H. (1999) 'Dangerous Severe Personality Disorder – an Independent View', *Prison Service Journal*, 126, 8–10.

Prins, H. (2001a) 'Whither Mental Health Legislation (Locking Up The Disturbed and the Deviant)', *Medicine, Science and the Law*, 41, 241–9.

Prins, H. (2001b) 'Offenders, Deviants or Patients – Comments on Part Two of the White Paper', *Journal of Mental Health Law*, 5, 21–6.

Prins, H. (2002) 'Psychopathic Disorder – Concept or Chimera', *Journal of Mental Health Law*, 8, 247–61.

Prins, H. (2005) *Offenders, Deviants or Patients?* (3rd ed.), London: Routledge.

Reznek, L. (1997) *Evil or Ill: Justifying the Insanity Defence*, London and New York: Routledge.

Riordan, S., Wix, S., Kenny-Herbert, J. and Humphreys, M. (2000) 'Diversion at the Point of Arrest: Mentally Disordered People and Contact With the Police', *Journal of Forensic Psychiatry*, 11, 683–90.

Riordan, S., Wix, S., Haque, M. S. and Humphreys, M. (2003) 'Multiple Contacts at the Point of Arrest', *Medicine, Science and the Law*, 43, 105–10.

Ritchie Q.C., J., Dick, D. and Lingham, R. 1994) Report of the Committee of Inquiry Into the Care and Treatment of Christopher Clunis, London: HMSO.

Rollin, H. (1969) *The Mentally Disordered Offender and the Law*, Oxford: Pergamon.

Roth, M. and Kroll, J. (1986) *The Reality of Mental Illness*, Cambridge: Cambridge University Press.

Rowlands, R., Inch, H., Rodger, W. and Soliman, A. (1996) 'Diverted to Where/ What Happens to Diverted Mentally Disordered Offenders?', *Journal of Forensic Psychiatry*, 7, 284–96.

Royal Commission on Capital Punishment (1953) Report, Cmd 8932, London: HMSO.

Sedgwick, P. (1982) *Psycho-politics*, London: Pluto Press.

Shaw, J., Tomenson, B., Creed, F. and Perry, A. (2001) 'Loss of Contact With Psychiatric Services in People Diverted From the Criminal Justice System', *Journal of Forensic Psychiatry*, 12, 203–10.

Simpson, A. I. F., McKenna, B., Moskowitz, A., Skipworth, J. and Barry-Walsh J. (2004) 'Homicide and Mental Illness in New Zealand: 1970–2000', *British Journal of Psychiatry*, 185, 394–8.

Singleton, N., Meltzer, H. and Gatward, R. (1998) *Psychiatric Morbidity Among Prisoners in England and Wales*, London: TSO.

Smith, J. and Donovan, M. (1990) 'The Prosecution of Psychiatric In-patients', *Journal of Forensic Psychiatry*, 1, 379–83.

Soothill, K. and Walby, C. (1991) *Sex Crimes in the News*, London: Routledge.

Stanley, N. and Manthorpe, J. (eds) (2004) *The Age of the Inquiry: Learning and Blaming in Health and Social Care*, London: Routledge.

Szasz, T. (1987) *Insanity, The Idea and its Consequences*, New York: Wiley.

Szasz, T. (1993) 'Curing, Coercing and Claims Making – A Reply to Critics', *British Journal of Psychiatry*, 162, 297–800.

Taylor, P. (2004) 'Mental Disorder and Crime', *Criminal Behaviour and Mental Health* (Special Supplement) 14(2), S31–S36.

Taylor, P. and Gunn, J. (1999) 'Homicides by People with Mental Illness: Myth and Reality', *British Journal of Psychiatry*, 174, 9–14.

Towl, G., Snow, L. and McHugh, M. (2000) (eds) *Suicides in Prisons*, Leicester: British Psychological Society Books.

Tumim, Judge Stephen (1990) Report of a Review into Suicide and Self-Harm in Prison Service Establishments in England and Wales, Cm 1383, London: HMSO.

Vaughan, P. (2004) 'An Evaluation of Psychiatric Support to Magistrates' Courts', *Medicine, Science and the Law*, 44, 193–6.

Vaughan, P., Austen, C., le Feuvre, M., O'Grady, J. and Sawyer, B. (2003) 'Psychiatric Support to Magistrates' Courts', *Medicine, Science and the Law*, 43, 255–9.

West, D. (1965) *Murder Followed by Suicide*, London: Macmillan.

World Health Organization (1992) *Classification of Mental and Behavioural Disorders: Clinical Descriptions and Diagnostic Guidelines*, Geneva: WHO.

Zigmond, T. (2002) (On Behalf of Royal College of Psychiatrists) 'Commentary on Draft Mental Health Bill', *Journal of Mental Health Law*, 8, 376–9.

7 Paedophilia prevention and the law

Dennis Howitt

Introduction

The precise number of paedophile sex offenders in the UK is not known (National Criminal Intelligence Service 2003). In 2004, there were 24,572 registered sex offenders in England and Wales – an increase of 12 per cent from the previous year. This means that there are 46 registered sex offenders for every 100,000 of the population (*The Daily Telegraph* 2004). Many of these had offended against adults and not children. Furthermore, the register only dates back to 1997. Given that the minimum period of registration is five years (and can be indefinite), the register is likely to accumulate numbers. However, according to the Foreign and Commonwealth Office (2004), there are 230,000 people in the United Kingdom involved in paedophile activity. The basis of this estimate is unclear, given that it is also claimed that only 3,400 paedophiles were serving sentences in 2004, with a further 18,000 registered under the Sex Offenders Act 1997. The number of victims is equally uncertain. Between 1980 and 2001 about 70,000 crimes of gross indecency with a child and unlawful sexual intercourse with a female child were reported (National Crime Intelligence Service 2003). If these were all carried out by different offenders then this amounts to 3,500 offenders or so a year. The extent to which this represents the tip of the iceberg is also hard to quantify. Of course, adults are known to report sexual victimization as a child at relatively high frequencies – a figure of 20 per cent or greater would not be particularly unusual for samples of women (Howitt 1992a). The figures vary enormously according to methodologies employed. Furthermore, definitions of abuse used in some studies may refer to behaviours which are not necessarily crimes under the law.

The history of adult–child sexual contact goes back to ancient times. Indeed, there is evidence of other cultures and eras having very different standards to our modern ones. Some even appear to have condoned certain forms of adult–child sexual contact (Howitt 1995a). However, for two decades, society has shown increased anxiety about paedophilic activities. There can be little doubting the public's antagonism towards sex offenders. It is demonstrated by public opinion surveys (Brown 1999) and, more dramatically, in arson attacks on sex-offender hostels and vigilante action against known or suspected sex offenders (Lovell 2001). Child protection organizations lobby government for legislation. The children's charity the National Society for the Prevention of Cruelty to Children was substantially involved in the development of the Sexual Offences Act 2003. Media pressure builds up at the time of especially newsworthy and dramatic child sexual killings such as the Holly Wells and Jessica Chapman murders committed by Ian Huntley in August 2002 at Soham, Cambridgeshire. The girls were ten years old. This may contribute to a false but dramatic image of paedophiles, which misleads more than it informs (Silverman and Wilson 2002).

What is a paedophile?

'Paedophilia' is a scientific term invented by the founder of sexological research, the psychiatrist Richard von Krafft-Ebing. The condition is described in his seminal book *Psychopathia Sexualis* (1886). Paedophilia is essentially a characteristic of individuals in which they have a sexual interest in adolescent, pubescent and younger people. Krafft-Ebing, like many others, believed that paedophilia is a long-term condition and that children are the primary sexual interest of a paedophile. By implication, this creates a separate category of people which does not have a primary or long-term sexual interest in children yet still offends against them. The problems of identifying just what it is which differentiates these 'secondary paedophiles' from 'primary paedophiles' are numerous and the distinction probably confuses understanding as much as it helps. Paedophilia is also a diagnostic category in the American Psychiatric Association's *Diagnostic and Statistical Manual of Mental Disorders* (4th edition) (APA 1994). Its status as a psychiatric diagnosis has no legal implications. It is not used as a defence so is of little relevance here. Paedophile is neither a legal category nor a legal term. Indeed, it is not illegal to have a sexual interest as such in children but it is illegal to act upon this interest in a number of ways. The illegal acts involve any direct contact abuse of a sexual nature, non-contact abusive behaviours such as indecent exposure or 'flashing', and making indecent images of children.

There are a number of subdivisions of paedophilia according to the preferred age group and gender of the child. However, more important is the distinction between those who molest children outside the family (extra-familial) and those who molest within the family (intra-familial). The latter could also be described as incestuous offenders although incest would be identified in terms of certain legal relationships rather than biological/genetic closeness alone. It is generally held that extra-familial offending is less common than intra-familial offending. Nevertheless, there is evidence that a high proportion of intra-familial offenders also offend outside of the family (Becker and Coleman 1988).

Some paedophiles specialize in a particular sex. Pederasty describes those oriented towards boys. Given that children as young as a few months are sexually abused, there is a need to identify the age group to which a paedophile is primarily attracted. The term hebephile, for example, refers to an individual primarily erotically interested in adolescents.

Conceptualisations of paedophilia, not surprisingly, have their origins in psychiatric perspectives. More broadly, the medical model of social problems (Howitt 1992b) encourages the view that paedophilia is an addiction like an addiction to drugs. Furthermore, unless checked, offending behaviour will escalate in intensity and frequency. The value of this analogy has yet to be evaluated. In this context, it is important to remember that increasing numbers of offenders are being created because of Internet child pornography offences. Many of these have no apparent history of sexually abusing children yet are treated in much the same way as contact offenders.

We will see that much of the legislation concerning sex offences against children appears to be directed against truly committed paedophile offenders. These are overwhelmingly male and presumed to be highly likely to repeatedly offend against children. Increasingly, all sex offenders against children are regarded as long-term problems despite some evidence that many are not. Furthermore, the image of sex offenders against children is considerably revised when we consider that a large proportion are themselves children and adolescents (NSPCC 2004). This, together with the evidence that paedophiles self-identify themselves as paedophilic by the time of late adolescence (Howitt 1995a), implies that young sexual offenders, often victims of sexual abuse themselves, ought to be a major focus of concern. That is to say, there is a need to regard paedophilia as part of a developmental process (Howitt 2004) and not due to perverse psychiatric anomalies of some older men and a few women.

Internet offending

Internet offending consists of two major categories of paedophile activity – Internet child pornography and Internet grooming. Neither has been extensively researched. Child pornography on the Internet is regarded as a major problem. There are a number of reasons why it has attracted attention:

- Child pornography may involve the abuse of a child, although this will vary in terms of how damaging it is to the victim. Nude photographs, for example, may or may not involve abuse. Paedophiles may use images of nude children from, say, baby product advertisements as a source of erotic imagery (Howitt 1995b). Such images are not the product of the sexual abuse of children. It is argued that downloading or viewing child pornography – because of the financial aspects of some use of child pornography – provides the financial stimulus for pornographers to create new imagery. Without the financial benefits, the argument goes, there is no incentive for producing further material.

- Viewing child pornography increases the likelihood that the individual will eventually abuse children directly himself – that is, become a contact offender. This is an example of the idea that viewing pornography is a stimulus to sexual offending. There is a great deal of research on this as applied to adult pornography (i.e. that not involving children) but a singular lack of evidence directly about child pornography as such for obvious reasons.
- By tracking down users of Internet pornography, it may be possible to uncover evidence of them directly abusing children known to them. At one extreme, there are paedophiles who photograph or film themselves or others abusing children to share over the Internet.

These are complex issues and there is little by way of convincing research concerning most of these matters. Internet offending could be tackled simply by blocking sites which contain offending material. It is possible to achieve this and recently both BT and Vodafone have indicated that they will do this. In the United Kingdom, the list of illegal sites is compiled by the Internet Watch Foundation. This is basically a self-regulatory body involving the Internet Service Providers, the police and others. Information on unacceptable material (illegal adult pornography, child pornography, and illegal racist material) is gathered from members of the public hot-lining the information. It is claimed that 15,000 sites have been found which are illegal under UK child pornography legislation. Shutting them down, in a sense, is a crime prevention measure. This may be misleadingly simple. Objective information about child pornography on the Internet is hard to come by. The material may be distributed in other ways. Offenders sometimes use Internet sites which host computer file distribution such as MP3 music files. Because the law about child pornography lacks mitigating or permissible reasons for having the material in one's possession, researchers are reliant on sources of information which cannot be independently verified.

Probably the most famous Internet pornography case in the UK is that of Operation Ore which was based on credit card details passed on by the FBI about subscribers to an 'adult pass' site which included two sites containing child pornography. The operation in the USA was known as Operation Avalanche. The FBI and others used the credit card list in the USA to contact men to offer them child pornography. As a result of purchasing this material 144 searches were organized (ABC News 2001). Relatively few of the clients of the site actually took up the offer of child pornography, which perhaps indicates that relatively few had an interest in that material. The purchasers of the child pornography were investigated further and 30 per cent of them were found to have known contact offences against children. Of course, this does not mean that 30 per cent of the subscribers to this site were contact abusers too (*Irish Examiner* 2004). We simply do not know how many of the clients of the site were actually interested in child pornography in the first place, and just how typical the 'purchasers' of the bogus child pornography were of Internet pornography offenders anyway. It is also unknown what proportion of contact offenders are also consumers of child pornography.

One vexed question is whether or not the Internet-only sex offender exists. This is a matter of theoretical importance (Howitt 1995b). Previously, there was virtually no evidence about the existence of men who are paedophiles in terms of having a sexual interest in children but never offend directly against any child. Indeed, when Howitt (1995a) discussed the matter for the first time, the only evidence that such men existed was from a suspect source. It concerned groups of men who attended for treatment to deal with their sexual interest in children but also claimed not to have actually abused a child sexually. It is easy to dismiss this evidence as merely the words of men who had a vested interest in not admitting their abusive behaviour. However, this is to assume that paedophiles cannot control their sexuality despite the evidence that heterosexuals and homosexuals can abstain from sex with other adults. Equally, given that considerable efforts are often made to find contact-offending by men arrested for Internet pornography offences, the number for whom no such contact-offending is found reinforces the possibility. It also weakens the escalation argument, which suggests that men who use child pornography are increasingly likely to seek out children to offend against.

Sheldon (2004) interviewed Internet-only offenders. These share some of the characteristics of contact-offending paedophiles. For example, they show similar cognitive distortions to contact offenders. This opens up the possibility that Internet-only offenders are a type of paedophile (since they are interested sexually in children) but are disinclined to offend directly against children. Others have pointed out that sexual fantasies do not necessarily lead to sexual acting out (Howitt 2004). For example, many normal men and women have sexual fantasies which they would never wish to fulfil in reality despite the fantasies being sexually stimulating. Indeed, one should regard the existence of non-acting out (i.e. non-offending) paedophiles as an optimistic possibility. It suggests that there may not be an automatic link between paedophile fantasy and paedophile offending. This, in its turn, may indicate that child sexual abuse is not necessarily the consequence of paedophile orientation.

Legislation and paedophilia

Taken on a long time-scale, the law dealing with adult sexual interest in children has largely revolved around the legal minimum age of consent (to sexual intercourse) and the (generally) closely related minimum age for marriage (marriageability). The age of consent and the minimum age of marriage are identical in most cultures with respect to heterosexual relationships. Homosexual relationships, comparatively, present a much more complex situation. Currently, gay marriage is only possible in a small number of legal jurisdictions, and the homosexual age of consent is historically unrelated to that for heterosexual couples. Recent legislation in the UK made the two ages of sexual consent identical. The age of consent to heterosexual intercourse has tended to increase historically whereas that for homosexual intercourse has tended to decline.

Legislation prohibiting sexual intercourse with girls under the age of 12 dates back to 1275 under English law. The age of consent gradually increased over the centuries to the present one of 16 years. Homosexuality was legalized in England and Wales in 1967 and in 1980 in Scotland. It is important to note that changes in the law occurred infrequently until recent years when legislation dealing with sexual activity with under age persons has proliferated.

What is legal at one time and in one place may be illegal at another. Furthermore, biological maturity is not the basis of the changes in the age of heterosexual consent since this latter has increased over the years, whereas the age of biological sexual maturity has declined. It has been argued that increases in the age of consent are a response to the demands of industrial societies for an increasingly educated workforce (Killias 1991).

Legislation related to paedophilia in recent years has a much more clearly articulated rationale than earlier legislation. Indeed, recent legislation targets not just the physical act of sexual abuse but also other aspects of the behaviour of paedophiles which lead to their offending. For example, 'grooming' is the term for the activities of paedophiles when contacting and 'befriending' children for eventual sexual purposes. As we will see, grooming has become targeted by defining it as an offence. In addition, legislation now requires the review and monitoring of sex offenders on release from prison. Another major development has been making criminal the use of the Internet to distribute, view, or download child pornography. All of these changes illustrate how activities which previously were merely pre-offence behaviours are now arrestable.

Contact and related sexual offences

The Sexual Offences Act (2003) is a significant development in the law on sex offending in Britain which came into effect on 1 May 2004. It replaced the Sexual Offences Act 1956. It is impossible to summarize the Act in a few words and only time will reveal the significance of the changes for reducing the sexual abuse of children. The Act does more than extend the severity of punishments and the range of punishable offences, it also seeks to protect particularly vulnerable groups and individuals. The Act considers young people under three age groups – those 12 years of age and under; those 15 years of age and under; and those 17 years of age and under.

12 year olds and under

Children of this age cannot, in law, give consent to sexual activity. Hence, there remains the concept of statutory rape for younger people who cannot legally consent to sexual intercourse. Penetrative penile sexual activities (of the vagina, anus, mouth) are classified as rape and may receive a sentence of life. Other forms of sexual assault (including penetration with any other body part or an object) or inciting a child in this age group to engage in sexual behaviour are punishable with up to 14 years of imprisonment.

15 year olds and under

The legislation includes an age differential when victims are under the age of 16 years and the offender is 18 years of age or older. This is not the first time that such an age differential has been incorporated into British law. The Offences Against the Person Act 1875 made carnal knowledge of a girl between 13 and 16 years of age illegal only when the man involved was 24 years of age or older. The development also fits in with the concern in the sexual abuse litera-ture which emphasizes the damaging nature of power differentials in abusive relationships – a big age differential implies power differentials throughout the feminist theory on child sexual abuse. Home Office advice accompanying the Act suggests that there is no intention unnecessarily to interfere with the mutu-ally consensual sexual activities of teenagers of a similar age. Furthermore, it is claimed that experts providing, say, sex education advice, are protected. The legislation concerning this age group also covers:

* causing and inciting under-16s to engage in sexual activities;
* engaging in sexual activity in the presence of a child, subject to require-ments of intent, knowledge and a motive of personal sexual gratification;
* causing a child to watch a sexual act – which may be pornographic images on videos – in order to obtain personal sexual gratification from this activity.

There is also legislation against other paedophile activity such as meeting a child following sexual grooming. Having communicated with an under-16-year-old at least twice, it is illegal to meet them or travel with the intention of meeting them in order to commit any of the offences discussed in the previous paragraph. Arranging things which might lead to or facilitate any of the forms of illegal activity described above is also an offence. Offenders under the age of 18 years are subject to this legislation except that the punishments are greatly reduced.

17 year olds and under

Another new development in the law is that the Sexual Offences Act 2003 seeks to protect under-18-year-olds. Offences involving indecent photographs of a 16- or 17-year-old are regarded as just the same as similar offences involving 14- or 15-year-olds. Limited exceptions are made for couples in a stable relationship or married and where consent was given, where no other person is featured in the photograph, and where the photographs are not shown to other people. Furthermore, there are now offences which result from using this age group for prostitution and in pornography.

A major development is legislation concerning adults in a position of trust *vis-à-vis* a young person of 17 years of age and younger – and some others who are vulnerable for reasons such as low intellectual ability. For example, teachers who have sexual relations with one of their 17-year-old students are now committing an offence and not simply risking their jobs.

Internet offences

Other legislation deals with the issues of Internet pornography. The foundation of modern law dealing with obscenity lies in the Obscene Publications Acts 1959 and 1964. There was further legislation under the Protection of Children Act 1978, which made it a criminal offence to take or permit another to take indecent photographs of a child under the age of 16 years. Furthermore, the distribution, showing, advertising or possessing for distribution of such photographs was also illegal. (The Criminal Justice Act 1988 made the mere possession of obscene materials involving children illegal.) The Act clarified to a degree the meaning of the term photograph but it was left to the Criminal Justice and Public Order Act 1994 to bring the electronic transmission of obscene photographs such as by e-mail attachments under the Obscene Publications Act 1959. The Criminal Justice and Public Order Act 1994 also brought computer generated or altered images under the legislation. Basically, this means that a computer manipulated image, which might deceive a viewer into believing that this was an actual indecent photograph of a child, was just as illegal as a real photograph. This is based on a different rationale from the usual one that child pornography depicts the actual suffering of a child abuse victim. Instead, the justification is that the viewer may be encouraged by the pseudo-image of child sexual abuse actually to abuse children. The current penalties for possession of child pornography are up to five years' imprisonment and twice this for distribution of child pornography.

Prison and prevention

There are a number of functions of imprisonment; punishment being the prime one. Imprisonment also provides opportunities for forms of rehabilitation – especially through the use of psychological therapies which have become increasingly available in prisons (sex-offender treatments), and which are also quite feasible in other contexts such as probation services.

Does prison work for paedophiles? One view is that paedophiles are persistent and frequent offenders whose offending goes largely unrecorded. This is clearly difficult to confirm or disprove by its very nature. Sometimes writers refer to a study which, on the face of things, suggests that the average sex offender commits many crimes, few of which are detected (Abel *et al.* 1987). It involved clients attending a sex offender clinic for assessment partly for court purposes. They were encouraged to divulge all of their offences. As is common, sex offenders of all types were combined for the research sample (e.g. the study would include adult rapists of adult women as well as paedophiles). Some remarkable figures emerged from the study. For example, the average number of offences admitted was 446 offences per man. However, a closer inspection reveals that the typical offender is very different. While the average (mean) number of claimed offences was high as we have seen, the median number of claimed rape offences was only one. In other words, at least half of the offenders only claimed one offence but a few offenders claimed huge numbers of victims. Sex offender issues are among the most highly politicised in the modern legal system and statistical data may be interpreted in a partisan fashion. There is older evidence that sex offenders in general tend to have few previous sex convictions (West 1987). However, Eliot *et al.* (1995) suggest that the figures are higher than this based on interviews with paedophile offenders in the UK. The issue, however, is not so much the number of offences but that some offenders show low frequencies of offending behaviour.

Basically, there are no satisfactory baseline data concerning paedophile behaviour. Probably, no feasible methodology could supply definitive data. We have no clear knowledge of frequencies, rates or any other aspect of paedophilia. That is to say, we have no yardstick by which to evaluate rates of re-offending by paedophiles after imprisonment compared to similar men who had not been in prison in order to assess prison's deterrent (and therapeutic) effect. Nevertheless, we know that reconviction is relatively uncommon for sex offenders – that is for sex offenders in general not specific individuals. The Home Office has issued figures indicating that 19 per cent of sex offenders are reconvicted within two years, which contrasts with the 52 per cent reconviction rate for all types of adult prisoners (Home Office 2004b). These are figures for any type of offence. The low levels of reconviction would be understandable if paedophiles in general are unlikely to re-offend. But, of course, the general assumption is that paedophiles simply get away with their offending much of the time and it is low detection rates not low re-offending rates which are responsible. One problem is explaining why paedophiles should be better than other offenders at avoiding arrest for other types of crime such as property and violent crime.

Hood *et al.* (2002) studied UK sex offenders who had been given a sentence of four or more years. Only determinate sentences were involved, which, presumably, excludes indeterminate sentences such as lifers. As such, we can assume that their offending behaviour was serious if not the most serious. Indeed, 59 per cent had been convicted of a penetrative offence or attempt at such (i.e. rape in the current definition of the term). Ten per cent had been convicted of incest, 26 per cent of a serious indecent assault or indecency, and the remaining 4 per cent had been convicted of unlawful sexual intercourse. The study followed these men for up to six years after release. The intra-familial or incest offenders were low on reconviction. None of them was re-convicted of a sexual offence and imprisoned – in fact only 2 per cent were re-imprisoned in the study period. This was for neither a sexual nor a violent crime. It is common to combine recidivism for sexual and violent crimes in such studies though it slightly muddies attempts to understand sexual re-offending. One reason for combining the two types of offence is that in some cases much the same offence is sometimes prosecuted as a violent case and other times prosecuted as a sexual case (Marshall 1994). Extra-familial offenders were more likely to commit a sexual offence for which they were re-imprisoned in a six year follow-up period – the figure was as high as 26 per cent. Reconviction for any sort of offence was detected in 11 per cent of the incest group and 47 per cent of the extra-familial group though these were not all sexual offences. Taken together, these various findings suggest that re-offending sexually is low for intra-familial offenders, higher for extra-familial offenders, and higher still for serious extra-familial offenders. Re-offending is not automatic, though one must remember that serious sex offenders are likely to be monitored in some form once they have left prison (see Multi Agency Public Protection Arrangements or MAPPAs later, for example). What appears to be true of sex offenders in general does not apply to offenders with the most serious offences against children.

In an attempt to understand the recidivism rates for sexual offenders better, Falshaw *et al.* (2003) carried out a study in the context of a community-based sex offender treatment programme – the Thames Valley Project. They took 173 sex offenders who had taken part in the Project's treatment programme. The minimum time of being at risk of re-offending was nearly four years. Two different national databases provided information on the criminal history of the men – the Police National Computer indicated three times the rate of re-offending than was found on the Offenders Index. In other words, recidivism rates varied markedly between the two databases. In addition, the Project had its own records of offending by its clientele. Combining all these three sources, re-offenders amounted to 12 per cent of the sample. This was 33 per cent more than the figures obtained from the Offenders Index and the Police National Computer. Interestingly, the researchers also had information from records about other behaviours indicative of sexual recidivism – for example, a sex offender who has been discovered in the vicinity of a school is exhibiting recidivism since this is a behaviour which is likely to lead to re-offending. Pooling all sources indicative of re-offending and signs of returning to paedophile behaviours, 21 per cent of offenders showed recidivistic behaviour of one sort or another. This was seven times the rate of re-offending as measured from the Offenders Index, and 2.33 times the rate of re-offending identified by the Police National Computer database. Of course, these offenders were on a community based project so the findings from them may not apply to other samples.

Reconviction studies simply cannot tell us anything about the effectiveness of prison as a deterrent. What the data do tell us is that reconviction is far from certain over quite a long period – especially if sexual offences alone are considered. Furthermore, even if prison is effective as a future deterrent, we do not know what it is about prison which has an effect. There is another problem in assessing the effectiveness of prison – that release is subject to risk assessment and on release virtually every sex offender would be on the Sex Offenders Register and monitored by a MAPPA. We will turn to these now.

Sex Offenders Registers and MAPPAs

In seconds, through the Internet, anyone can check whether a name is listed on sex offender registries in the United States of America. Megan's Law is federal legislation which in 1996 required communities to be informed about serious sex offenders in their midst. Seven-year-old Megan Kanka had been abducted and murdered in New Jersey in 1994 by a convicted sex offender living close by. Megan's Law was in fact a strengthening of an earlier US law (the Jacob Wetterling Act) which permitted but did not require the release of such information. In some states of America, community information legislation had predated Megan's Law. Considerable latitude remains with the individual state concerning just how the principles of the federal law are enacted. According to Lovell (2001), there is state-to-state variation in terms of the ways in which risk assessment procedures are used; the methods by which the community is informed about the presence of sex offenders in its midst; and the penalties for vigilante actions against the registered offender.

Megan's Law is primarily about the requirement to inform local people about the presence of sex offenders within their community. The law does not require that information about all sex offenders registered is communicated to the community or even that all members of the community are informed. As indicated, precisely what is required varies from state to state. Recipients receiving the information are required to use it responsibly.

Following this and defying a considerable media and public outcry demanding community notification, the British government has resisted the idea of a 'Sarah's Law'. Sarah's Law refers to a concerted attempt by the newspaper, *The News of the World*, to create legislation permitting community notification of serious sex offenders. This was a response to the abduction and murder of Sarah Payne in 2000 by a local man, Roy Whiting, who had a previous criminal history for the abduction and indecent assault of another nine-year-old girl. Indeed, he was one of the first offenders to be placed on the Sex Offenders Register and noted to be one of the most dangerous predatory paedophiles. However, sex offender registration legislation in the United Kingdom does not require or allow the provision of information to the community concerning the whereabouts of serious sex offenders. Multi Agency Public Protection Arrangements (MAPPAs) were introduced by the Criminal Justice and Courts Services Act 2000. This Act required the police and probation services to work together in order to manage the risks posed by dangerous sex offenders in the community. The Criminal Justice Act 2003 added the prison service to the list of responsible authorities alongside the police and probation services. These responsible authorities are also expected to involve other local agencies such as social services, health services and housing services. There is assessment of the risk posed by offenders by the police or probation services using standard risk assessment methods approved by these services.

So, in this way, information about sex offenders and, in particular, those sex offenders judged to be the most risky can be discussed in the context of a variety of agencies and appropriate action taken or protection plans drawn up. Sex offenders (MAPPAs are not solely about sex offenders) are identified from the Sex Offenders Register (which should include everyone convicted or cautioned for certain sexual offences). Furthermore, Sex Offenders Orders may be applied for under the terms of the Sexual Offences Act 2003 by police who are concerned about the behaviour of a particular individual. Recipients of such an order must register themselves on the Sex Offenders Register. But the Sex Offenders Register is not the only source of information about offenders. Any offender convicted of a sexual or violent crime and given a year or more custodial sentence will be under the purview of the MAPPA – even if their sexual offence did not require them to be placed on the Sex Offenders Register. Indeed, the MAPPA may consider anyone about whom they have concerns, such as an offender whose time on the Sex Offenders Register has finished.

In addition to these, there is another level of control and constraint on sex offenders. The Serious Sex Offenders Unit at the National Criminal Information Service monitors paedophiles using intelligence on sex offenders. Offenders seeking to avoid prosecution by offending in other countries are prevented from doing so since registered sex offenders are not allowed abroad for more than three days without notifying the police. UK residents and nationals may be prosecuted in the UK for sexual offences carried out abroad.

So how effective is registration? In the UK, 93 per cent of offenders actually register their whereabouts. This is an impressively high figure compared to data from the USA which suggests a lower level of 80 per cent compliance with the requirement to register (Expert Law 2003). The penalty in the UK for failing to register is up to five years in prison. Reasons for the difference are difficult to ascertain. The lower risk of vigilantism in the UK because names are not released to the community may be one reason for offenders registering in high numbers. However, it could simply be that the mechanisms and procedures for registration are better in the UK. For example, offenders may be more clearly informed of the requirements and consequences. Whatever the reason, such high compliance rates tend to undermine the suggestion that UK offenders go underground to avoid detection.

Out of the 25,000 on the register, 26 offenders committed a serious sexual or violent offence while on their MAPPA programme in 2004 (*The Daily Telegraph* 2004). This amounts to an annual fall of 46 per cent from the figures for the previous year. One could say that this is indicative of success as so few re-offend. However, it also makes it clear that the most dangerous individuals at any time may well not be on the Sex Offenders Register as these numbers are a small fraction of the total number of sex offences against children annually.

One of the imponderable but frequent findings of research into sex offenders is the evidence about their previous and later convictions. Basically, research reveals that many sex offenders do not specialize in sex offending in the sense that their previous and later convictions are for non-sexual offences – sometimes these are violent offences but more commonly for other offences such as ones against property. Quite how these trends should be interpreted in terms of prevention of sex offending against children is not clear. One obvious suggestion, though it risks appearing fatuous, is that there should be a register of offenders rather than a register of sex offenders! In that way, more of the persons who are a risk to children could be identified. The problem with this is the relative infrequency of sexual offences against children compared with violent and property types of crimes. Although the previous and future conviction patterns are frequently for property and violent offences, there may be an explanation for this superficially curious trend. It is possible that the different types of offence may share a common origin in childhood experiences. Swanston *et al.* (2003) found evidence that sexual abuse may have a causal influence on self-reported crime in general amongst young people and not simply sexual crime.

Risk management

Risk assessment and risk management are related but different concepts. Risk assessment involves an estimation of the likelihood of further offences if a person is released into the community and the likely seriousness of these offences. Risk management refers to the procedures used to reduce the chances that the risk will become a reality. Management does not boil down to a single strategy but a range of strategies which may be considered in a particular case. Not releasing an offender from prison may be regarded as an example. A sex offender who is electronically tagged may in many cases be effectively deterred from re-offending but not entirely prevented. Police checks for workers in educational establishments can also be seen as a risk management strategy for offenders released back into the community. Again it is less than perfect and is dependent on the quality of the records and the checking procedures.

Risk assessment requires the identification of risk factors. Risk factors are basically any variable or set of variables which differentiates offenders who are likely to re-offend from those with little or no likelihood of re-offending. These factors are not necessarily the causes of re-offending behaviour but they do correlate with it. For example, the greater the number of previous convictions the more likely is a future reconviction. Previous convictions have no direct causal influence on subsequent offending behaviour. Nevertheless, previous convictions probably are associated with factors which do influence re-offending – for example, the strength of paedophile urges or the offender's inability to control them.

Evidence about risk factors in sexual offending against children tends to reveal a fairly consistent and, perhaps, somewhat mundane list. These include factors such as:

- offending begins earlier in life;
- previous conviction for sexual offences;
- sexually offending against male victims;
- multiple victims.

(Loucks 2002)

A major problem in risk assessment is that no factor is a foolproof predictor of re-offending – or not re-offending for that matter. As a consequence, mistakes will be made. Some offenders will be predicted to re-offend but do not re-offend, and others will be predicted not to re-offend but nevertheless do re-offend. Diagnosticity or specificity is a term which indicates the power of a predictor to classify accurately re-offenders and non re-offenders. Of course, the balance between releasing someone who re-offends as opposed to keeping someone in prison who would not have re-offended had they been released is a matter of judgement and political will.

There is little systematic information about how influential risk factors are in forensic decision making. For example, the Parole Board decides on the early release of offenders back into the community. This has been studied by Hood and Shute (2002). Especially pertinent here is the aspect of their work which compared 'objective risk assessment' methods developed by the Home Office based on statistical criteria with the actual decisions of the Parole Board. This 'objective' measure (ROR score – risk of re-offending) was calculated by the researchers based on available evidence and was not part of the Parole Board's procedures. Intriguingly, for non-sexual offenders there was a strong relationship between the decision made about releasing the prisoner on parole – those with the highest ROR score were the least likely to be paroled. In contrast, there was no relationship between risk of re-offending and the Parole Board decision concerning sex offenders. The Simple Actuarial Risk Classification Procedure for Assessing Long-Term Risk of Sexual Offenders is a measure of the likelihood of recidivism for serious sexual offenders. According to Hood and Shute, this is highly regarded as a means of predicting recidivism. Once again, this measure had no relation to Parole Board decisions – high risk offenders as measured by the Simple Actuarial Risk Classification Procedure were no less likely to be released than low risk offenders. The risk as assessed by this measure is actually adjusted according to whether the prisoner has successfully completed a sex offender treatment programme. Having taken such a treatment programme was associated with the Parole Board releasing the offender.

However illuminating these findings are, we need to know more about the actual risks being managed. Hood, Shute, Feilzer and Wilxox (2002) report a follow-up of 162 sex-offender prisoners for four years (and some for longer) as part of a study of Parole Board panel decision making. They distinguished offenders in terms of the age of their victims (adults versus children) and, for the offenders against children, whether the offence was intra-familial or extra-familial. There were a number of important findings. The first is that intra-familial offenders did not re-offend sexually or violently in up to a six-year period after release. Re-offending for any sort of offence (and, to stress, none of these were sexual or violent) was 7.8 per cent after four years and 11.4 per cent after six years for those who had originally sexually offended against a child family member. These figures are for those who were re-imprisoned.

There were proportionately more extra-familial offenders who re-offended. After four years 9.1 per cent of these had re-offended sexually, 15.2 per cent had re-offended for a sexual or violent offence and had been re-imprisoned. These figures increased to 26.3 per cent for sexual offences and 31.6 per cent for any sexual or violent offence for the sample who could be followed up for six years. Interestingly, there was a degree of sexual switching in that a substantial minority of offenders against children switched to offences against adults on re-offending. Similarly, those with an initial sexual offence against adults switched to sexual offences against children on re-offending. The proportion switching is between 30 and 40 per cent approximately. However, since we do not know the actual ages of the victims involved we should be careful not to assume too much – the adult victims might have been not much older than the child victims.

One factor which seems to ensure that a sex offender will remain in prison and not be given parole is the denial of the offence (Hood and

Shute 2002). Nevertheless, of the deniers who were released by the panel, fewer than 2 per cent re-offended, compared with18 per cent of the admitters. One possible interpretation of this is that denial indicates difficulty in defining oneself as a sex offender which may also act as a deterrent to re-offending. There is reason to believe that this trend to deny deniers release has declined since the decisions made in the Hood and Shute study were investigated. This is because of legal judgements which prevent denial being used as the sole criterion of likelihood to re-offend (BBC 1999).

There is little to suggest in all of this that sexual offenders against children are released to re-offend against children because of lax risk assessment and decision making procedures. Quite the reverse seems to be true – that is, many more sex offenders against children are kept in prison who are unlikely to re-offend than those who are let out and go on to re-offend. Of course, one could take away the risk entirely by allowing no sort of early release for sex offenders against children. At this crude level, risk assessment clearly needs a decision about the level of risk (re-offending) that is acceptable. Decisions about the releases made by the Parole Board in the UK are subject to criteria decided upon by the Home Secretary.

Since the 1970s, it has become increasingly accepted that paedophiles and other sexual offenders can be treated using psychological and other therapies. Overwhelmingly, Cognitive Behavioural Therapy groups, possibly supplemented by individual psychotherapy, are the preferred method. Cognitive Behaviour Therapy essentially works on the thought processes or cognitions which lead to offending behaviour. A multi-faceted view of offending is adopted which assumes that a variety of different psychological processes may lead to offending. Examples of such processes would include a lack of empathy for the victim, belief that children desire sex with adults, lack of social skills, deviant fantasy, and depressive thought processes. Treatment involves a mixture of group work in which members of the group may challenge what the offender is saying, homework and similar preparation involving dealing with offending issues, role play, and a number of other procedures. The precise mixture involved in a treatment programme will differ. However, it is increasingly the trend for programmes to be standardized throughout the organization. For example, the STEP programme has been used throughout the British Prison Service since 1991 in various forms (Beech *et al.* 1998). Cognitive Behaviour Therapy is primarily oriented towards offence reduction – it is directive and unaccepting of the offending behaviour. It is quite different in this way from more traditional forms of psychotherapy which are much more client-oriented (Howitt 1995a). Examples of client-oriented approaches to the treatment of sex offenders are rare (e.g. Holland once had such a programme for paedophiles – see van Zessen 1991). Behavioural therapies are the main psychological alternatives to Cognitive Behavioural Therapy. In Behaviour Therapy the task is to change behaviour by conditioning techniques which involve relearning or unlearning, for example fantasy deconditioning in which the offender masturbates to his deviant fantasy until over-satiation occurs and the fantasy's power to arouse is hopefully extinguished. Purely behavioural therapies are somewhat rare.

Given that offence reduction is the goal of Cognitive Behaviour Therapy, there are relatively few studies which investigate the impact of therapy on re-offending. More common are investigations of the influence of Cognitive Behaviour Therapy on the thought processes associated with offending. That is, the impact of the treatment on things like distorted beliefs about childhood sexuality, sexual knowledge, attitudes to women, and the like are evaluated. The problem with this, of course, is that it is an assumption that changes in such measures will lead to changes in offending behaviour. More pertinent is evidence of re-offending after leaving prison. Re-offending is clearly different from reconviction, which has led to some debate as to the value of reconviction rates in assessing the success of psychotherapy. Only a proportion of re-offenders will be reconvicted though it is uncertain quite what this proportion is. We also need to remember that reconviction information is generally obtained from data bases which themselves may suffer a degree of inaccuracy. However, it is difficult to argue with any confidence that errors or biases in reconviction as an index of re-offending will differentially affect treated and non-treated paedophiles.

It should also be added that treatment is not offered to all prisoners. For one reason, as part of Cognitive Behavioural Therapy offenders are assessed for suitability for treatment. Those deemed not suitable for treatment quite clearly are different from those offered treatment. A review of practices in Minnesota (1994) found that treatment establishments offered no treatment to between 25 per cent and 50 per cent of those assessed. Offenders were unlikely to be offered treatment if they were in a significant state of denial of the offence, if they were a significant security risk, and where their intellectual ability was low. There are two ways of looking at this. One is that assessment helps target resources where they are likely to be effective. The alternative is to suggest that assessment weeds out those unlikely to improve with therapy. Whatever the truth in this, the assessment process makes it a little difficult to evaluate the success rate of any form of sex offender treatment which involves it. Equally problematic are those who do not complete treatment. This may be for a variety of reasons but they include offenders who are asked to leave the programme for one reason or another – such as a violation of the rules or requirements, non-cooperation and so forth. How should we classify failures to complete treatment? One could just count them as part of the evaluation of the treatment programme. If they re-offend then the programme did not work for them. On the other hand, one could say that they did not meet the expectations of the programme so should not be counted in the therapy category at all. Once again, the argument is hard to clinch in either direction. One interesting finding is that non-completion of treatment is actually one of the predictors of re-offending (Hanson and Bussiere 1998). Quite why that should be is open to interpretation.

Finally, we should consider that it is unlikely that all sex-offender treatment is of the highest quality even when the same framework is being employed. The management, delivery and follow-up systems may vary in quality. Hence, one should be careful about generalizing from the more effective regimes to all sex offender treatment of a similar sort.

So, any data on the effectiveness of sex offender therapy have to be set against a complex backdrop of other factors. There are a number of evaluations of the effectiveness of treatment though little to indicate precisely what aspects of treatment lead to the alleviation of re-offending. Hanson *et al.* (2002) analysed the results of over 30 studies of the effectiveness of sex offender treatment on reconviction. On average, 12 per cent of sex offenders re-offend sexually if they have received psychological therapy in prison, compared with 17 per cent who do not receive therapy. General recidivism is influenced in much the same way. Cognitive Behaviour Therapy seems to be among the most effective.

Conclusions

To what extent is the flurry of new legislation sufficient to deal with the problem of the sexual abuse of children? New laws, in themselves, are no guarantee of progress on crime reduction. Cynics might argue that legislation may divert attention from the failings of government and of the child protection system. Current British legislation related to sexual offences against children does far more than punish adult sexual activity with children. It incorporates a much more sophisticated understanding of the nature of paedophile activities than ever the law did in the past. This partly reflects the enormous strides that have been made in the field of sex-offender research in the last twenty years. Virtually everything worthwhile that we know about sex offenders is that recent. The advances in legislation are indicative of an increased willingness of government to work with child protection agencies and other sources of expertise when drafting and planning legislation.

Legislation has begun to pre-empt abuse by implicitly recognizing the importance of the grooming process in paedophile activity. Sexual abuse of children rarely conforms to a pattern of forcible abduction but instead involves a fairly complex and lengthy process of grooming children for their eventual sexual abuse. The law now identifies minimum criteria which define when grooming for sexual purposes has taken place. Of course, much sexual abuse takes place within the family where it is difficult to distinguish grooming for sexual purposes from other aspects of intra-familial intimacy. In a quite different way, but to the same ends, the law now seeks to control paedophile activities in other countries – for example by severely curtailing the freedom of those on the Sex Offenders

Register to travel abroad where they may be able to abuse children with impunity. Furthermore, it is possible to prosecute in the United Kingdom for the sexual abuse of children irrespective of where in the world the abuse took place.

Conceptualisations of where the risk of sexual abuse lies have also changed significantly in recent legislation. It is only in the last few years that it has been clearly accepted on the basis of research that many acts of abuse take place in the context of schools, child-care organizations and similar settings. The image of paedophiles as loners approaching children in parks and other public places is not only a partial picture, but it also diverts attention away from those very settings in which many children are vulnerable. So those in a position of trust (such as school teachers or those caring for children with learning difficulties, for example), are singled out in the legislation by extending the protection of the law to under-18-year-olds in such cases.

A major difficulty with previous legislation was its inability clearly to differentiate between young people's natural sexual interest in one another and exploitative sexual approaches of adults towards adolescents. The new legislation makes it clear that the latter is unacceptable by penalizing heavily the sexual activities of 18-year-olds and older with adolescents under the age of 16 years. So, in a sense, the legislation accepts that society has changed in the last few decades to be more accepting of the sexuality of under age persons while, at the same time, indicating that adolescents may be vulnerable to the sexual attentions of adults. Furthermore, the new legislation protects 16- and 17-year-olds from various forms of sexual exploitation (prostitution and pornography, for example) by targeting those who might coerce such young people into these sexual activities.

Even just a decade or so ago, concerns were expressed about the way in which sex offenders could be convicted, serve their sentences and then return to the community without undergoing any sort of treatment or therapy which might change their behaviour. When back in the community, very little would be done to monitor their activities. This is no longer true. Now large numbers of sex offenders undergo treatment programmes while in prison, and the Sex Offenders Register and the Multi Agency Public Protection Orders not only allow for more monitoring but also positively require the police and others to do so.

The criminal justice system has moved a long way from simply prosecuting for the sexual abuse of young people and punishing offenders. The law has extended its attentions to activities prior to the actual sexual abuse to long periods of time after an offender has been released from prison.

It is probably more important to identify what it is that the law overlooks than simply to recapitulate the law's achievements further. It is an obvious comment, but nevertheless important, to point out that most of the law and social policy related to paedophile activity addresses what needs to be done about offenders known to the criminal justice system. Sex offenders seem not to have particularly high recidivism rates and the monitoring of offenders on the Sex Offenders Register seems to be effective as far as can be judged from available information. The problem is that children are also at risk from adults who are not known to the criminal justice system as sex offenders. Concentrating on known offenders does little to help the prevention of sexual abuse by others.

There is a sense in which the risk being managed in the criminal justice system is that to the system itself. The furore surrounding cases in which the system fails to prevent re-offending is evidence of the pressures. Preventing re-offending is not the same as preventing offending. The two things have very different requirements. We need to know a great deal more about how to prevent youngsters turning into young sex offenders and finally becoming an adult sex offender, for example. We know that sex offenders often have a history of being sexually abused in their childhood (Howitt 1995a). This suggests the importance of stopping the sexual victimization of children to break this abusive cycle. Of course, there is much work done on this by social services and charities in this area. A good example of an integrated programme between a variety of agencies is Stop it Now (2004). Knowing the high numbers of sexual offences committed by children and adolescents, many against other children and adolescents, makes it imperative that youthful sex offenders are a major focus of concern. There is child protection work that focuses on the young sexual offender. For example, The AIM project is one such initiative. Starting offending at a young age is a serious risk factor in re-offending (Loucks 2002). Strengthening service provision in this areas may have long-term benefits.

Finally, there is the question of whether there is sufficient opportunity for paedophilic men, perhaps who have not offended or even wish to avoid offending, to gain therapeutic and other forms of help and support. By assuming that everyone with a sexual interest in children is on an inevitable slide into offending encourages containment and punishment strategies. Perhaps, for some of the men, there is a choice to make between offending and not offending. To the extent that this is a possibility, then there would seem to be a need for clear and unproblematic routes into therapy and treatment for them.

Bibliography

ABC News (2001) 'An avalanche of child porn' 14 November 2001: http://abcnews.go.com/sections/business/TechTV/TechTV_Avalanche_Porn_011 114.html (accessed 17 August 2004).

Abel, G. G., Becker, J. V., Mittelman, M. S., Cunningham-Rathener, J., Rouleau, J. L. and Murphy, W. D. (1987) 'Self reported sex crimes of non-incarcerated paraphiliacs', *Journal of Interpersonal Violence*, 2, 3–25.

APA (1994) *Diagnostic and Statistical Manual of Mental Disorders* (4th ed.), Arlington, VA: American Psychiatric Association.

BBC News (1999) 'Rape case tycoon released', 7 December 1999: http://news.bbc.co.uk/1/hi/uk/554522.stm (accessed 16 August 2004).

Becker, J. V., and Coleman, E. M. (1988) 'Incest', in V. B. Hasselt, R. L. Morrison, A. S. Bellack, and M. Hersen (eds) *Handbook of Family Violence*, New York: Plenum Press.

Beech, A., Fisher, D. and Beckett, R. (1998) 'STEP 3: An evaluation of the prison sex offender treatment programme', Home Office: London.

Brown, S. (1999) 'Public attitudes to the treatment of sex offenders', *Legal and Criminological Psychology*, 4 (2), 239–45.

Daily Telegraph, The (2004) 'Sex offenders register grows by 15 per cent', 28 July 2004: http://www.telegraph.co.uk/news/main.jhtml?xml=/news/2004/07/28/uoffend.x ml&sSheet=/portal/2004/07/28/ixportaltop.html

Elliot, M., Browne, K. and Kilcoyne, J. (1995) 'Child sexual abuse prevention – what offenders tell us', *International Journal of Child Abuse and Neglect*, 19, 579–94.

Expert Law (2003) 'Megan's Law': http://www.expertlaw.com/library/pubarticles/ megans_law.html

Falshaw, L., Friendship, C. and Bates, A. (2003) 'Sexual offenders – measuring reconviction, reoffending and recidivism', *Findings*, 183.

Foreign and Commonwealth Office (2004) 'Drugs and international crime: Sex offences against children': http://www.fco.gov.uk/servlet/Front?pagename= OpenMarket/Xcelerate/ShowPage&c=Page&cid=1044901626358 (accessed 16 August 2004).

Hanson, R. and Bussiere, M. (1998) 'Predicting relapse: A meta-analysis of sexual offender recidivism studies', *Journal of Consulting and Clinical Psychology*, 66, 348–64.

Hanson, R. K., Gordon, A., Harris, A. J. R., Marques, J. K., Murphy, W., Quinsey, V. L. and Seto, M. C. (2002) 'First report of the Collaborative Outcome Data Project on the effectiveness of psychological treatment for sex offenders', *Sexual Abuse: A Journal of Research and Treatment*, 14(2), 169–94.

Henniker, J., Print, B. and Morrison, T. (2002) 'An inter-agency assessment framework for young people who sexually abuse: principles, processes and practicalities', *Child Care in Practice*, 8(2), 114–26.

Home Office (2004a) *Research, Development and Statistics Directorate*, London: http://www.homeoffice.gov.uk/rds/pdf (accessed 16 August 2004).

Home Office (2004b) 'Reconvictions of prisoners discharged from prison in 1996', Prisons: Research Development Statistics: http://www.homeoffice.gov.uk/rds/ prischap9.html (accessed 16 August 2004).

Hood, R., and Shute, S. (2002) 'The parole system at work: a study of risk based decision making', Home Office Research Study 2002: http://www.homeoffice. gov.uk/rds/pdfs/hors202.pdf (accessed 16 August 2004).

Hood, R., Shute, S., Feilzer, M. and Wilcox, A. (2002) 'Sex offenders emerging from long-term imprisonment', *British Journal of Criminology*, 42, 371–94.

Howitt, D. (1992a) *Child Abuse Errors*, London: Harvester Wheatsheaf.

Howitt, D. (1992b) *Concerning Psychology*, Milton Keynes: Open University Press.

Howitt, D. (1995a) *Paedophiles and Sexual Offences Against Children*, Chichester: Wiley.

Howitt, D. (1995b) 'Pornography and the paedophile: is it criminogenic?', *British Journal of Medical Psychology*, 68(1), 15–27.

Howitt, D. (2004) 'What is the role of fantasy in sex offending?', *Criminal Behaviour and Mental Health*, 14, 185–91.

Irish Examiner (2004) 'Child porn hysteria targets the innocent and ignores the victims': http://www.irishexaminer.com/text/story.asp?j=326717884812&p= 3z 67y7885z3x&n=326717885267 (accessed 17 August 2004).

Killias, M. (1991) 'The historic origins of penal statutes concerning sexual activities involving children and adolescents', *Journal of Homosexuality*, 20(1/2), 41–6.

Loucks, N. (2002) 'Recidivism amongst serious violent and sexual offenders', Social Research: http://www.scotland.gov.uk/library5/justice/rsvo-00.asp (accessed 16 August 2004).

Lovell, E. (2001) *Megan's Law: Does it protect children?*, London: NSPCC.

Marshall, P. (1994) 'Reconviction of imprisoned sexual offenders', Research Bulletin 36, 23–9, London: Home Office.

National Criminal Intelligence Service (2003) 'United Kingdom threat assessment of serious and organised crime: 9. Sex offences against children, including online abuse': http://www.ncis.co.uk/ukta/2003/threat09.asp.

NSPCC (2004) 'Young Abusers Need Help To Avoid Crime Tag, Says NSPCC', 26 July 2004: http://www.nspcc.org.uk/html/home/informationresources/crimetag MAPPAs.htm (accessed 17 August 2004).

Office of the Legislative Auditor (1994) *Sex Offender Treatment Programs*, St Paul, MN: State of Minnesota.

Sheldon, K. (2004) 'A new type of sex offender?', *Forensic Update*, 79, 24–31.

Silverman, J. and Wilson, D. (2002) *Innocence Betrayed: Paedophilia, the Media and Society*, Cambridge: Polity Press.

Stop it Now (2004) 'An innovative approach to preventing child sexual abuse': http://www.stopitnow.org.uk/ (accessed 17 August 2004).

Swanston, H. Y., Parkinson, P. N., O'Toole, B. I., Plunkett, A. M., Shrimpton , S. and Oates, R. K. (2003) 'Juvenile crime, aggression and delinquency after sexual abuse', *British Journal of Criminology*, 43:4, 729–49.

Van Zessen, G. (1991) 'A model for group counseling with male pedophiles', *Journal of Homosexuality*, 201/2, 189–98.

West, D. (1987) *Sexual Crimes and Confrontations: A study of victims and offenders*, Aldershot: Gower.

8 Crime as pollution

Proposal for market-based incentives to reduce crime externalities

Graham Farrell and John Roman

Introduction[1]

Noise pollution and industrial pollution are well-known phenomena. The more technical term for such pollution is 'externalities'. In both instances, the producer of the pollution creates a social cost that is borne by others. Unwilling recipients, such as residents on a noisy airport flight-path or downstream recipients of water pollution, bear the cost. For some types of pollution, such as greenhouse gases dispersed in the atmosphere, society as a whole bears the cost of the emissions.

That crime can also be examined as a form of pollution is the subject of this chapter. It is proposed that various agents, whether manufacturers of frequently stolen products, or owners and managers of premises that are crime prone because of poor design or policies, can produce costly criminal opportunities for which other parts of society bear the cost. In furthering the study of 'crime as pollution' (Roman and Farrell 2002), this chapter discusses the nature and definition of externalities, and seeks a preliminary mapping of how the notion of pollution applies to different types of crime. Crime reduction that utilized rewards and market-based incentives as proposed herein would be adopting a radically different philosophy to 'traditional' punitive approaches to crime control and criminal justice. The chapter also undertakes a preliminary examination of control instruments that have been developed in environmental economics. A range of instruments has been proposed for climate control, and these are examined for possible lessons for crime reduction.

With regard to the implementation of crime-reduction efforts based around an understanding of crime as pollution, the possibility of an Enhanced Crime Doctrine is considered. It is adapted from the existing Enhanced Injury Doctrine applied to the motor vehicle industry whereby, since it is highly predictable that many traffic crashes will occur, vehicle manufacturers are accountable for safety standards to reduce any additional (enhanced) injury. Since aggregate levels of crime can be predicted with reasonable accuracy for many crime types, it is argued that it should legally behove crime polluters to recognize this and adopt anti-crime measures. Since many of the teething problems associated with such an approach have been overcome in relation to motor vehicle injuries, this approach may pave the way for rapid progress for the prevention of crime pollution.

A couple of simple examples of crime pollution will set the scene. First, mobile phone manufacturers make millions in profits. Yet, theft and robbery of mobile phones produces the equivalent of many millions in lost property, pain and suffering to victims, investigation and criminal justice costs. However, mobile phone companies and telecoms networks typically do not cover any of the costs of crime resulting from their products. If they more fully incorporated the anticipation of crime, manufacturers would incur only small increased costs, while society would experience a reduced crime rate and a significant net benefit. Second, alcohol manufacturers and licensees make millions from sales of alcohol at bars and clubs. Bars and clubs are the sites of frequent alcohol-related crime and disorder. Assaults and disorder produce massive costs to society in terms of damage to victims (physical and emotional, with significant health system costs) as well as costs of vandalism and property damage, and the costs to taxpayers of policing and criminal justice. Yet, alcohol producers and distributors incur few of the costs that are the result of sales of their products. At relatively little cost to licensees, changes to the design and management policies of bars and clubs could be introduced to reduce such crimes significantly. The costs of the crime reduction effort would be massively outweighed by the overall benefit to society.

The next section explores more traditional forms of pollution and their control. This is followed by a closer examination of crime as pollution and potential crime reduction approaches.

Controlling traditional forms of pollution

A variety of instruments has developed to control pollutants. To control noise pollution, there are restrictions on decibel levels, on time and place (no loud noise after 11 pm in residential areas), and requirements for sound-proofing. To reduce air and water pollutants, regulations on the time, place and level of emissions have been similarly adopted. Taxation of industry to pay for pollution is known as a Pigouvian Tax after economist Arthur Pigou (1877–1959) who is credited with the proposal. Breaches of regulations can result in punitive fines. Technological innovations such as catalytic converters are sometimes mandated or otherwise encouraged. In addition, in some arenas, incentives such as tax-breaks for good behaviour are becoming increasingly common.

The scope of regulation or other response depends upon the particular externality. Local ordinances may be appropriate for local problems, and national laws or regulations for others. In contrast, greenhouse gases are frequently argued to require an international response because the external cost is shared around the world, as the gases diffuse in the Earth's atmosphere. In an effort to address this, the Kyoto Protocol to the United Nations Framework Convention on Climate Change is currently a controversial effort to introduce international regulation (see, for example, Barrett and Stavins 2002). Since February 2005, the Kyoto Protocol has legally obliged industrialized nations to reduce worldwide emissions of greenhouse gases to 5 per cent below their 1990 levels by 2012.

Less traditional types of pollution

Yet, noise and industrial pollution are just the well-known tip of the externality iceberg. In other walks of life, some of society's more hidden externalities have begun to be recognized. A building designed such that people cannot escape in the event of fire, or a comfy chair that is not made from fire-retardant material, is now acknowledged to produce a negative externality; that is, a risk to life and limb. As a result, there are fire regulations, minimum safety standards for buildings, product safety checks and Safety Commissions. In general, many types of consumer product meet more stringent standards than in the past, thus reducing overt risk of injury to consumers. Consumer pressure groups have become increasingly widespread, thus increasing market pressure on polluters and inducing political pressure to develop protective legislation. Overall, recent years have seen a shift away from *caveat emptor* towards product liability and consumer safety.

The role of litigation

Where political pressure and lobbying are insufficient, or where pollution is flagrant yet unrecognized, lawsuits have played an important role in promoting consumer protection legislation. The Ford Pinto car is an infamous example from the United States. The Pinto was a fire risk whose poor design was responsible for deaths that could have been avoided. The car design was eventually changed so that the petrol tank was protected by a shield and located where it would not be prone to puncture by the rear axle (see Cullen *et al.* 1987). Stephens and Stephens (2000) list 24 instances of legislation that have improved car safety. Such legislation has been particularly prominent in the United States, but because of that country's widespread economic influence, many of the benefits have spread to the UK and elsewhere, and this is arguably true for many areas in addition to motor vehicle manufacture.

Legislation prompting manufacturers to improve car safety

1 Several cases filed in California in the early 1960s together with resulting publicity by Ralph Nader contributed to cessation of production of the Corvair with its unstable rear suspension system.

2 'Paddle Door Latch' litigation in Iowa and Pennsylvania in the mid-1960s contributed significantly to the introduction of recessed door handle designs in current use today.

3 Crashworthiness cases beginning as early as *Larson* v. *General Motors* in 1968 have substantially contributed to the development of what the automotive industry refers to as energy-absorbing 'crush zones'.

4 Litigation beginning as early as 1969 arising out of excessive roof crush in rollover accidents has been a substantial factor in the improvement of roof strength including what General Motors currently refers to as its 'rugged safety cages'.

5 As a result of the Ford Pinto fire litigation, Ford added a fuel tank shield to prevent puncture by the rear axle bolts and discontinued its drop-in fuel tank design in which the top of the fuel tank also serves as the floor of the trunk.

6 Two adverse verdicts in 1979 forced Ford Motor Company to eliminate an 'illusory park' position hazard that had resulted in a number of park-to-reverse design defect injuries.

7 Litigation in 1980 arising from a side impact with a steel pole, resulting in severe injuries to a police officer, substantially contributed to the incorporation of side impact door beams.

8 Litigation in the early 1980s contributed to the discontinuation of the Firestone 500 tyre.

9 Adverse verdicts in Florida and California in Ford Motor Company Pinto fire cases significantly contributed to increasing the collision speed of crash tests to more accurately reflect real-world collisions.

10 Litigation in the mid-1980s contributed to the identification and correction of the Audi sudden acceleration problems.

11 Several substantial verdicts resulting from rollovers caused by instability problems in the Jeep CJ-5 and CJ-7 led to the development of the Jeep Wrangler with its substantially wider track and lower centre of gravity.

12 Litigation arising out of a Minnesota woman's collision with the rear of a tractor trailer rig helped spur new regulations improving the safety of underride guards.

13 The fuel tank location litigation in the 1980s contributed to the relocation of all front wheel drive fuel tanks and many rear wheel drive fuel tanks to a more protected position in front of the rear axle.

14 Combined with the 1986 Report of the National Transportation Safety Board, a series of suits against the automotive industry arising from severe abdominal injuries, lumbar spine fractures and paraplegia from rear seat lap belts ultimately resulted in the transition to significantly safer three-point lap belt/shoulder harness seat restraint systems.

15 A series of successful lawsuits in the late 1980s contributed to the discontinuation of the windowshade slack-inducing device in GM and Ford restraint systems.

16 A large verdict in *Ketchum* v. *Hyundai* led to the discontinuance of the 1988–9 Hyundai shoulder harness only restraint system.

17 A substantial verdict in Colorado in *Miller* v. *Solaglas* in 1991 led the entire aftermarket glass industry to revise its practices to require glued-in aftermarket windshield glass.

18 Litigation arising out of a series of injuries from collapsing seat backs in rear-end collisions including adverse verdicts against General Motors in Arizona and Illinois led GM to adopt more realistic seat back strength standards in the early 1990s.

19 Litigation and resulting publicity involving the instability of the Suzuki Samurai caused it to be pulled from the market.

20 Following extensive litigation involving General Motors side-saddle C/K pickup fuel tank design including the large punitive damage verdict in *Moseley* v. *General Motors* in 1993, essentially all fuel tanks are now located within the protective confines of the frame rail.

21 A substantial punitive damage verdict against General Motors in Alabama in 1996 significantly contributed to design improvements in the General Motors Type III door latch.

22 A series of lawsuits combined with pressure from the National Highway Traffic Safety Administration led to redesign and voluntary replacement of door latches in the Chrysler minivan.

23 More recently, litigation in Missouri involving the 'electronic gas-brake' joystick device in vans specially equipped for handicapped drivers has resulted in the incorporation of several safety design modifications recommended by the plaintiff's expert.

24 Litigation arising from injuries caused by overly aggressive airbags together with pressure from NHTSA (National Highway Traffic Safety Administration) has led to the development of safer and less aggressive airbag systems.

Stephens and Stephens (2000)

An aside is warranted here, on the seemingly widely held opinion in the UK and elsewhere that the USA is an overly litigious society. However, even from this cursory glimpse at the subject, it is apparent that the legal process has produced significant benefits, in terms of consumer protection, that would not have been otherwise realized. It is likely that public opinion is biased against such litigation if it is tainted by a few seemingly absurd high-profile cases such as Stella Liebeck's prosecution of McDonald's, where the jury tried to award nearly $3 million after Liebeck scalded herself with hot coffee in February 1992.[2]

Monitoring and enforcement agencies

The enforcement of anti-pollution measures takes various forms. Monitoring and enforcement agencies administer and/or enforce legislation. Such agencies include the Environment Agency in the United Kingdom and the Environmental Protection Agency in the United States.[3] Efforts to restrict potentially damaging products are widespread. Toys with parts on which children could choke are banned. Imports from a source country without the same level of regulation are closely checked and, if necessary, rejected. A Consumer Product Safety Commission exists to oversee the development and enforcement of control instruments to tackle these externalities.

The philosophy of control

The usual formal definition of externalities is that they are goods people care about that are not sold in a market. They are not sold but they are received anyway, for better (positive externalities) or for worse (negative externalities). Policy is typically concerned with reducing negative externalities or pollutants. Strategic frameworks exist to tackle negative externalities. Broadly speaking, however, command-and-control instruments (restrictive regulations and fines) are being supplemented by, or even making way for, market-based instruments such as tradeable permits. Command-and-control strategies are characterized by their punitive nature that can disrupt market incentives and economic growth. In contrast, market-based incentives seek to reward good practice, thereby harnessing market forces to reduce externalities without the threat to economic growth (see Portney and Stavins 2000).

When located solely in the terminology of criminology and criminal justice, command-and-control measures can be characterized as *ex post* punishment and market incentives as *ex ante* rewards. However, this may not capture the key distinction. The fact that incentives harness market forces is arguably the critical difference between the approaches to control. It is via market forces that incentives seek to promote efficiency by increasing the motivation of those responsible for pollution. Efficiency is increased because the pollution is avoided in the first place (rather than produced then followed by punishment). Such motivation has shifted the goal from being one of seeking to avoid punishment to one of proactively seeking to reduce pollution. Command-and-control techniques can be used in conjunction with market incentives, and the precise combination would be determined by the presenting pollution problem and its context.

Market-based instruments include the use of tradeable permits and the encouragement of research and development for new technologies. Tradeable permits work on the basis that potential polluters are 'allowed' to produce a certain amount of pollution but no more. Those who fail are allowed to purchase (trade) additional permits from those who successfully keep within their prescribed limits. Hence, over-polluters pay extra while safe practices produce extra profit. This produces an incentive to stay within limits and to promote practices that lower emissions further in order to free up tradeable allowance. Research and development can be encouraged via the use of encouragements, particularly patents. Patents allow those who make significant new developments that are widely adopted to licence and benefit from them, thus recouping and potentially benefiting from the investment in research.

Developing and introducing techniques such as tradeable permits and other incentives for crime reduction will require significant effort and political skills. However, having traditionally relied upon regulation and punishment, the possibility of a crime reduction philosophy based around incentives may prove an exciting prospect that warrants further examination and experimental testing.

Crime as pollution

Many of the categories of pollution discussed so far are defined as crimes in certain circumstances. It might, therefore, be concluded that the relationship between crime and externalities has been fully charted and its implications realized. However, this would be a wrong conclusion. Most of the activities discussed above (air and noise pollution, fire safety and consumer product safety) were only legally proscribed after they were recognized as externalities. In contrast, the focus here relates to behaviours that are already legally proscribed as crime but where the role of externalities goes largely unrecognized. There is a fundamental difference between the notion of 'crime as pollution' and that of 'pollution as crime'.

The simplest examples of crime pollution are probably those with close parallels in the consumer safety examples discussed above. Products that are poorly made in such a way as to effectively encourage crime are the easiest to fathom. Cars with door locks that can be opened by a bent coat hanger (an accusation often levelled at the 1970s Ford Cortina) could be said to encourage crime. A more recent example is afforded by mobile phones. The rapid growth of mobile phones in the 1990s led to a mini-crime wave of robbery and theft resulting in 'CRIME U.K.' according to the *Daily Mirror* newspaper and 'Panic on the Streets' (BBC 2002). The phones were highly portable, highly valuable and easily stolen items that made, to use the terminology of Routine Activity Theory, particularly suitable targets. Robbery and theft increased not because the youth population suddenly became more deprived, less well off or less educated, but because a very good criminal opportunity presented itself. However, it is possible that this criminal opportunity did instigate many new criminal careers.

Violent crime and disorder can be viewed as pollution in many instances. Assaults, robberies and disorder in and around bars and nightclubs are arguably externalities caused by profit-seeking alcohol manufacturers, retailers (and even, perhaps, local governments who receive taxation).

Perhaps a case could even be made that alcohol manufacturers hold some liability for domestic violence. Alcohol is certainly commonly understood to be present in many instances. Of course, alcohol is frequently used as an excuse for domestic violence but most commentators would deny that it can justifiably be cited as a cause. However, if the alcohol industry as a whole were taxed and the resources poured into services for victims/survivors of domestic violence, it is likely that many commentators would view this as an advance on the current situation, and would not require any reduction in the culpability of a violent offender. This is only raised here as a possibility that warrants further discussion. The intention here is to raise the possibility that, since alcohol is a commonly cited factor in domestic violence (if not an excuse), then the industry which is the primary beneficiary might, in some fashion, be made to return some of its profits to the victims who incur a major cost which few would hold to be unrelated.

Child pornography, and hence perhaps child sexual abuse, are arguably facilitated by the Internet. The Internet and e-mail facilitate the advertising, exchange and purchase of illegal pornography (and other illegal products and services) of various types. It has also been suggested that the Internet facilitates the illegal sex trade as well as the illegal drugs trade and other forms of crime and organized crime. Perhaps Internet Service Providers (ISPs), who benefit financially from subscriptions, could be considered as crime polluters. If their service promotes illegal activities, a case could be made that they should be held responsible. At the very least, it could be argued that ISPs should be more formally encouraged to rapidly develop monitoring and tracing technologies that deter and detect. While there may be some public pressure on major ISPs to do so (so that many have password protection to reduce the possibility of minors accessing certain types of site), it is likely that legislation which recognizes e-crimes as pollution caused by the Internet and by ISPs (as those who profit), will accelerate this process. Perhaps the process could be incentivized so that 'safe' ISPs benefit from their improved software and practices.

A tentative and preliminary list of crime types, possible polluters, and possible solutions is presented in Table 8.1. It is extremely preliminary, and at this stage represents more of an attempt to brainstorm the issue than to develop a comprehensive list. It is certainly not intended to be exhaustive but, rather, to set the ball rolling. It is also recognized that some of the elements it contains may, upon closer examination, prove to be erroneous or to require significant revision. This is normal in the development of a concept that is likely to require many iterations of revision.

How is crime pollution recognized? The first step in examining a crime type appears to be the identification of possible polluters. Often, but not necessarily always, there is a link via the question of 'who benefits?' directly or indirectly from this type of crime. The identification of possible control mechanisms is a next step. Whether or not control mechanisms can incorporate market incentives, which should be more efficient than traditional command-and-control techniques, is a different question. Some combination of approaches seems the most likely possibility – that is, stick and carrot in combination to produce maximum effect.

Table 8.1 Preliminary list of sources of crime pollution by crime category.

Crime type/area	Possible polluter(s)	Why is it pollution?	Comments/Possible Measures
Vehicle Crime			
Theft of and from vehicles	Vehicle manufacturers	Savings on production costs which avoid built-in anti-theft design and measures.	Minimum crime safety standards and testing akin to those for crash safety.
Theft of and from vehicles	Car park designers, owners, managers	Savings on barriers to reduce access, on CCTV, on staffing, on design.	Safer Parking Scheme (new version of Secured Car Parks) extended to minimum crime-safety standards and practices.
Theft of and from vehicles	Car owners	Failure to lock car is negligent.	System of fines for negligent owners (as used in Austria and elsewhere).
Property Crime			
Residential and commercial burglary	Architects and builders	Failure to incorporate safe designs and standards.	Legislation to promote safer designs.
Theft and robbery of hot products	Product designers and manufacturers	Production of lightweight, valuable, easily stolen products (DVDs, iPods). Savings on design and production costs.	Mobile phones caused mini-crime wave of robbery and theft in UK. Phone manufacturers and providers benefit but do not bear the crime cost.
Street crime	Architects and builders	Saved tie and energy by avoiding need to incorporate crime risks.	Street layouts to promote surveillance.
Street crime	Local government authorities?	Absence of suitable street lighting?	Painter and Farrington suggest lighting reduces crime and can be very cost-effective.
Credit card fraud	Credit card companies, banks, financial institutions	Huge benefit from credit card business but little attention to increased fraud.	Mandatory photo-ID credit cards (reduced fraud in Sweden by 70%), mandatory chip and pin, mandatory identification of unusual patterns of use.

(continued on next page)

Table 8.1 (continued)

Crime type/area	Possible polluter(s)	Why is it pollution?	Comments/Possible Measures
Internet fraud	Internet Service Providers, Internet retailers, e-commerce and auction sites	Huge benefit from e-commerce but little (or belated) attention to crime risk.	Increased accountability of ISPs, perhaps incentives for research and development of tracking and detection software.
Crime in shopping areas and transport nodes	Architects, builders, owners and managers	Layout is formulated to maximise sales or other goals with little regard for crime potential.	Layouts to promote surveillance and reduce dangerous areas (as with Felson et al. study of Port Authority Bus Station)
Bank robbery	Architects and designers	The cost of robbery is not only the financial cost to bank but is also the risk and trauma to staff victims and the public.	Historically, security has been a key role of bank design. Imagine if it was not considered!
Commercial robbery	Designers, shop owners and managers	Poor designs can encourage robbery.	Mandatory crime-proof checks akin to fire safety standards.
Shoplifting	Shop designers, owners and managers	Responsible for aspects of design and shop layout. If poor layouts encourage shoplifting it may encourage novice offenders, with society paying the crime cost of future offending.	Mandatory standards for shop layout and practices.
Personal crime and disorder			
Child pornography	Internet Service Providers (ISPs)	ISPs benefit from subscriptions, but also facilitate exchange of illegal porn. Society pays the cost in terms of crime.	Increased accountability of ISPs, perhaps incentives for research and development of tracking and detection software.
Stalking	Telecoms companies and ISPs	Mobile phone and email are increasingly used for stalking.	Encourage companies to track and detect stalking behaviour.

Table 8.1 (continued)

Crime type/area	Possible polluter(s)	Why is it pollution?	Comments/Possible Measures
Inner-city grime caused by chewing gum on streets	Chewing gum manufacturers	Manufacturers profit from sales while society incurs the cost of extensive gum-grime littering the street.	Manufacturers should pay for clean-up costs, encourage environmentally friendly disposal of gum (e.g. gum-tree boards).
Youth crime and disorder	Parents?	Parents save time and effort expended on children?	The UK has increased parental liability and accountability in recent years through fines.
Domestic violence	Alcohol manufacturers and licensees?	Alcohol often pays a role (but should not be allowed as an excuse for) domestic and other violence. Manufacturers and licensees profit but victims and society pay the cost of personal crimes.	Enforced responsibility of licensees. Perhaps taxes and fines used to fund domestic violence services.
Snatch theft	Bag manufacturers	Some bags are easier to snatch, to dip into, or to cut open.	Bags can be designed to avoid snatch, dipping or ripping? Perhaps production guidelines, quality controls or standards should be considered?
Organised crime Drug dealing and money laundering	Financial institutions	Financial institutions benefit from transactions and investment from drug money laundering and organized crime.	Asset freezing and seizures. Regulation of financial transactions.

Note:
Please note that this list is tentative. Some of its suggestions are possibly inflammatory (such as holding parents responsible for the crime of their children) – but the intention is to promote thinking about crime externalities and begin to chart the territory rather than produce a definitive framework.

Table 8.2 Costs of crime (£) for two crime types.

	Robbery/ mugging	Wounding (serious and slight)
Security expenditure	0	2
Insurance administration	40	-
Property stolen or damaged	310	-
Emotional and physical impact on victims	2,400	12,000
Lost output	420	2,000
Victim Services	6	6
Health services	190	1,200
Criminal Justice System (incl. police)	1,400	2,700
Total average cost	4,700	18,000
Total UK cost	2,000 million	15,600 million

Source: Brand and Price (2000).

Who benefits from crime?

The possible list of polluters is large once the penny drops. It appears that a necessary, though perhaps not sufficient, means of identifying polluters is to ask 'Who benefits?' and 'Who pays?' in relation to particular crime types. Identifying the scale of the pollution involves examining the difference between the benefits and the costs. Some crimes produce far greater overall social cost than others, particularly when intangible costs (pain and suffering) as well as police and criminal justice costs are incorporated.

Car manufacturers may save (benefit) on production costs by excluding some anti-theft devices. Yet their savings are likely to be small when compared with the overall cost to the victim and society from car crime (particularly when emotional and psychological damage are considered as well as fear of crime and insurance costs). The beneficiaries from alcohol-related crime and disorder are alcohol manufacturers and retailers. Retailers may fail to follow safe practices regarding alcohol sales, may promote rapid consumption of alcohol via 'happy hours' and other promotions (thus boosting sales), and thereby maximize their profits while incurring little of the overall cost of resultant crimes. Since many crimes will take place off the licensed premises, retailers argue that they are not their responsibility, while victims can incur major costs in terms of lost property, and perhaps physical damage that may result in hospital bills, psychological damage and even lost productivity and wages due to absence from work. The improved measurement and understanding of the costs of crime, which has occurred as part of the growth of cost–benefit analysis within criminal justice, is possibly fundamental in promoting an understanding of crime as pollution.

The role of cost–benefit analysis

The identification of crime externalities is located within the field of cost–benefit analysis (Roman and Farrell 2002). The field of cost–benefit analysis has made significant steps forward in relation to criminal justice in recent years. Of particular relevance are advances in the measurement of the costs of crime (see Cohen 2000 for a review; and Brand and Price 2000 for UK national estimates). The latest estimates are based on Willingness-to-Pay (WTP) or contingent valuation estimates (Cohen *et al.* 2004). WTP uses a survey asking respondents how much they would be willing to pay to avoid crime, and such methods have not been used previously in this context.

A key insight deriving from recent advances in cost estimation method-ology has been the greater understanding of both the types of cost item relating to crime as well as their cost to victims and society. Table 8.2 shows the various cost components for only two crime types. The data are taken from Brand and Price's influence study (Brand and Price 2000). Note that these cost estimates are now viewed as relatively conservative and that those produced by the method adopted by Cohen *et al.* (2004) are some-times many times greater.

While cost–benefit analysis may be a necessary vehicle for the further-ance of the specification of the costs of crime (and hence of the extent of pollution), it is not sufficient to ensure the implementation of such efforts. The next section considers issues relating to implementation via a discus-sion of the possibility of an Enhanced Crime Doctrine.

An 'Enhanced Crime Doctrine'

In consumer product legislation, the Enhanced Injury Doctrine is promi-nent. Citing the influential case of *Larsen* v. *General Motors* of 1968, Whelan (1999) captures the essence of the doctrine in relation to the liability of USA car manufacturers for injuries to vehicle occupants:

> Larsen [v. General Motors] held that collisions are foreseeable to vehicle manufacturers and therefore cars must be reasonably crash-worthy. Hence, injuries caused by the lack of crashworthiness are separate and apart from the accident-caused injuries inasmuch as the manufacturer has a duty to design for foreseeable crashes, which occur 'with or without the fault of the victim'.
>
> (Whelan 1999)

This doctrine suggests that, even though some crashes may be caused by ('with or without the fault of') the victims, the manufacturers know that crashes will occur and are obliged to minimize damage. The same principle should arguably apply to consumer goods, since manufacturers know that some of them will be stolen. Therefore, regardless of whether theft occurs 'with or without the fault of the victim', manufacturers should have a responsibility to design products in ways that minimize risk and the resul-tant cost of crime. An Enhanced Crime Doctrine would be the appropriate criminological parallel. In relation to stolen consumer products, it could run thus:

> The theft of certain types of products is clearly foreseeable. Hence, manufacturers should have a duty to design for foreseeable theft and resale which occurs with or without the fault of the victim. Therefore, frequently stolen consumer products must be reasonably difficult, unattractive, or unrewarding propositions for theft and resale.

Yet crime pollution is more widespread than solely via consumer products. It would also apply to bars and clubs with high rates of assaults, disorder and other crimes. Such crimes are similarly predictable, and so the appropriate enhanced crime doctrine would be along the lines of:

> In and around licensed premises, certain types of assault, disorder and other crimes are clearly foreseeable. Hence licensees should have a duty to design and practise business for foreseeable assault, disorder and other crime. Such premises must have designs, policies and practices that ensure they are reasonably free from such crimes.

The same Enhanced Crime Doctrine could be applied to other types of businesses, and perhaps public and private spaces. The identification of a potential polluter is the prerequisite to the formulation of the appropriate Enhanced Crime Doctrine.

Implementing crime–pollution reduction

Whereas most people talk of aiming to avoid reinventing the wheel, Paul Ekblom refers, in his driest tone, to the need to avoid reinventing the flat tyre. This captures the need to avoid known bad practices, but more importantly, the fact that 'new' policies which fail to learn from previous ones often turn out worse. In the present context, the Enhanced Injury Doctrine may prove a useful model for an Enhanced Crime Doctrine in several practical ways. The issue of how to implement anti-crime-pollution measures is a critical aspect for any progress in crime reduction. When discussing the possibilities of making polluters pay for crime reduction, Ekblom (2005) notes 15 obstacles to overcome in his section 'Making it Work'. Ekblom's list includes the need to establish:

- Principles. (How would we decide if a company is responsible?)
- Levels of fines. (How much do they pay?)
- A level playing field. (Are competing companies all equally liable?)
- Whether or when an industry or an individual company is liable.
- What to do with any money raised from fines.

However, there may already be established frameworks to answer these questions and more. Crime reduction might avoid the need to reinvent the wheel if it can poach proven methods, techniques and practices that are derived from the Enhanced Injury Doctrine and elsewhere. This is neither cynical nor lazy: it is good practice to learn from success and mistakes elsewhere. Others have been tackling these practical questions for many years and have made significant progress in overcoming them. Crime reduction should overtly seek to plunder such sources of knowledge and good practice.

The architecture of control instruments

Instruments are the policies and tactics for the control of pollution. They take different forms. Barrett and Stavins (2002) review the architecture of the various types of instruments developed in environmental economics for climate control. The instruments are (briefly, but hopefully not too rudely) summarized in the list below. The specifics of the various proposals will not be discussed here, and the reader is referred to Barrett and Stavins for the complete review and to the additional original sources.

Fourteen designs (architectures) for climate control instruments adapted to crime reduction

Barrett and Stavins (2002) reviewed 14 types of proposal for environmental control instruments. Here, the 14 are simply taken and, where appropriate, switched to read as if they were crime reduction instruments while retaining key references from the climate control literature:

1 Producer emissions limits and market-based trading incentives (Kyoto Protocol to United Nations FCCC, 1992).
2 As (1) but with fixed-price permits available. Proceeds of permit sales fund research on safe design and crime risk management (Aldy *et al.* (2001), and others).
3 No emissions commitments or market-based instruments; incentives for safe design and management research, developing common standards for technology and management (as a way to ensure participation) (Barrett 2003, 2001a, b).
4 A portfolio of policies: development of design and management standards (aimed at long-term emission reduction), and incentives for technology innovation and diffusion; emissions targets (small at first then increasing); crime tax to fund research (Benedick 2001).
5 Emissions trading – no fixed limits; permits for business-as-usual emissions. Periodical purchase (and retirement) of emissions allowances (Bradford, 2001).
6 Negotiation on a set of standards to achieve lower emissions (within industry or crime type?) A harmonized crime tax (Cooper 1998, 2001).

7 Experimentation with multiple 'case studies' of policy instruments including: coordinated measures; emissions tax; tradeable emissions permits; hybrid system (Hahn 1998).

8 Price-based approach with two markets for tradeable permits: annual market and perpetuity (endowment) market (McKibbin and Wilcoxen 1997, 2000).

9 Crime tax system harmonized through dynamic cost–benefit analysis; import duties on non-compliant goods and services; graduated fines increase over time (Nordhaus 1998).

10 A 'Marshall Plan' of mutually agreed actions (e.g. by key manufacturers in an industry emitting criminal opportunities) (Schelling 1997, 1998, 2002).

11 Two-step plan: first, introduce low crime taxes (for easy implementation) with broad coverage – broad and shallow approach; second, gradually build depth of impact on crime pollution (Schmalensee 1996, 1998).

12 Three-part architecture: a) Initial broad coverage with taxes 'means tested'; b) Moderate yet rigid short-term targets, then ambitious yet flexible long-term targets (to induce technological and other change and to adapt to learning); c) Market-based tradeable permit instruments possibly with government safety-valve (further sales) (Stavins 2001).

13 A Clean Development Mechanism (CDM) – big polluters receive credit for assisting smaller ones; voluntary participation in emissions permit trading; mechanisms for voluntary accession to emissions quota system; automatic graduation to emissions quota system for companies (etc.) beyond a certain size (Stewart and Weiner 2001).

14 Tradeable emissions permits initially targeted at key polluters (above a relevant threshold), with quotas or growth-targets for others (Victor 2001).

Barrett and Stavins synthesize the information from the various proposals for climate control. They identify four key factors which are presented here as they contain lessons for any possible crime reduction enterprise along these lines. It is concluded that the most successful instruments will have:

- moderate short-term goals;
- provision for later expansion beyond key polluters;
- the use of market mechanisms to maintain economic incentives (tradeable permits; hybrid quota-tax schemes) and encourage technological responses;
- incentives for participation and compliance.

While this is a gross simplification of the Barrett and Stavins work, the intent here is to unashamedly steal lessons that may inform the development of crime reduction.[4] Moderate short-term goals are necessary because everything cannot change at once. There will be little support for immediate extensive change. This is also why the second factor, that is, provision for later expansion, is also critical. Assuming that crime-pollution-reduction instruments are considered, their development would need to be cautious at first. The low-hanging fruit of crime types and legislation that will encounter little political opposition would be approached at first (that is, crime reduction probably shouldn't start with the gun control lobby in the USA). Crime types where existing measures are akin to anti-pollution measures should be identified and developed. Many of these exist already; efforts to promote safe building designs for residences and businesses, as well as secure car parks, have become increasingly widespread. The UK's Secured Car Parks Scheme has, after a decade, grown into the Safer Parking Scheme, continuing as an initiative of the Association of Chief Police Officers (British Parking Association 2005). Secured By Design (ACPO Crime Prevention Initiatives Limited, 2005) already seeks to apply security standards and the principles of designing-out-crime to residential and business premises and areas as well as schools, railway stations, caravan parks, children's play areas, and sheltered accommodation. Such efforts have shown to be effective in at least one evaluation of anti-residential burglary initiatives (Armitage 2000). Extending such efforts to incorporate a more extensive pollution approach, perhaps initially with market incentives at the fore (more carrot than stick, at least at first) would seem appropriate. This fits well with Barrett and Stavins's third factor cited above; that is, the incorporation of market mechanisms where possible as well as incentives to encourage participation and compliance.

It is also possible that other aspects of knowledge relating to crime analysis might be fruitfully integrated into the approaches used in climate control. It is known that crime clusters along various dimensions. Crime is disproportionately committed by prolific repeat offenders, disproportionately experienced by repeatedly victimized targets (whether persons, places or other targets), and crime is concentrated geographically into hotspots. Accommodating such knowledge into instruments in ways that focus them upon these crime clusters is a possibility that should be considered if it does not occur as a natural part of the process.

The role of the police service

Currently, the police service deflects much responsibility away from local or national government and other community agencies. The police are effectively the organizational whipping boy, and receive criticism for crime that is, in the framework proposed herein, more appropriately categorized as an externality produced by others. A preferable role for the police might be as enforcers of legislation against crime-pollution. This would shift some of the police role to being more akin to that of quality control and a trading standards agency. Whether or not such work fell within the role of the traditional police agency or led to the establishment of a new crime-pollution agency, is a different question. In the long run it would be hoped that it would lead to a decline in demand for traditional police work. In the short to medium term, however, it would undoubtedly be viewed as competing for existing limited resources. Perhaps a separate crime-pollution agency to develop, administer and enforce anti-pollution efforts against crime, would be more appropriate.

Conclusion

This chapter has continued work begun in Roman and Farrell (2002). That study noted how crime is an instance where market failure is common. Many agents in society (such as manufacturers and businesses) have little or no economic incentive to act in ways that reduce crime risks for others. They may, rather, save production costs or business costs in ways that, whether inadvertently or not, serve to effectively increase the risk of crime to others. Hence the normal market mechanism, which often serves to protect consumers, frequently fails when it comes to crime. The result is that crime costs to society are immensely greater than if the criminal opportunities had been stemmed at source.

Crime reduction seeking to tackle externalities must do so in ways that do not otherwise hinder the market. Crime reduction should not, for example, increase the costs of businesses in ways that make them less profitable. It is useful to reiterate the statement from Roman and Farrell about the need for caution in developing crime reduction measures based on this approach:

> [C]learly, such an approach should not be so interventionist so as to interfere with the market, its incentives and its profits. Reducing market efficiency is, firmly, not the aim of these proposals. The avoidance of a specific instance of market failure as it relates to crime – where manufacturers impose large external costs on society in order to reap small rewards for themselves – is a more desirable objective.
>
> (Roman and Farrell 2002: 78)

Crime control is traditionally punitive. It uses fines and other punishments across a range of custodial and non-custodial sentences after detecting perpetrators. The possibility of introducing a different orientation to crime control philosophy may be an exciting prospect. Market-based incentives, that is, using combinations of rewards and incentives (such as tax breaks and tradeable permits) to encourage crime reduction activity of various sorts, may produce an actual and perceived shift in the philosophy of crime control. More practically, it could present the possibility for efficient and effective crime reduction efforts that are developed and implemented by those who might be more appropriately viewed as the root causes of crime – that is, those agents who generate criminal opportunities or facilitate crime in various ways that often go unrecognized. The further exploration of the nature of crime-types as forms of pollution, the drafting of appropriate legislation and the introduction of experimental trials of various market incentives, may be the appropriate next steps.

Notes

1   Acknowledgements: Earlier versions of this work were presented to the American Society of Criminology in Denver, November 2003, and to the Midlands branch of the British Society of Criminology, at the Galleries of Justice, in Nottingham on 31 March 2004. We thank Kate Moss for the latter of those two opportunities.
2   Even this case is more complex than many people believe from the poorly informed anecdotes – see Greenbaum (2005).
3   The UK's Environment Agency is at http://www.environment-agency.gov.uk. The US EPA is at http://www.epa.gov.
4   We apologise to Barrett and Stavins for the brevity of coverage of their extensive review, as well as for any possible misrepresentation incurred in its transfer to this context. It is our worry that the brevity of this section does not adequately convey the respect that their work warrants.

Bibliography

ACPO (Association of Chief Police Officers of England and Wales) Crime Prevention Initiatives Limited. 2005. 'Secured By Design' at http://www. securedby design.com/ (accessed March 2005).

Aldy, Joseph E., Orszag, Peter R. and Stiglitz, Joseph E. (2001), 'Climate Change: An Agenda for Global Collective Action', Prepared for the conference on *The Timing of Climate Change Policies*, Pew Center on Global Climate Change, Washington, DC.

Armitage, R. (2000) 'An Evaluation of Secured By Design Housing within West Yorkshire', *Policing and Reducing Crime Unit Briefing Note 7/00*, London: Home Office.

BBC News (2002) 'Panic on the Streets' BBC News online, 21 February 2002, http://news.bbc.co.uk/1/hi/uk/1833953.stm

Barrett, S. (2001a) 'International Cooperation for Sale', *European Economic Review* 45(10), 1835–50.

Barrett, S. (2001b) 'Towards a Better Climate Treaty', *Policy Matters*, 01–29, November, Washington, DC: AEI-Brookings Joint Center for Regulatory Studies.

Barrett, S. (2003) *Environment and Statecraft: The Strategy of Environmental Treaty-Making*, Oxford: Oxford University Press.

Barrett, S. and Stavins, R. (2002) 'Increasing Participation and Compliance in International Climate Change Agreements' *International Environmental Agreements: Politics, Law and Economics* 3(2003): 349–76.

Benedick, R.E. (2001) 'Striking a New Deal on Climate Change', *Issues in Science and Technology* 18(1), 71–6.

Bradford, D.F. (2001) 'Succeeding Kyoto: A No-Cap but Trade Approach to GHG Control. Version 02a', Princeton University and NYU School of Law, September 5.

Brand, S. and Price, R. (2000) *The Economic and Social Costs of Crime, Home Office Research Study 217*, London: Home Office (http://www.homeoffice.gov.uk/rds/pdfs/hors217.pdf)

British Parking Association (2005) 'What is the Safer Parking Scheme (SPS)?' and 'Is the SPS the Same as the Secured Car Parks Scheme?' (http://www.britishparking.co.uk/pages/secure/secure1.htm) (accessed March 2005).

Cohen, M.A. (2000) 'Measuring the Costs and Benefits of Crime and Justice', *Measurement and Analysis of Crime and Justice*, Vol. 4 of Criminal Justice 2000, Washington DC: National Institute of Justice.

Cohen, M.A., Rust, R.T., Steen, S. and Tidd, S.T. (2004) 'Willingness-to-pay for Crime Control Programs', *Criminology* 42(1), 89–109.

Cooper, R. (1998) 'Toward a Real Treaty on Global Warming', *Foreign Affairs* 77(2), 66–79.

Cooper, R. (2001) 'The Kyoto Protocol: A Flawed Concept', *Environmental Law Reporter*, 31 (December), 11, 484–92.

Cullen, Francis T., Maakestad, William J. and Cavender, Gray (1987) *Corporate Crime Under Attack: The Ford Pinto Case and Beyond*, Cincinnati: Anderson Publishing.

Ekblom, P (2005) 'The "Polluter-Pays" Principle and Crime Reduction', unpublished manuscript, Home Office Central Intelligence Hub, London: Home Office.

Felson, M., Belanger, M.E., Bichler, C.D., Bruzinski, C.D., Campbell, G.S., Friecol, C.L., Grofik, K.C., Mazur, I.S., Regan, A.B., Sweeney, P.J., Ullman, A.L. and Williams, L.Q. (1996) 'Redesigning Hell: Preventing Crime and Disorder at the Port Authority Bus Terminal', in R.V. Clarke (ed.), 'Preventing Mass Transit Crime', *Crime Prevention Studies*, 6, 5–92.

Greenbaum, J. (2005) 'McDonald's Hot Coffee Lawsuit and Beyond: The Tort Reform Myth Machine', Common Dreams News Centre, 22 January 2005 (http://www.commondreams.org/views05/0122–11.htm).

Hahn, R.W. (1998) *The Economics and Politics of Climate Change*, Washington, DC: American Enterprise Institute Press.

McKibbin, W.J and Wilcoxen, P.J. (1997) 'A Better Way to Slow Global Climate Change', *Brookings Policy Brief*, No. 17, Washington, DC: Brookings Institution.

McKibbin, W.J and Wilcoxen, P.J. (2000) 'Moving Beyond Kyoto', *Brookings Policy Brief*, No. 66. Washington, DC: Brookings Institution.

Nordhaus, W.D. (1998) 'Is the Kyoto Protocol a Dead Duck? Are There Any Live Ducks Around? Comparison of Alternative Global Tradeable Emissions Regimes', Working Paper, Department of Economics, Yale University, New Haven, CT, July 31.

Portney, P. and Stavins, R. (2000) *Public Policies for Environmental Protection*, Washington DC: Resources For the Future Press.

Roman, J. and Farrell, G. (2002) 'Cost–Benefit Analysis for Crime Prevention: Opportunity Costs, Routine Savings, and Crime Externalities', in N. Tilley (ed.) 'Evaluation for Crime Prevention', *Crime Prevention Studies*, 14, 53–92.

Schelling, T.C. (1997) 'The Cost of Combating Global Warming: Facing the Trade-offs', *Foreign Affairs* 76(6), 8–14.

Schelling, T.C. (1998) *Costs and Benefits of Greenhouse Gas Reduction*, Washington, DC: AEI Press.

Schelling, T.C. (2002) 'What Makes Greenhouse Sense? Time to Rethink the Kyoto Protocol', *Foreign Affairs* 81(3), 2–9.

Schmalensee, R. (1998) 'Greenhouse Policy Architecture and Institutions', in William D. Nordhaus (ed.) *Economics and Policy Issues in Climate Change*, Washington, DC: Resources for the Future, pp. 137–58.

Stavins, R. N. (2001) 'Give Bush Time on Climate Change', *Boston Global*, 4th April.

Stephens, John L. and Stephens, James S. (2000) 'Can Trial Lawyers Really Help Make Cars Safer?' FindLaw at http://library.lp.findlaw.com/articles/file/00586/004776/title/Subject/topic/Torts/%20Personal%20Injury_Motor%20Vehicle%20Accidents/filename/tortspersonalinjury_2_6256.

Stewart, R.B. and Wiener, J.B. (2001) 'Reconstructing Climate Policy: The Paths Ahead', *Policy Matters*, 01–23,Washington, DC: AEI-Brookings Joint Center for Regulatory Studies, August.

Whelan, Paul W. (1999) 'Enhanced Injuries and the Restatement of Tort Thirds' FindLaw at http://library.lp.findlaw.com/articles/file/00665/006761/title/Subject/topic/Transportation_Motor%20Vehicles/filename/transportation_2_6384.

Victor, D.G. (2001) 'International Agreements and the Struggle to Tame Carbon', July 4 (cited in Barrett and Stavins 2003).

9 Managing offenders and reducing crime

Government responses to persistent offenders and the development of the National Offender Management Service

Steve Goode and Stephen Brookes

Introduction

This chapter examines two major policy initiatives which aim to reduce crime in the community through the targeting and effective management of offenders. Taking into account the context of current legislation and links with policy initiatives, it contends that a focus on the offender is one critical element of a range of government policies to reduce crime. It describes two such initiatives; the first is both practitioner based and locality driven, being underpinned by inter-agency strategies designed to target the small core of offenders who are responsible for causing the most crime, disorder and fear in their local communities. The second initiative is organizational and details the ongoing reform of the correctional services and in particular the merging of the prison and probation services within the National Offender Management Service. The focus of this merged organization is on offender management and the development of a marketplace for improved services for offenders from the public, private and independent sectors.

The chapter begins with a brief contextual examination of the law and of policy-making in relation to both crime reduction more generally and tackling offenders specifically. It then focuses on how legislation and policy are turned into practice on the ground, before moving on to the more detailed discussion of the two policy initiatives. Some comments are offered in relation to 'what works' in dealing with offenders. The chapter also notes that whilst not all practioners or academics have welcomed the growth of integrated corrections, the challenge for government is to achieve the proper balance between custody and other community penalties to ensure a minimum level of recidivism. This can only be achieved if efforts to prevent and deter, catch and convict, and resettle and rehabilitate offenders are properly managed. If this is successful, confidence in the criminal justice system is more likely to be improved whilst at the same time bringing more offenders to justice.

The context of tackling and managing offenders: an informed agenda?

Central government develops policies on crime reduction and in an ideal world those policies should be framed within the context of well-tested criminological theory. This does not always happen for at least two reasons. First, the field of criminological theory is beset with contradictory approaches and findings and it is often difficult to point to any one approach with confidence. Second, even if one accepts a particular criminological theory with confidence, it does not necessarily follow that policy makers will embrace that theory within either policy or legislation. This has significant implications in determining how to deal with crime more generally and criminals more specifically.

It is suggested that the two examples described in this chapter help to address this issue in two ways. First, the merging of the probation and prison services will doubtless provide a much stronger opportunity to introduce and develop different approaches to dealing with offenders. Second, the three strands of the priority and prolific offender strategy – namely the focus on prevention and deterrence; the emphasis on catching and convicting; and finally the importance of rehabiliting and resettling offenders – should give some confidence that policy makers are indeed both listening and responding to aspects of what works in criminology. Both examples offer the potential for a seamlessness within policies that hitherto has not existed.

Every crime policy makes certain theoretical assumptions about crime that have to be supported in order for a person to believe that the policy will work. It could be argued that criminology should be in a position to inform policy-making. As a professional academic discipline, criminology did not exist in Britain until 1935. Garland (1988) contends that, by convention, modern scientific criminology is said to have begun with Lombroso's criminal anthropology in the 1870s. Although criminological developments in Britain did not develop from the Lombrosian tradition, it is important to note that the focus on the characteristics and behaviours of offenders has always been present – perhaps not as radically (or, as Garland would argue, naively) as Lombroso's description of the atavistic man – but most certainly as a central part of criminal policy-making. How have the policies shaped the agenda in relation to dealing with offenders and how has criminology assisted in informing that agenda?

Vold and Bernard (1986) suggest that every theory of crime implies policies about how best to handle the crime problem. The authors argue that, in principle, policy ought to be derived from theory. In reality, practical measures often do not wait for theoretical grounding. Rather, they suggest that policies which seem necessary at the time are implemented, and theoretical explanations come along afterwards to rationalize and justify what has occurred. In this situation people tend to believe in one theory of crime or another because its policy implications are consistent with what they believe should be done about crime. A similar point has been made by Garland (2002: 26) who observed that crime policies that were adopted and succeeded did so because 'they characterize problems and identify solutions in ways that fit with the dominant (political) culture and power structure upon which it rests'.

Vold and Bernard (1986: 349) define 'crime policies' as 'the different ways in which the organized state responds to the serious social problems described by the term "crime"'. In doing so they describe a typology of crime policies in the following ways:

- Some deal with individual offenders.
- Other policies attempt to change the social conditions in the communities that offenders come from or the physical environment in the communities where offenders commit their offences.
- Still more policies address social and political conditions in society at large.

This seemingly simple description of what 'crime policies' means starts to emphasize the complexity of crime, its causes and potential solutions.

To what degree, therefore, can criminology have a real impact on the ground? The complexity of criminological theory has been described as being of little help in dealing with crime in the real world. Clarke and Eck (2003: 9), for example, suggest that this is because it finds causes in distant factors, such as child-rearing practices, genetic makeup and psychological or social processes. However, the same authors point to the utility of environmental criminology because this deals with the immediate situational causes of the crime event.

For policy makers to focus on only one or two theories, or indeed self-postulated reasons for crime, can result in unintended consequences. Young (1994: 78) identified one such example from the late 1970s and early 1980s – a time when tough regimes for offenders were favoured by politicians both in the USA and in Britain – which he described as 'an etiological crisis on the left with regard to the causes of crime; a parallel intellectual crisis on the right over the failure of policing and prisons and a fiscal crisis'. To summarize: more money was being pumped into law and order and the building of new prisons but crime was still rising. Similar views in relation to the political economy of crime have been made by other commentators. Taylor (1997: 295) has also acknowledged the Left Realist argument and referred to the attention that was being paid to the continuing contradiction between the massive increase in the prison population in the 1980s and the escalation in crimes of violence, robbery and other disruptive and disorderly behaviours on American streets.

Political priorities also change over time and during the lifetime of each priority it is possible to align them to different paradigms within criminology. This view is assisted by Young's (1994: 78) summary of four recent paradigms:

1   Left Idealists see the causes of crime as being rooted in the deprivation of the poor and the greed of the rich. A focus on social conditions and social policy is necessary.

2   For the New Administrative Criminologists, crime is not caused by social conditions – it is opportunistic, being committed where situations arise which present possibilities for crime and when those who are minded to commit crime avail themselves of those opportunities. The focus therefore should be on the situations that enable crimes to occur and to target those who are minded to commit the crimes.

3   Right Realists claim that crime is caused by a breakdown in social order and further that policing is effective, not through a direct effect on the control of crime but rather in maintaining social order. Where disorder is not controlled, the neighbourhood enters a spiral of decline. The focus therefore is on maintaining social control.

4   Left Realism contends that the causes of crime are too complex for one explanation and that different approaches are required at different times and in different situations.

It could be argued that the first three paradigms were instrumental in shaping political influence and government policies in the mid- to late twentieth century and also led to the etiological and fiscal crisis referred to by Young (1994). However, this chapter contends that the fourth paradigm is either directly, or at the very least indirectly, influencing political direction today and this will be discussed further within the context of current policies and practices to target persistent offenders and the effective management of offenders.

From policy to practice

In policy terms a focus on the offender is critical and is one of three elements described by environmental criminologists as 'the crime triangle'. Derived from one of the main theories of environmental criminology – Routine Activity Theory – Cohen and Felson (1979) state that predatory crime occurs when a likely offender and suitable target come together in time and space, without a capable guardian present. Clark and Eck (2003) take this one step further by linking the crime triangle to another useful analytic tool which is a classification of the three main kinds of recurring problems that confront crime. In addition to repeat victims and repeat places the authors also refer to repeat (or persistent) offenders. The need to focus on persistent offenders is therefore critical in the fight to prevent and reduce crime.

   The importance of the persistent offender has always been recognized but hitherto the focus has been on sentencing as opposed to targeting. As Pyle (1995: 42) has argued: 'Since at least the middle of the last century a predominant theme of sentencing has been the principle of cumulation. Under such a scheme, for each new offence committed the sentence is increased above the previous level.' It is beyond the scope of this chapter to describe legislative changes in relation to sentencing – many of which have altered – rather, it focuses on the more pragmatic approaches to targeting such offenders.

Equally, policy needs to address those longer-term approaches that seek to influence and change either potential or actual offender behaviour. So, what effect has criminology had on the development of current legislation and policies in relation to offending both in the short and medium term, and has legislative policy acted to reduce crime? A key milestone is the implementation of the Crime and Disorder Act 1998 and the publication of the first ever national crime reduction strategy. The legislation introduced statutory Crime and Disorder Reduction Partnerships (CDRPs) in every local authority area. The responsibility of these partnerships is described comprehensively elsewhere in this book (see for example Moss, Chapter 1, and Brookes, Chapter 3). In November 1999, the government published the first national crime reduction strategy (Home Office 1999). A number of key priorities were included, the first of which was to raise the performance of the CDRPs and the police. It also identified as priorities the reduction of burglary; property crime; vehicle crime; and dealing with anti-social behaviour and disorder. Importantly, it also identified the need to deal effectively with both young and adult offenders and victims and witnesses, thus bringing into its remit the role of criminal justice agencies as well as the police and local authorities.

A plethora of White Papers and policy changes were subsequently introduced which sought to integrate government policy-making and service delivery within what has been called the 'modernizing government agenda'. This agenda (also discussed in more detail in Chapter 3) places a 'culture of delivery' at the heart of the government's change programme. It provides a focus on what it describes as moving away from the 'one size fits all' approach to providing a service around the needs of the customer, including patients, pupils, passengers as well as the wider general public (HMSO 2002).

In relation to criminal justice specifically, the White Paper 'Criminal Justice: The Way Ahead' (Home Office 2001a) followed a number of themes. It recognized that crime has a pervasive and corrosive effect on society and suggested that confronting these issues is a task beyond the criminal justice system alone. 'It requires concerted action across Government, in local communities, in schools and in homes' (HMSO 2001a: 5).

Its overall aim was to ensure that the criminal justice system works as a modern, coherent and joined up system and it recognized the role that CDRPs could play (HMSO 2001a: para. 3.185). The need to reduce crime through these efforts and by targeting persistent offenders was reinforced throughout the paper. Supporting research illustrated that a small group of 100,000 offenders were responsible for 50 per cent of all crime (HMSO 2001a: para. 1.29).

The White Paper led to further major reviews within the criminal justice system. Integration of criminal justice agencies was initially slow but the creation of Local Criminal Justice Boards (LCJBs) is now providing a much stronger focus on integrating criminal justice activity with crime reduction efforts. This is particularly the case in relation to the prolific and priority offender strategy and much more opportunity now exists with regard to the creation of the National Offender Management Service.

At a wider level than crime or criminal justice, one of the major planks of the modernizing government agenda is the New Commitment to Neighbourhood Renewal (Home Office 2001c). In the foreword to this policy paper the Prime Minister stated:

> When we came into office, we inherited a country where hundreds of neighbourhoods were scarred by unemployment, educational failure and crime. They had become progressively more cut off from the prosperity and opportunities that most of us take for granted. Communities were breaking down. Public services were failing. People had started to lose hope. That's why I asked the Social Exclusion Unit to work on developing a new and integrated approach to reversing this decline.
>
> (Home Office 2001c: 5)

The action plan set out a new approach to renewing poor neighbourhoods in an effort to narrow the gap between the most deprived neighbourhoods and other areas. It is an integrated programme focusing upon all social conditions including housing, the physical fabric of neighbourhoods, unemployment, crime and also poor public services. It recognized that in such neighbourhoods there are few services – too few GPs, too little policing. The programme – targeted in the 88 most deprived areas of the country – provides a real opportunity for integrated action and supports the view described earlier in relation to left realism for the need for a framework of interventions based on the best of all approaches but tailored to suit local need.

Also of prime importance is the need to engage the community in crime reduction activity in an attempt to build civil renewal. This is a key government priority and one which has direct relevance to the discussion of offender management. The need to increase confidence in the criminal justice system could be said to be critical given public perceptions of the criminal justice system (CJS). In the latest British Crime Survey (BCS) three-quarters of respondents were confident that the criminal justice system respected the rights of people accused of a crime but in other respects the report stated that 'overall confidence in the CJS was not generally high' (Home Office 2004d: 9). In a recent report which summarized findings in respect of public confidence in the CJS, it was evident that almost a third more respondents (63 per cent) were confident about the way crime was being dealt with in the area where they lived, compared to 47 per cent who were similarly confident about the way crime was tackled across England and Wales generally (Page *et al.* 2004: 1). Respondents were also asked to choose (from a list of 20 suggestions) the functions of the system which they thought were essential but in which they had low confidence. Two of the functions which were consistently reported as essential but in which confidence was low was 'stopping offenders from committing more crime and bringing people who commit crimes to justice'. It is possible therefore to see that the views of the public are also important issues for policy makers and have on occasion been acknowledged as such. For example, (as described by Brookes in Chapter 3) the former Home Secretary has argued that: 'Government depends upon active participation by citizens in order to achieve the goals pursued on their behalf' (Blunkett 2001: 1). David Blunkett's ideology was translated into Home Office policy and will be detailed further in this chapter. It was not simply restricted to Home Office policies but also those of the Office of the Deputy Prime Minister. Developing social capital, fostering greater engagement in local decisions, and taking action to promote inclusion are all included in the ten-year vision for local government (ODPM 2004). This therefore is the background against which the management of offenders and the reduction of crime in respect of this can be placed. Specific strategies which have been formulated to deal with this are now discussed.

Central strategy: improving the targeting and management of offending

It is increasingly evident that the approach of targeting persistent and priority offenders is central to the Home Office strategy of reducing crime, although there remains recognition that initiatives should be led locally with ownership of specific approaches being the responsibility of CDRPs. Although CDRPs have specific responsibility, the co-ordination of such approaches in the 42 police areas in England and Wales is now the responsibility of what are known as Local Criminal Justice Boards. Membership of these boards comprises Chief Officers from all the criminal justice agencies (the police, courts, Probation, prisons, Crown Prosecution Service and Youth Offending Service). Central oversight remains strong, with accountability expected from the Chair of the Local Criminal Justice Board to the National Criminal Justice Board, with broadly the same constituent members at a national level as at area level.

The first inspection of persistent and prolific offender strategies was completed in 2004 (HMCIC *et al.* 2004) and the findings were broadly encouraging, including as they did some of the following:

- all criminal justice agencies supported the concept of prioritising work with a small number of offenders;
- there was evidence that intensive interventions can have a positive crime reduction and rehabilitative effect;

- there was evidence of good partnerships and positive outcomes between the police and the Probation Service where a limited number of persistent and prolific offenders were supervised;
- the majority of interventions concerned offenders whose behaviour was thought to cause significant fear of crime;
- there was a 'win–win' effect in which offenders were either rehabilitated or returned to prison for breach of their order.

There were also some reservations in the Inspectors' findings, including:

- the majority of offenders were at the lower end of the offending scale (for example, persistent shoplifters) and were therefore not eligible for post-custody supervision;
- some persistent offenders were not felt to be a 'priority' by local partnerships;
- the cost of such schemes to the majority of practitioners outweighed the benefits.

(HMCIC *et al.* 2004).

Inspectors argued for an improved performance focus for all criminal justice agencies. This was particularly the case in relation to the Crown Prosecution Service and the courts where persistent and prolific offenders had previously not been prioritised. Local Criminal Justice Boards were considered to be the responsible agency to co-ordinate joint performance monitoring of activities in this field and such guidance has now been issued.

The executive function is also well defined with a planning and performance framework devised by the newly created Office of Criminal Justice Reform, which has a direct link to the Cabinet Office and the Prime Minister himself, who regularly hosts criminal justice 'stock-takes' to check progress on major crime and criminal justice government strategies. This therefore is the current situation with regard to government strategy to improve the targeting and management of offenders. It is pertinent at this point to focus more specifically on particular projects which have been designed to manage persistent offenders and to reduce crime in the community.

The community focus: a case study

The importance of pioneering 'local' or neighbourhood developments which have shaped or had a major influence on government approaches to reducing re-offending should not be under-estimated. The 'Tower Project' in Blackpool was established in January 2002 and an independent evaluation of this project was commissioned in November 2002. This was carried out by the Applied Criminology Group, University of Huddersfield in 2003.

The Tower Project was described as a persistent offender targeting initiative with a particular focus based upon an assertive and intensive supervision model that combined drug treatment and lifestyle support with police disruption and targeting tactics – a 'carrot and stick' approach (Applied Criminology Group 2003).

The project aims were to reduce the offending behaviour of a targeted group of persistent drug-related offenders, with an expectation of bringing down the average illegal drug use of this group by 30 per cent. In 2002 Blackpool had seen a rise in criminality because of a significant escalation in the use of crack cocaine and heroin. The project recognized the broader social care issues and not simply criminal justice considerations. For example, there was a significant delay in offenders accessing drug treatment services (12–18 months' waiting time).

External interest in the scheme, which after six months had targeted 38 offenders, was considerable. The potential for marked crime reduction was seized upon by the Government Office for the North West and the Police Standards Unit and was quickly being heralded as 'good practice' (Applied Criminology Group 2003). One suggestion for this premature championing could potentially be that it accorded with the 'policy beliefs' rather than 'what works' approach – such as that suggested by Vold and Bernard (1986) in the introduction to this chapter.

Reduction in crime was, however, significant with drops in both 'burglary of dwelling houses' and 'theft from vehicles', with little evidence of displacement of crime to other police areas. There were some caveats with an increase in shop theft which could however have been attributed to an influx of summer visitors to the Blackpool area. Overall a reduction in crime was estimated to be in the region of 30 to 40 per cent. The influence of other police initiatives to reduce crime was not, however, independently calculated and it was not altogether clear which approach had been most successful or indeed the nature of the interrelationship between different aspects of police intervention. Nevertheless, the unique nature of the Towers Project was recognized and could be described as a 'crackdown consolidation' approach. That is, a sustainable long term intervention which followed on from more short term police approaches, which is a supportable crime reduction strategy (Chenery, Farrell and Pease 1997).

The scheme had elements of the Burnley Dordrecht scheme which has been independently evaluated elsewhere (Chenery and Pease 2000). The central element here is the linking of targeted policing of prolific offenders with intensive probation supervision and timely interventions at the point where the offender was released from prison or when a community penalty had been made.

Moving on from this, the question remains as to whether the probation and prison services are organizationally geared up to providing a seamless approach to reducing crime by both persistent offenders and others or whether, in a transfer of responsibilities from a custodial to a community context, crucial focus and attention is lost. So, what does work with offenders?

What works: re-embracing positive work with offenders

During the Thatcher years, the concentration on punishment left rehabilitation and resettlement issues very much in the shadows of penal developments akin, it is suggested, to the over-concentration on prisons and policing and the resultant etiological crisis. The emphasis was on punishment and retribution with elements of training as indicated in the 'short sharp shock' approach employed in detention centres run under military lines and akin to 'boot camps' developed in the United States. There was little support for positive developments within the probation service and this was reflected by commentators who embraced both national expectations but also had an overview of local services throughout England and Wales. The Chief Inspector of Probation, writing in his 1993 Annual Report, was in a critical mood about the efficacy of probation service work with offenders, commenting that: 'Unfortunately too many users of Probation Services and the public appear unconvinced that current forms of supervision are either sufficiently rigorous to constitute adequate punishment or sufficiently effective to reduce criminal behaviour' (Home Office 1993:1).

Although this was not a positive statement about the crime-reductive potential of statutory probation services, it did recognize that community sentences were punishments in their own right and not just alternatives to prison incarceration. In the 1970s the focus as regards community penalties, particularly for young offenders, was whether they were too demanding with the inherent care and treatment being intrusive and not justified by the seriousness of the offence (Thorpe *et al.* 1980). Bottoms and McWilliams (1979) argued that probation interventions should be seen not as treatment at all but as a non-custodial penal measure offering a humane alternative to coercive measures. 'Just deserts' thinking had recently begun to dominate sentencing debates generally where punishments were based on the principles of proportionality as regards the seriousness of the offence.

However, a search for interventions that governed future re-offending rather than simply responding to past offending had not been completely lost and in the late 1980s the influence of other countries' thinking on correctional services began to influence provision in England and Wales. For example, in Canada psychologically oriented services began to develop, based on intensive supervision (Ross *et al.*1988) and some general principles began to emerge. Rayner (2000) describes these principles in the following way:

A   Target high-risk offenders, who are otherwise likely to continue to offend, rather than low-risk offenders who may gain little benefit or be harmed.

B   Focus on criminogenic need – that is, those characteristics of offenders or of the circumstances which have contributed to their offending.

C   Use programmes that are highly structured, making clear and explicit demands and following a logical sequence determined by learning goals.
D   Use a directive working approach so that participants know what they are meant to be doing.
E   Use broadly cognitive behavioural methods to provide opportunities to learn new thinking and behaviour.
F   Locate in the community.
G   Ensure programme integrity – that is, the programmes are delivered as intended with procedures to ensure this.
H   Use committed and effective management.
I   Employ appropriately trained staff who believe they can be effective.
J   Provide adequate resources for continuity.
K   Have integral evaluation and feedback.

These principles now form the basis for the accreditation of new programmes for offenders which are to be applied in both the prison and probation settings. Some interventions were adapted from programmes run in the USA and Canada but a national accreditation panel was established in 2000 by the Home Office to ensure that programmes used for offenders either in prisons or probation would be, as far as possible, those which had the best demonstrable prospect of effectiveness in addressing offenders' problems and helping them reduce their offending. This is not to say that New Labour policies have left behind the populous toughness of the previous Conservative regimes but there is a genuine commitment to crime reduction and the use of evidence-based effective methods to achieve this (Rayner 2000).

It is interesting to note at this point that it could be argued that these efforts are drawing together a framework of interventions that comprise the pragmatism of the new administrative criminologists (targeting high-risk offenders); the socially centred Left Realists (focusing on criminogenic needs); the more determined Right Realists (targeted sentencing directed towards targeted persistent offenders) and the free-thinking Left Realists (drawing the various processes together within an integrated framework).

The next section examines in some detail the radical organizational reform that has resulted in the creation of the National Offender Management Service (NOMS).

Organizational reform and modernization: a case study

In the introduction to his review of Correctional Services entitled 'Managing Offenders, Reducing Crime', Carter (2003: 1) remains critical of 'joined up' approaches to reducing crime, commenting that:

> We have found an urgent need for different parts of the criminal justice system to work closer together. At its simplest each part of the system has little regard for the consequences of its actions on other

parts. This means that resources are not always used effectively. Further, few of the players are focused on the overall aim of crime reduction.

It is the latter comment that is the most pertinent to the discussion in this chapter. This criticism of all criminal justice agencies is explicit and potentially damning. Carter believes that all criminal justices agencies have become preoccupied with their own policies, procedures and standards and have forgotten their unique and combined contribution to crime reduction. His solutions are multi-faceted, including the bringing together of the prison and probation services into one organization. This suggestion has formed the basis of the newly created National Offender Management Service which has for the first time, a single person – the Chief Executive – accountable to Ministers for both punishing offenders and reducing re-offending. In addition, a strengthening of market forces is also seen to be a central part of the new landscape, in that the newly created National Offender Manager will also be responsible for reducing re-offending, supported by 10 Regional Offender Managers from each government region and from Wales, who will direct and ensure offender management both in prisons and on community penalties and also commission new services from the public, private and voluntary sectors.

Other aspects of the report mirror parallel developments in criminal justice, including the establishment of the Sentencing Guidelines Council. The powers of this new body are concerned primarily with improving consistency in sentencing, with information and analysis being made available to sentencers about what combinations of prison or community sentences are most likely to reduce re-offending and the best use of 'capacity' in Correctional Services – an area which has traditionally not been one that sentencers have addressed. Better targeting of Correctional Services reflects the increasing knowledge base of what is effective in community penalties, an area which is beyond the scope of this chapter.

The introduction to this chapter highlighted the emphasis that the government had in relation to the targeting of persistent offenders in the White Paper 'Criminal Justice: The Way Ahead' (HMSO 2001a). To reiterate, this paper outlined that 100,000 or about 10 per cent of all active criminals were responsible for half of all crime. Fast-tracking through the courts; the improvement of enforcement by the probation service and better follow up of short prison sentences to avoid the quick return to a life of crime and drug abuse were all emphasized. The report was to anticipate Carter's (2003) comments in wishing to build on the achievements of the prison and probation services but highlighting the need for better integration of services both within correctional agencies and beyond in establishing a more holistic approach to reducing re-offending from health, education, employment and housing agencies.

Not all practitioners and academics have welcomed the Carter approach and have pointed out the limitations or unintended consequences of reforms to sentencing. Nellis (2004) describes what he sees as the process by which the probation service has become a quasi profession slowly acquiring internal managerial structure and operating as part of the state bureaucracy but without a high public profile. He further describes how the creation of a National Probation Service in 2001 was seen as an opportunity to accelerate existing modernization processes within the probation service. His argument is sequential considering that positive developments in changing community service to community punishment orders in 2001 reflected increasing centralization and a move away from local communities. This argument does not however take account of the priority of a local approach to crime reduction in the persistent offender strategies described earlier in this chapter and is thus a major omission. His comments about the Home Office (2001b) review of sentencing, 'Making Punishments Work' are, however, more salient. He contends that in future there is less likelihood of a marked differentiation between community and custodial sentencing, which in itself downplays the need for a clear distinction between two separate organizations such as the prison and probation services and instead prompts the creation of an over-arching offender management service.

Faulkner (2004) is less equivocal, commenting that although the Carter Report provides a framework and an opportunity for what is potentially the most radical reform of the penal system for 125 years, serious reform will depend on the determination and the enthusiasm with which the government, the prison and probation services and other agencies put the report's proposals into effect. He further questions some of the proposed new structures, arguing that a regionally based commissioning of new services represents a transformation of the services as they exist at present, particularly as they have been thus far nationally focused as to their structure, policies and standards. This perspective however arguably gives little significance to the strong local tradition of community responses to crime that have been described in this chapter.

Faulkner also sees developments such as the move to greater local autonomy – demonstrated by the regional commissioning role – being closely allied with the Prime Minister's vision for public service reform. This includes giving more power to the public and designing public services around the individual, which in Faulkner's view would be the offender rather than the arguably equally legitimate claims of victims. Faulkner supports Carter's proposals for a reconstruction of the prison estate with older and smaller prisons being replaced by larger and more modern buildings but with their design and creation being determined by Regional Offender Managers.

Faulkner makes some interesting comments about the link between offender management and the concept of civil renewal or active citizenship, as proposed by the former Home Secretary (Blunkett 2003a). Again, this emphasizes the local context of crime and follows the tradition of indirect reparation where individual offenders pay something back to communities in respect of the damage they have created by their crimes. The vision of the former Home Secretary is characterized by creating a 'sense of owner-ship' on the part of communities where individuals can do something positive about crime. Faulkner, like Blunkett, believes that the proposed reforms in the traditionally court-based criminal justice system and attempts to change the silo mentality of traditional Correctional Services, should benefit local communities and contribute to improving public confidence whilst also increasing what David Blunkett calls 'social capital' (Blunkett 2003b). Faulkner remains cautiously optimistic, commenting that the success of civil renewal as applied to offender management will demand sustained commitment from those on whom it depends.

Nash (2004) speculates that the establishment of the National Offender Management Service might be regarded as effectively signalling the end of the independent probation service. He also believes that this is the culmi-nation of the process of ending penal welfare and postulates that enforcement of court orders is incompatible with assisting offenders who have a wide range of personal, social and economic problems. This is a polarized view and denies the multi-faceted aspects of probation supervi-sion evident in persistent and prolific offender schemes. Nash takes as his example the Intensive Change and Control Programme (ICCP) where surprisingly he believes collaboration with the police service would trans-form probation supervision as the police may identify stolen goods or other illegal items. Again this is not a new approach and any probation officer in the last 20 years who failed to respond to known offending by those they supervised would be vulnerable to both internal discipline by their employers and would lose, on behalf of the wider service, the confidence of both the courts and the communities of interest or geography they serve. Such joint working with the police merely formalizes long standing exchanges of information between two parties in the criminal justice system.

Tonry (2004: 4) describes the crime control policy in England and Wales in recent years as both 'tumultuous and schizophrenic' and comments that 'many have expressed frustration over apparently incessant and discon-nected changes and pessimism about the likelihood that further changes would be beneficial'.

Tonry has expressed concern that White Papers subsequent to the Criminal Justice Act 2003 were not always evidence based. He supports, for instance, the proposals that some persistent offenders would not receive imprisonment in the first instance for their offences but instead may be given something short of an immediate prison sentence – for example 'custody minus', a form of a suspended prison sentence but with the full range of conditions available as any other community sentence. Tonry's concern is that any breach of such an order would lead to immediate imprisonment. A significant amount of offenders breach such conditions and this issue was not highlighted in the government's proposals which stated that: 'Automatic imprisonment of all of them will increase and not decrease the prison population' (Home Office 2001b: 10).

In Tonry's view this is not evidence based but purely based on a 'tough' political stance towards offenders. However, there are indications in the early draft of guidelines issued by the newly established Sentencing Guidelines Council that this problem is recognized as a breach of such a new hybrid order and may lead to additional conditions and not necessarily to an immediate prison sentence.

Tonry (2004: 32) is less convincing in his belief that persistent or prolific offenders do not merit serious attention, despite the evidence that they commit the majority of crime, commenting that: 'Nuisance offenders exist everywhere but only in England have they become a major and chronic policy preoccupation.'

Tonry believes the majority of such offenders are young; have drug problems that tie them into a crime-dominated life until their dependency is broken; have a range of personal, family and economic problems, including unemployment, mental health or disability; and lack the necessary skills for sustainable employment. He supports in this context the work of the Social Exclusion Unit which addresses a wide variety of initiatives of a social, educational or treatment nature to target persistent offenders, including greater use of diversion or restorative justice (Social Exclusion Unit 2002). What therefore does the future hold under the new regime currently coming into operation?

Towards the future: structural change in correctional services and keeping a focus on crime in the community

This chapter contends that in spite of the ongoing changes to the structure of those agencies dealing with offenders, this is not a fundamental shift in emphasis in terms of the longstanding aims of the correctional services in England and Wales. Currently offenders are more likely to go to prison than they were ten years ago. For example, statistics from magistrates' courts show that the use of imprisonment in Dorset has increased by 285 per cent; in Northamptonshire by 326 per cent and in Hampshire by 282 per cent, with only four areas being under 100 per cent (Dyfed Powys 33 per cent; Warwickshire 85 per cent; Devon and Cornwall 66 per cent and Nottinghamshire 75 per cent) (Home Office 2004e). If the earlier comments in relation to the economics of crime policy are taken into account, there is clearly much more improvement needed. Although more recent crime trends have been encouraging one could still argue that both etiological and fiscal crises remain.

The challenge for government is to seek from sentencers a proper balance between the use of prison and other community penalties. Creating a more effective working arrangement between the prison and probation services is sensible if the revolving door of return to community, crime and back to prison is to be avoided. Social exclusion and regeneration initiatives combined with a wish to empower communities to take responsibility for crime and their own offenders are not unconnected agendas, particularly in the context of the response to persistent offenders, which by its very nature must be locally driven for the reasons outlined in the introduction to this chapter.

If the new Regional Offender Managers employed by the National Offender Management Service are to achieve their aims, they must commission the right type and volume of services to reflect local needs and they must consider the dangers of attempting to provide the same services in each of their regions for fear of being accused of what has been termed 'postcode justice'. The comments of criminologists and other commentators suggest that providing such services from the market place might decrease the humanistic and constructive approach to working with offenders that is evident in the combination of approaches employed in the Towers Project previously described in this chapter. There is, however, no strong evidence for this as both the independent and voluntary sectors have a long history of ethics and moral values in their work and increasingly the private sector recognizes its broader social responsibilities, both in corporate governance terms and also in the sponsoring of joint ventures with both the public and independent sectors.

Delivering new services designed to further reduce levels of re-offending and the incidence of crime is a perpetual concern for government, particularly as regards the behaviour of the most persistent offenders. The National Offender Management Service has the responsibility to achieve these aims. By galvanizing the imagination and innovation of a range of providers, it has the potential to improve quality and value for money whilst preserving what is best and sustainable from present arrangements in the prison and probation services. All new and existing provision needs to dovetail with present and future strategic partnerships in criminal justice and crime reduction. Any new approach will be under considerable scrutiny over the new few years, both by internal and external stakeholders as well as a wide range of practitioners and academics. Given the need to increase confidence in the criminal justice system the scrutiny of the community should not be overlooked either.

The Coulsfield Inquiry (2004) into alternatives to prison is concerned that the market place might not work so well in relation to community penalties because small providers might not be as cost effective and will be put off by the formality of tendering processes. In addition, the report argues that regional procurement might not meet the needs of specific groups in the criminal justice system such as women and ethnic minorities. These are genuine concerns but there is no doubt that a pure model of 'contestability' – that is, a competitive value for money exercise to determine who *should* provide services – needs to be balanced with the opportunities of local people to decide on the projects and initiatives which would benefit them and offenders. Like aspects of contestability, this notion is also highly attractive to Home Office ministers who wish to build public confidence and understanding of community penalties in England and Wales, where such sentences do not have the characteristics of prison sentences, particularly for high-profile offenders or persistent/prolific offenders.

This chapter has sought to highlight the importance that government places on tackling and managing the offender. Hitherto, policies have tended to reflect individual theoretical propositions about 'what works' in reducing offending, but the importance of tackling and managing offending and its impact on reducing crime has only really come to fruition in more recent years. The two examples highlighted in this chapter to target offenders through the persistent offenders' strategy *and* to manage them seamlessly through the creation of the National Offender Management Service are exciting opportunities, but the real test will be in their implementation and impact.

Bibliography

Applied Criminology Group (2003) *The Towers Project,* University of Huddersfield.

Carter, P. (2003) *Managing Offenders, Reducing Crime – A New Approach,* Home Office Strategy Unit, London: HMSO.

Blunkett, D. (2001) *Politics and Progress: Renewing Democracy and Civil Society,* London: Politico Publishing.

Blunkett, D. (2003a) *Civil Renewal: A New Agenda,* London: Home Office.

Blunkett, D. (2003b) *Active Citizens, Strong Communities: Progressing Civil Renewal,* London: Home Office.

Bottoms, A. and McWilliams, W. (1979) 'A Non-Treatment Paradigm for Probation Practice', *British Journal of Social Work* 9(1), 159–202.

Chenery, S., Farrell, G. and Pease, K. (1997) *Consolidating Police Crackdowns: Findings from an Anti-Burglary Project,* Home Office: Police Research Paper 113/97.

Chenery, S. and Pease, K. (2000) *Evaluation Report on the Burnley/Dordrecht Initiative,* (unpublished).

Clarke, R. and Eck, J. (2003) *Become a Problem-Solving Crime Analyst,* London: Jill Dando Institute of Crime Science.

Cohen, L. and Felson, M. (1979) Social Change and Crime Rate Change, *American Sociological Review,* 44, 588–608.

Coulsfield, J. (2004) *Independent Inquiry into Alternatives to Prison,* London: Esmée Fairbairn Foundation.

Faulkner, D. (2004) 'A Moment of Opportunity: Some Reflections on the Carter Report and on the Government: Accompanying Statement. Reducing Crime, Changing Lives', *Vista,* 9(1), 2–7.

Garland, D. (1988) 'British Criminology Before 1935', *The British Journal of Criminology,* 28(1), 1–17.

Garland, D. (2002) *The Culture of Control: Crime and Social Order in Contemporary Society,* Oxford: Oxford University Press.

Her Majesty's Chief Inspector of Constabulary, Her Majesty's Chief Inspector of Probation, Her Majesty's Chief Inspector the Crown Prosecution Service, Her Majesty's Chief Inspector of the Magistrates' Courts Service, Her Majesty's Chief Inspector of Prisons, Audit Commission (2004) *Joint Inspection Report into Persistent and Prolific Offenders,* London: Home Office Inspection Directorate.

HMSO (2002) 'Better Government Services: Executive Agencies in the 21st Century', London: Office of Public Sector Reform and HM Treasury.

Home Office (1993), *HM Inspectorate of Probation Annual Report 1992–1993*, London: Home Office.

Home Office (1999) *Crime Reduction Strategy*, London: HMSO.

Home Office (2001a) 'Criminal Justice: The Way Ahead', Cm 5074, London: Home Office.

Home Office (2001b) 'Making Punishments Work: Report to a Review of the Sentencing Framework for England and Wales', London: HMSO.

Home Office (2001c), 'A New Commitment to Neighbourhood Renewal: National Strategy Action Plan', London: HMSO, Social Exclusion Unit.

Home Office (2004a) 'Prolific and Other Priority Offender Strategy, Initial Guidance, Prevent and Deter', London: HMSO.

Home Office (2004b) 'Prolific and Other Priority Offender Strategy, Guidance Paper 2, Catch and Convict Framework', London: HMSO.

Home Office (2004c) 'Prolific and Other Priority Offender Strategy, Supplementary Guidance, Rehabilitate and Resettle Framework', London: HMSO.

Home Office (2004d) 'Crime, Disorder and the Criminal Justice 02/04 System – Public Attitudes and Perceptions to Crime in England and Wales 2002/2003' Supplementary Vol. 2, London: HMSO.

Home Office (2004e) 'The Use of Custody in the Magistrates Court by Probation Family Area', London: Home Office (unpublished).

Nash, M. (2004) 'Glorious Past or Bright New Futures? Turning Probation into Corrections', *Vista*, 9(1), 40–4.

Nellis, M. (2004) *Into the Field of Corrections: The End of English Probation in the Early 21st Century?*, University of Birmingham (unpublished).

ODPM (2004) 'The Future of Local Government: Developing a 10-year Vision', London: ODPM, July 2004.

Page, B., Wake, R. and Ames, A. (2004) 'Public Confidence in the Criminal Justice System', Home Office Research Development and Statistics (RDS) Briefing Paper 221.

Pyle, D. (1995) *Cutting the Costs of Crime: The Economics of Crime and Criminal Justice*, London: Institute of Economic Affairs.

Rayner, P. (2002) 'What Works: Have we Moved On?' in Ward, D., Scott, J. and Lacey, M. (eds) *Probation: Working for Justice*, Oxford: Oxford University Press.

Ross, R., Fabiano, E. and Ewles, C. (1988) 'Reasoning and Rehabilitation', *International Journal of Offender Therapy and Comparative Criminology*, 32(1) 29–35.

Social Exclusion Unit (2002) *Reducing Re-Offending by Ex-Prisoners*, London: ODPM.

Taylor, I. (1997) 'The Political Economy of Crime', in Maguire, M., Morgan, R. and Reiner, R. (eds) *The Oxford Handbook of Criminology* (2nd edn.), Oxford: Clarendon Press.

Thorpe, D., Smith, D., Green, C. and Paley, J. (1980) *Out of Care*, London: Allen and Unwin.

Tonry, M. (2004) *Punishment and Politics: Evidence and Emulation in the Making of English Crime Control Policy*, Cullompton: Willan Publishing.

Vold, G. and Bernard, G. (1986) *Theoretical Criminology*, Oxford: Oxford University Press.

Young, J. (1994) 'Incessant Chatter: Recent Paradigms in Criminology', in M. Maguire *et al.*, *Oxford Handbook of Criminology* (1st edn), Oxford: Clarendon Press.

10 The future of crime reduction

Kate Moss

Change is inevitable ... except from a vending machine.

In this concluding chapter, an attempt will be made to select some of the points made by chapter authors and address their implications. Whilst all of the preceding chapters deal with a broad range of different topics – from central and local government responsibilities for crime prevention, through policing; mental disorder; paedophilia; offender strategies; management of places and crime as a pollutant to a provoking discussion of risk; incentivization and rehabilitation as the underpinning factors for crime reduction – at the most general level, three conclusions appear to be held in common:

1   All conclude that legislation can work to reduce crime in certain circumstances.
2   None conclude that the crime reductive impact of legislation is currently being fully realized.
3   Insofar as the chapters make bold recommendations for change, these often address aspects of economic and social life outside the conventional boundaries of criminal law.

In Chapter 1, Kate Moss clarifies recent problems in bringing legislation to bear on crime reduction. She uses two examples: first, section 17 of the Crime and Disorder Act 1998 (CDA) (which enjoins local partnerships to consider the crime consequences of all their decisions) and second, the implementation of the Data Protection Act 1998, alongside section 115 of the CDA, which sought to facilitate data sharing for the purposes of crime reduction. She notes that these provisions reflect a welcome change in perspective towards an emphasis on the integration of social arrangements to limit the supply of and demand for criminal opportunities. She identifies a number of problems which have collectively meant that the legislation has not fulfilled its potential. These include the lack of detailed guidance provided, the lack of an underlying awareness of the criminological literature suggesting the (not always obvious) factors which are criminogenic, and the anomalies created by section 17's non-applicability to central government, whose bizarre consequences are evidenced in her recounting of the *Aquarium Entertainments* case.

As for Moss's second point, the disclosure of crime-reductive information among members of local Crime and Disorder Reduction Partnerships, she concludes that in practice partnerships have agonized about what data can legitimately be shared and on what basis, with police data protection officers varying greatly regarding how they interpret the statute and senior officers or managers not taking active roles in promoting data sharing – probably because of a lack of knowledge of the issues. The result of this in most cases has been a presumption against the sharing of data. Moss's central conclusion is that what has been lacking are the guidance and underpinning knowledge which provide the context of the legislation. She argues that guidance, education and the extension of section 17 to apply to central government are necessary conditions for transforming rhetoric into reality.

In Chapter 2, Martin Seddon deals with the design and management of places and their link with crime. He performs the useful function of tracing town planning legislation and locating its roots in public health considerations. Whilst noting fortification of homes in the distant past, he opines that planned towns were 'practical attempts at social engineering with the objectives of relieving urban congestion and creating harmonious communities in a pleasant environment, [but] the connection between crime and design was not directly made'. The exclusion of crime from the social ills to be ameliorated by place design was perhaps a consequence of the traditional emphasis on offender change, notably by religious and temperance means, as the preferred route to crime reduction. Once the supply of crime opportunities afforded by a location came to be recognized, the crime reduction agenda in place design has always been playing catch-up in relation to other social purposes. The detailed tracing of the social purposes behind, and the specific forms of, town planning are useful, in the present writer's view, for two reasons. First, they specify the social purposes behind planning, often with less empirical justification than could be brought to bear on place manipulation for the purposes of crime control. Second, it makes clear which specifics need to be changed, and how, to best serve the purposes of crime reduction.

In Chapter 3, Steve Brookes constructively but provocatively details the interplay between policy creation and policy implementation, and the local–national dimension along which fault lines may develop. He structures this debate by asking three questions. First, to what extent has legislation effectively structured local authorities to enable them to play a meaningful role in crime reduction activity? Second, to what extent does legislation currently enable local authority executives to make decisions and choices based on locally determined needs whilst also satisfying national priorities? Third, how effective is the support provided by legislation to improve the safety of communities?

Although expressed more diplomatically by Brookes, the simplified answers seem to be respectively: 'not much', 'a lot but not enough' and 'not very'. Brookes observes that:

> An organization does what it is measured on and, in the case of local authorities this relates ... recently ... to the Comprehensive Performance Assessment (hereinafter referred to as 'CPA'). CPA was introduced to assist local councils in improving local services for their communities. It aims to identify how well a local authority delivers its services; how well it is run; and how this impacts on the services it delivers. Whilst community safety is now an integral feature of CPA, this has not always been the case. This has resulted in the CDA being very much the poor relation in comparison with local government legislation in respect of the setting of priorities.

Brookes also comments on the multiplicity of targets under Public Spending Agreements, leading to individual crime targets being overlooked. Brookes's line here supports arguments in both Chapters 1 and 2 about how crime reduction as a social purpose has been late on the scene and not fully integrated into structures and policies.

Brookes's listing of the legislation and organizational change directed primarily or incidentally at crime and disorder reduction is useful in that it reminds us how much has been done over the last decade. His challenge to local leadership to give community safety its 'place in the sun' highlights how much could be done without any further legislation.

In Chapter 4 Ken Pease widens the debate by insisting on a dual-track approach to crime reduction. He makes the point that the legislative or other means are incidental, but that the policy ends whose consequence would be crime reduction are, to paraphrase him:

- controlling fertility, reducing the number of children born of impulsive liaisons;
- designing education and social policy so that adolescents (adolescent boys in particular) can reasonably anticipate reproductive success in the middle term;
- incentivizing central government, designers and the private sector to embrace crime reductive design;
- targeting prolific and persistent offenders, for whom dispositions and affordances have combined to yield high frequencies of crime, while introducing safeguards to ensure that such targeting takes place accurately (a necessary qualifier he deems to be missing from current policy, notwithstanding much Home Office activity directed to such offenders).

Pease controversially eschews approaches based on:

- the manipulation of risk and hygiene factors in early childhood;
- the rehabilitation of convicted offenders;
- drugs as causal of crime.

The Pease chapter is helpful in broadening the canvas of policy purposes with crime reduction consequences. It may also turn out to be prescient in alerting us to the emergence of heredity–environment interactions in establishing criminal dispositions, and in introducing the term 'affordance' to the debate, referring to the perception of opportunity as more crucial than opportunity itself.

In Chapter 5, Steve Everson traces changes in the practice and governance of policing over the last 30 years. He observes that the changes have been largely government driven, and have possibly been insufficiently sensitive to changes in the resulting relationships between the police, with its monopoly power on the exercise of legitimate force in civil society and the public. He concludes:

> Assuming that there is both intention and commitment to retain, or indeed regain, the traditional British concept of 'policing by consent', then a major effort is required to repair the damage inflicted upon the system over the past two or three decades. The police–public dynamic requires effective and professional contact to underpin 'policing by consent' – that is to say, a requirement for meaningful contact with victims, witnesses and members of the public in their everyday demands for reassurance, support and advice. It may require a radical re-think about the role of the police and may even challenge some traditional concepts. Whatever that outcome may be, it should be one that is considered and planned rather than a consequence of a series of random events and interventions, however well intentioned each may have been, which is leading inexorably to a potentially irreversible change in the style of policing of the United Kingdom.

In Chapter 6 Herschel Prins provides a scholarly account of the manner in which 'the law has a part to play in reducing the extent of known mental disorder in offenders', without any necessary suggestion that by doing so offending would be materially diminished – the relationship between mental disorder and crime being described by Prins as 'equivocal'. He rails against 'over-speedy recourse to inadequately thought through legislation' and concludes:

> The relationship between mental disorders, criminality and the law is complex. In addition, both mental disorders and serious criminality tend to arouse powerful emotions, particularly those of fear. Such fear is exacerbated by the media, and 'moral panics' … are common and unhelpful phenomena. To all of this we must add political sensitivities

... [Hasty] legislation produces difficulties for all those who have to implement it; and this in turn may lead to their best efforts being disparaged by the general public. Both mental disorders and crime require calm approaches; today, sad to relate, these are not always in evidence.

Prins's wise and measured approach suggests, although he does not say as much, that legislation which seeks to address crime reduction should regard mental health considerations as marginal. Crime is not typically the product of a mentally disordered mind, and the mentally disordered should not be the scapegoats of misguided attempts to behave as though this were the case. As ever, hard cases make bad law.

In Chapter 7 Dennis Howitt addresses the fraught topic of paedophilia and the law. Dealing with Internet images, he remains agnostic about the value of shutting down illegal websites unless there is evidence that the same material would not otherwise be distributed by different means (the displacement argument). He also speculates about the existence of a group of men with paedophilic interests but who never engage in contact offences against children. Commentating on the Sexual Offences Act 2003, Howitt remains unsure of what effect, if any, the legislation will have on paedophilic offences. He outlines other legislation dealing with Internet pornography. Addressing the question of whether prison 'works' for paedophiles, he notes that researchers are hampered by the lack (for fairly obvious reasons) of baseline data on rates of offending among paedophiles. He concludes:

> Reconviction studies simply cannot tell us anything about the effectiveness of prison as a deterrent. What the data do tell us is that reconviction is far from certain over quite a long period – especially if sexual offences alone are considered. Furthermore, even if prison is effective as a future deterrent, we do not know what it is about prison which has an effect.

Considering the effect of registration on the Sex Offenders Register (and other forms of 'flagging' a paedophilic history), Howitt observed a reduction in recorded offending of those on the Register in comparison with the preceding year. He notes:

> One could say that this is indicative of success, as so few re-offend. However, it also makes it clear that the most dangerous individuals at any time may well not be on the Sex Offenders Register as these numbers are a small fraction of the total number of sex offences against children annually.

On balance, Howitt finds discretionary release to be cautious:

There is little to suggest in all of this that sexual offenders against children are released to re-offend against children because of lax risk assessment and decision-making procedures. Quite the reverse seems to be true – that is, many more sex offenders against children are kept in prison who are unlikely to re-offend than those who are let out and go on to re-offend.

He notes that the best assessments of the efficacy of treatment of sex offenders suggest only modest success, but is cautious given the difficulties of evaluation of the programmes in question. Howitt's most emphatic conclusion concerns the balance of effort directed towards known and unknown offending:

> The problem is that children are also at risk from adults who are not known to the criminal justice system as sex offenders. Concentrating on known offenders does little to help the prevention of sexual abuse by others.

In Chapter 8, Graham Farrell and John Roman draw parallels between the supply of crime opportunities and pollution as more conventionally understood. This is a theme which has previously been linked with the work of Paul Ekblom. Farrell and Roman do signal service by fleshing out these ideas into a form readily translatable into a legislative programme. Because the theme chimes with some current thinking within the Home Office but is developed imaginatively, it may prove particularly influential. One of the most original elements of the chapter is the possibility of an Enhanced Crime Doctrine. Farrell and Roman state that this is:

> adapted from the existing Enhanced Injury Doctrine applied to the motor vehicle industry whereby, since it is highly predictable that many traffic crashes will occur, vehicle manufacturers are accountable for safety standards to reduce any additional (enhanced) injury. Since aggregate levels of crime can be predicted with reasonable accuracy for many crime types, it is argued that it should legally behove crime polluters to recognize this and adopt anti-crime measures.

In some senses, this approach merely systematizes an incentive system already in place – for example, licences to sell alcohol may be withdrawn if the licensee ignores or is reckless about crime and disorder resulting from the way in which he or she conducts the business. In other senses, it promises heated debate. In essence, people in the course of their business invariably create a social cost that is borne by others, but this is typically more direct in respect of pollution than in the case of the supply of criminal opportunities. Factories spewing toxic waste into waterways are *ipso facto* culpable. By contrast, iPod devices have distinctive earpieces, and this alerts potential robbers to the existence and value of what is available to steal. This may be criminogenic, but it needs the agency of a robber for the crime to occur. Universities are criminogenic by bringing together large numbers of young people with varying levels of 'street smarts', and providing a Union bar at which they can get drunk before venturing home through inner city streets to insecure rented accommodation in which they keep their computers and entertainment electronics. Where do externalities stop? This is in no way to detract from the sophisticated and important analysis offered by Farrell and Roman; simply to note that legislation along the lines advocated will be mightily controversial.

In Chapter 9, Steve Goode and Stephen Brookes examine two major policy initiatives which aim to reduce crime in the community through the targeting and effective management of offenders. The authors support the recent decision to integrate the prison and probation services into a single National Offender Management Service. Discussing programmes for targeting prolific and persistent offenders, Goode and Brookes accurately identify the Blackpool Tower Project as the *primus inter pares* of its type. The chapter hints at what was clear in the relevant evaluation report; namely that the crime reduction achieved was primarily a function of a police crackdown which pre-dated the Tower project, with (at best) modest effects added by the project itself. There are many reasons for applauding the Tower Project, but it falls short of making the case that integrated working between police and probation services has yet advanced to the point where it achieves significant crime reduction.

In spite of their variances, what all of these chapters tell us is that legislation is not necessarily a good way, or the only way, of reducing crime and in many cases it is difficult to ascertain whether indeed it has had this effect at all or whether reductions in crime are actually incidental to the implementation or interpretation of existing law. A further difficulty is that both law and central government crime policies change fairly often and a knock-on effect of this is that it is frequently difficult for agencies to respond quickly to these changes and for the judiciary to interpret Parliament's wishes in this respect. Perhaps more important is the fact that the sort of crimes that can be committed are changing all the time and it is difficult to stay ahead of this since the law cannot pre-empt what crimes will be possible in the future but can only act subsequently to legislate to make something a new crime. By the time this happens, further new crimes are being committed or are possible. The law therefore plays 'catch-up' and will continue to do so unless changes are made to the way in which we think about preventing crime and the mechanisms which we use to do so. Part of the problem here is the difficulty in persuading policy makers about what sorts of things they should be concentrating on. Moreover, another issue is knowing what research would be most beneficial to the reduction of crime. Finally, there needs to be recognition that legislating to reduce crime is only one aspect of a much broader spectrum of more imaginative thinking that should be going on in relation to the prevention of future crime. Some criminologists have tried to develop work in this area, such as Morgan and Newburn (1997) and Bayley (1994). The problem with this sort of work is that the focus has been on future responses to criminality rather than on what changes in actual crime there might be. Pease (in a personal communication) likens this approach to that taken by science fiction writers who concentrate on changes in how the criminal justice system might operate but not on how crime might change. So, is it possible to be more pre-emptive about reducing crime, but who should we be looking to for advice about this?

Crime reduction and criminology

Unsurprisingly, as a criminologist, the author contends that legislators, policy makers and practitioners should all be looking to criminologists for advice about crime reduction. Although criminology as a broad discipline is hard to define, what all criminologists attempt to do is to apply scientific methods to the study of crime in order to suggest ways of reducing or preventing it. There may have been a time when criminology as a discipline concentrated too much on issues such as what do to with the criminal and why particular criminals committed particular crimes. It might even be true to say that criminology shrank from the future because it is awkward to predict what future crimes might be possible and even more awkward if those predictions turn out to be wrong. This would be embarrassing. Another reason is that most criminologists need funding to facilitate research. Whilst it is true that funding for research does exist, those who allocate it – and the Home Office is a good example of this – don't generally give it to people to study things that haven't happened yet. However, if you want to carry out evaluations there is usually a lot of money for that sort of work. As Goode and Brookes argue in Chapter 9, policies often follow policy makers' own beliefs and personal agendas rather than being informed by criminological debate or findings.

Dissatisfaction about these issues first became more prevalent in the 1970s, with a group of British writers which included, most prominently, Jock Young, John Lea and Roger Matthews. These criminologists felt that the political climate of the time was shifting dramatically and that the result was that criminology was slipping away from them. They felt there was too much emphasis on certain aspects of crime and small-scale interventions and that the Home Office was monopolized by what they called 'administrative criminologists' who were serving a conservative 'law and order' agenda. They felt that there was too little emphasis on the victims of crime, that too much weight was being given to official statistics and that crime was not being considered as a real problem.

They made some uncomfortable observations about both women and ethnic minorities in relation to their respective contributions to crime. For example, they argued that women, who were only in the 1970s finding a place in the labour market, had been under-represented massively as offenders but that as they were becoming integrated into the workplace, so their crime rate started to rise quickly because women wanted their slice of the economic cake and, if they couldn't get it legitimately, they might turn to illegitimate means. They were also ahead of their time in feeling that too much emphasis had been placed on the offender, that the criminal justice system protected the offender, making it harder to prove guilt, harder to press charges and harder to send people to prison or give them other punishments. They felt that the victims were given a raw deal.

In their 1986 book *Confronting Crime*, Roger Matthews and Jock Young commented that:

> the tide is turning for radical criminology. For over two decades it has neglected the effect of crime upon the victim and concentrated on the impact of the state – through a process of labelling – on the criminal. ... It became an advocate for the indefensible: the criminal became the victim, the state the solitary focus of attention, while the real victim remained off-stage.
>
> (Matthews and Young 1986:1)

They advocated a balance of intervention at all levels to achieve a more comprehensive solution based on the diagram in Figure 10.1.

Using this diagram, these Left Realists asserted that crime is a function of four factors:

1   the state which creates crime and labels individuals and groups as offenders;
2   the victim who experiences crime either because of a lack of defence or because of a precipitation towards crime as a result of personality or lifestyle;
3   society which exercises the various forms of social control;
4   the offenders who are important in terms of how many there are, how many crimes they are committing and of what type.

Controlling crime using the square basically meant that Left Realists advocated intervention at every part of the square. This would include things like trying to employ offenders or educate them away from crime; helping victims through target hardening; mobilizing the state, for example to provide more effective policing; and better mobilization of society against crime in general. Basically, Left Realists felt that they were different because, rather than looking at explanations for crime in very narrow terms, they looked at them in a much wider way.

In the last few decades of the twentieth century things have undoubtedly changed. Society has become characterized by its increasing secularity

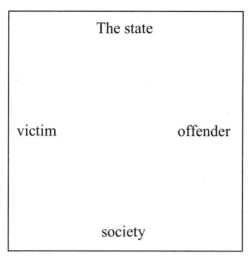

Figure 10.1 The square of crime.

and by its greater emphasis upon science. We have come to live in a much more fragmented and diverse world than ever before and this has sometimes been referred to by social scientists as 'the post modern condition'.

Criminology and post modernity

Taylor, Walton and Young's (1973) 'New Criminology' characterizes some of the thinking about the post modern age. They and others wanted to challenge orthodox positivist forms of thought and even called for the abolition of the power to criminalize what they saw as human diversity. They were concerned with the enlarged power of the state and with state monopolies over many things and they felt that this was not a good thing. This kind of thinking also fitted in at the time with Foucault's conceptualization of power. Such a state of affairs was a great fear among academics and writers of the time, but in actual fact something different politically was just around the corner – something they perhaps had not expected.

Post modernity was actually expressed in new Conservative ideals alongside Thatcherism and Reaganomic ideologies: shrink 'big' government; get the government off the backs of the people; tax cuts; the dismantling of state monopolies and greater emphasis on diversity of interests. It became characterized by a moral certainty that had been lacking for some time. It became a backcloth against which social scientists and criminologists all over the world felt able to recognize the new complexities and ambiguities of society and to begin to acknowledge that different explanations and discourses about crime and criminality were possible at different times and for different people. The search for the objective view of reality in criminology was slowly replaced by recognition that there are multiple complex realities which are open to different interpretations by politicians, academics and the public. It is against this backcloth that in 1997 New Labour was elected.

New Labour's new politics fitted in with the idea of post modernity in that it had considered policies from a wide range of different perspectives, and attempted to build new moral certainty by accepting that good ideas can come from both the Left and the Right. This is both ideological and pragmatic since it was the only way Labour was ever going to get back into power (and acknowledges that Tony Blair's self-confessed hero was Margaret Thatcher). For the future of criminology these developments might have appeared beneficial since, in theory at least, it meant that more diverse research might be undertaken and accepted by a much wider range of people. In practice, however, this has not happened since the government is arguably only looking for quick fixes in criminology and crime reduction and not long-term sustainable results. It is only concerned with outcomes in spite of the fact that it preaches flexibility in dealing strategically with crime. This approach makes it difficult for criminologists to undertake the most innovative or ground-breaking research and also hinders imaginative thinking, not least because policy makers need to be persuaded that this sort of approach is merited. So where do we go from here?

Thinking more imaginatively about crime prevention

In spite of this, there are some criminologists who are not shrinking from the future. Pease (2000) comments that in line with more recent trends in policy making, and specifically section 17 of the CDA, referred to by Moss in Chapter 1, we should all feel more responsible about preventing crime. There will, of course, always be sceptics who say 'Why should we bother?' Pease (2000) refers to these as the non-believers in taking responsibility and puts the author in mind of the elected member of a particular local council who argued that he shouldn't have to have a burglar alarm or a gravel drive to deter potential offenders since it was the responsibility of the offenders not to commit crime. For those of us who live in the real world, we know that this cannot be the case. Other sceptics often use the argument of displacement – that the crime will only go elsewhere or other people will commit it – an argument which, according to Barr and Pease (1990 and 1991), is not necessarily supportable.

If we required still more reason to feel responsible about preventing crime, we have only to look at how successful we currently are at dealing with crime and offenders. For example, recent figures from the Prison Reform Trust (2004) indicate that 71 per cent of those aged under 21 who are sent to prison are reconvicted within two years. Added to this, it currently costs approximately £24,000 per year to fund one prison place. This is a lot of money to pay for failure and arguably this money could be better spent elsewhere.

There could be no better argument for taking more responsibility for crime and also for not neglecting the future. One of the more heartening things that has happened recently with regard to this was that the Department of Trade and Industry included a Crime Reduction Panel amongst those in its Foresight Panel which met to explore the changes in science and technology which might facilitate crime reduction. The two Foresight Reports (2000a and 2000b) foresaw a number of trends, including:

- new technology allowing individuals to commit crimes previously beyond their means;
- crime exploitation of the electronic world;
- location aware and chipped valuables having the potential to shrink the universe of stealable things;
- people will increasingly become the target of offenders thwarted in their pursuit of goods.

Because of these issues, any recommendations for the future of crime reduction should take account of how the future of crime will be shaped. Legislation can't hope to keep up with these trends so we must look to other, more imaginative ways of preventing and reducing crime. This is the real future of criminology and in a sense means that criminology must either reinvent itself or gear up to face the challenges of the twenty-first century in new ways. How can it do this?

The way forward must surely be to engage with other disciplines, and of course businesses, to encourage people to take responsibility for reducing crime and to demonstrate that there are economic and social incentives to do so. For example, if the cost of crime could be demonstrated to the National Health Service, alongside ways of reducing this cost, this would incentivize crime reduction in a sphere which traditionally distances itself from crime prevention. In other spheres, such engagement has already started happening; for example, with design culture and to a certain extent in relation to buildings, architecture and the environment as a whole. The crux of this is the acceptance of a change in thinking about reducing crime, and some examples of this follow.

Engaging with design: changing the environment

Environmental criminology, as Seddon points out in Chapter 2, is concerned with where and when crimes occur. There has been a renewed interest in this since the 1970s when a greater emphasis was placed on trying to find out if knowing more about such issues could help us to reduce the opportunities for crime. However, the idea in itself is not particularly new.

In the nineteenth century, Guerry (1833) and Quetelet (1828 and1846) looked at conviction rates in different geographical areas. The Chicago Ecologists (Park 1921) were also interested in spatial characteristics of crime and used geographical forms of analysis such as the concentric circle theory to do this at the beginning of the twentieth century.

These and other later studies typified much of the research of the time in that they tried to bring together three different theoretical perspectives to explain criminal behaviour. These were:

1   the ecological approach (why people live where they do);
2   the deviant subculture approach (why people behave in particular ways in particular areas);
3   the social reaction (or labelling) approach (what effect labelling certain people in particular ways has on them. For example, those from working class areas being labelled in a particular way and feeling stigmatized as a result).

Recent criminologists have looked specifically at the notion of how our environment shapes crime and whether we can actually make recommendations to design the areas in which we live in order to reduce crime. After all, it is all very well talking about where the crime is; more important are the recommendations for change that can be made. Preventing crime through environmental design has become more popular in recent years but is not a new idea. This has been referred to in both the chapters by Moss and Seddon. This idea captured modern criminologists' imagination in the mid-1960s and early 1970s subsequent to Jane Jacobs's book (1965) *The Death and Life of Great American Cities*. This contribution was the forerunner to much of the later work in this area and Jacobs's notion was that mixed land use provided more 'eyes on the street', resulting in lower crime and lower fear of crime. She emphasized diversity as the key to safety, her reasoning being that multi-functional areas would attract a continual flow of people throughout all times of the day and evening. She argued that the more people who use the streets, the more opportunity exists for informal surveillance. One drawback to this hypothesis is that it assumes that the individuals using those streets would 'care' about the property within them. This may not always be the case.

Newman's (1972) seminal work on crime and the environment suggested that part of the explanation for urban crime lies in the breakdown of the social mechanisms that once kept crime in check, combined with the inability of communities to come together in collective action. His solution was to restructure the residential environments of the cities so that they could again become liveable and controlled – not necessarily by the police but by a community of people sharing a common terrain. Newman's notion of defensible space argues that the physical design of a neighbourhood can either release or inhibit people's latent sense of control and responsibility over the space that they live in, the intervening variable being informal social control. What do we mean by this? Neighbours questioning strangers, watching each other's property, and apprehending individuals who should not be there would be examples of such control.

Newman advocated the adoption of certain actions to foster this, including territoriality, natural surveillance, a safe image and a safe milieu. The notion of environmental criminology really took off in the 1980s with work by the Brantinghams (1981) and Wilson and Kelling's (1982) 'Broken Windows'. They looked particularly at the idea of the environmental management of crime which can be implemented in relation to existing places and situations. Theoretically, such environmental management asserts that where you have an area with particular crimes, if those crimes go unchecked, this will lead to more offences, either of the same type or the same offences plus others too. This argument is particularly relevant when applied to anti-social behaviour and other offences such as drunkenness, vagrancy and vandalism.

It was Wilson and Kelling who took up this point in their 1982 article, describing urban America in the following way:

> A piece of property is abandoned, weeds grow up and a window is smashed. Adults stop scolding rowdy children; the children, embolden, become more rowdy. Families move out, unmarried adults move in. Teenagers gather in front of the corner store. The merchant asks them to move, they refuse. Fights occur. Litter accumulates. People start drinking in front of the grocery store; in time an inebriated drunk slumps to the sidewalk and is allowed to sleep it off. Pedestrians are approached by loiterers.
>
> (Wilson and Kelling 1982: 29)

The hypothesis here is that incivilities lead to crime which leads to further incivilities. Environmental management as referred to by Seddon in Chapter 2 strives to remove the primary incivilities and therefore break the cycle of crime and further incivility. Examples are cleaning the streets of litter, removing graffiti, removing signs of vandalism, repairing property and not allowing it to fall into further disrepair.

The debate concerning appropriate land use continues and most recently has been characterized by the Conservative leader Michael Howard in relation to travellers whom he claims are using the Human Rights Act 1998 to avoid planning regulations. Commenting to the BBC on 24 March 2005, Mr. Howard contended that travellers were currently able to bend planning laws, building where they liked, thanks to the Human Rights Act, and elucidated a five-point action plan to tackle this misuse of land, including a review of the Act to ensure that it does not clash with laws against unauthorized land development.

Twenty-first-century design against crime

One of the most recent innovations in crime prevention through environmental design was the Secured by Design (SBD) initiative. This was a national police initiative and award scheme designed to promote the use of crime prevention measures at the developmental stage of building, covering aspects of both design and physical security. The scheme was endorsed by the Association of Chief Police Officers (ACPO) and backed by the Home Office (then) Crime Reduction Unit.

Some information about SBD can be found on a dedicated website at http://www.securedbydesign.com but basically what SBD advocates is as follows:

- that new buildings can be built to a design which incorporates security at the outset; or
- that older buildings can have their security levels updated to the SBD standard.

SBD focuses on a number of aspects of designing out crime in residential areas, including physical security, surveillance, access and egress, management and maintenance and territoriality. The principles of SBD basically mean that:

- if the fabric of an environment is designed correctly, you need less effort to maintain it;
- design endures across the lifetime of a building or location; we have the choice of building relatively crime-free or relatively crime-ridden environments.

The success of secured by design is demonstrated in research by Armitage (2000) whose work proved consistently that SBD houses are burgled less and that people feel safer in these neighbourhoods. This has also been proven in practice, for example by the Royds initiative, referred to in 'Safer Places' (ODPM 2004). This is an area of Bradford with one of the highest rates of burglary in the country – seven times the current national average. After the refurbishment of the estate to SBD standards, not one of the 1,596 dwellings had been forcibly entered in five years. The quality of life in the area has been transformed and this regeneration has since won numerous local and national awards.

In spite of the proven success of the SBD initiative, some planners are opposed to SBD because they know very little about it. Others are not necessarily opposed to it, but do not feel it is that important because it is one of the crime and disorder considerations which have been marginalized by the 'Safer Places' (ODPM 2004) guidance. Added to this, it is often stereotyped as damaging aesthetics when it frequently does quite the opposite by producing safe, sustainable facilities. The bottom line is that until SBD is written into planning guidance or is incorporated into building regulations, it will continue to be ignored or marginalized. If SBD continues to be marginalized then the outcome could be poor. The

Maidenbower case study from Sussex (also referred to in 'Safer Places' (ODPM 2004)) concerning 3,600 residential units also shows how SBD and non-SBD can be compared. Only 119 dwellings belonging to the council were approved for build as SBD. The rest were not built to SBD because the developers did not want the extra cost. Six years on, the SBD area is virtually crime free compared with the non-SBD area which suffers badly from all forms of crime, graffiti and anti-social behaviour. Residents who own the private (£300,000 houses) are now asking why the local authority housing is so superior to their own. Secured by Design should therefore be incorporated into building regulations.

We need to act now in order to redress the balance between development and crime and disorder which is facilitated by the environments in which it is happening. After all, an area from which people or businesses flee because of crime or the fear of crime, where the remedy is costly and police led, is just as doomed as an area that cannot be used because it is polluted. Moss (2002) has recommended that the following actions should have been or still could be taken:

- To write SBD into a relevant government document as being obligatory. The ideal opportunity for this would have been the revised 'Planning out Crime' Guidance recently updated in 'Safer Places' (ODPM 2004) by the Office for the Deputy Prime Minister. Arguably, this represents a missed opportunity.
- To follow the approach taken by the Home Office in its Property Crime Reduction Action Team (PCRAT) Report (Home Office 2001), and within a government document include a link which seeks a design against crime assessment for (in the first instance) publicly funded buildings. Linking this across to the private sector would be even more ideal.
- To incorporate SBD principles into revised building regulations.
- Good design with safety and security built in is cost effective. Every burglary prevented saves society money. Using environmental crime prevention techniques, we can prevent more crime and the misery it causes.

In line with changes in relation to the law and management of places which has been referred to in Chapter 2 by Martin Seddon, the Office for the Deputy Prime Minister recently produced the 'Safer Places' (ODPM 2004) guidance. Criticism of the lack of commitment to the concepts of planning and designing out crime and the reluctance to extend these sorts of responsibilities to central government were also referred to in Chapter 1 by Moss. Following the publication of this guidance, there remain areas which have not been fully integrated. The first of these is in relation to sustainability where it could still be argued that not enough emphasis on sustainable approaches to planning and designing out crime has been given by the guidance. This is a pity – for a number of reasons.

First, if the fabric of an environment is designed correctly, it needs less effort to maintain it. Second, design endures across the lifetime of a building or location; we have the choice of building relatively crime-free or relatively crime-ridden environments. Third, some approaches appear to have high sustainability – for example the Secured by Design Initiative (Armitage 2000). For others, notably CCTV, there is evidence of diminishing effect with time. Fourth, that individual elements of decay lead to an accelerating process is the central proposition of the 'Broken Windows' hypothesis (Wilson and Kelling 1982; Kelling and Coles 1996).

There is undoubtedly a climate now in which people are thinking more about crime reduction. Awareness is being raised and there is also movement within the private sector to make public limited companies more liable at board level. In line with this, new guidelines should not be static and should have a dynamic for growth in this respect.

Recent engagement between criminologists and the design culture has produced innovative ideas which would never have been anticipated a decade ago. Perhaps one of the best examples of this is the work which has recently been carried out by Central St Martin's College of Art and Design, the most topical of which can be found in Gamman and Pascoe (2004) and Gamman *et al.* (2004). Most of this work revolves around changing the design of products in order to maximize crime-reductive effect, such as the application of crime prevention through environmental design principles to bicycle parking provision. One point importantly made is that whilst it is clear that innovative design can help to reduce crime, it remains critical to preserve a pleasing visual image in relation to environmental crime prevention techniques such as alley gates in order to dispel the myth that to prevent crime requires 'fortress design'. Changing the public's perception about issues such as this will advance the cause of crime prevention. Again, it all comes down to changing the way we think about things.

Identifying risk: changing the way we think about risk

Although some interest has been generated about looking more closely at heightened risk factors, this is another idea which has yet to take off entirely. In Chapter 4, Pease highlights that the manipulation of risk factors for crime-reductive purposes has not been fully realized. There are few examples where risk has been used as an identifying factor by which to highlight where crime reductive measures should be most usefully placed. However, one example is in the East Midlands where a particular interest in information sharing between agencies and how this could work to reduce crime kick-started a regional focus on ways in which this could be facilitated. Initial funding was given to all local authority areas by the regional Government Office to provide analytical capability both in the form of hard kit and software and also in relation to training and the appointment of analysts. Two years into this project, in 2002, a report was commissioned by the Government Office East Midlands (GOEM) to evaluate its impact. This demonstrated the need for a more strategic and evidence-led approach to information sharing. Alongside this it was also felt that there was a need to encourage Crime and Disorder Reduction Partnerships (CDRPs) to have a greater involvement in and ownership of the strategic development of specific crime-reductive projects and a need to determine what data, over and above that which was currently available, should be obtained as a matter of urgency to inform an evidence-led response to particular crime problems in Nottingham. One such problem identified for further research was domestic burglary. This was pertinent for several other reasons also. For example:

- domestic burglary had been identified as a key priority;
- there was a need to move to evidence-led crime reduction since there was little evidence of this at the time of the project;
- there was a clear need for an agenda for action in relation to this problem for which Nottingham had the highest rate in England and Wales;
- it was felt that the CDRP should have a greater involvement in and ownership of the strategic development of specific crime-reductive projects;
- there was a need to determine what sort of data (over and above that which was currently available) should be obtained as a matter of urgency in order to inform an evidence-led response to domestic burglary in Nottingham;
- there was a need to continuously monitor and evaluate these processes in terms of performance management and results.

The Nottingham Burglary Risk Index, or BRIx Project as it became known, suggested that two residential pilot areas should be chosen for the focus of a project to develop a risk index for domestic burglary. In relation to these areas, such a risk index relies on a number of different strands of data being gathered from different agencies in order to inform this approach. Aside from this and the core data which was potentially available from the police and GOEM, it was suggested that there was also a body of data which should realistically be gathered from locational survey work and a victim study carried out within the two areas in question.

The intention of the project was to draw up a risk assessment instrument based upon accepted and proven risks rather than those that could best be described as anecdotal or experiential. In this case the bases for this were three individual pieces of academic research; namely Budd's (1999) work on domestic burglary; research on repeat victimization by Farrell and Pease (2001); and the Winchester and Jackson (1982) Environmental Risk Index. Combining these elements in a manner which informed the gathering of specific data and which also formed the basis of empirical survey work which was later carried out provided the foundation of the burglary risk assessment instrument. In order to achieve this, it was necessary to collect data specific to those identified risks previously highlighted in these academic works.

The ultimate aim of this research was to provide agencies with knowledge, based upon the risk index, regarding how much of the identified risk was conferred by factors over which those agencies may have had stewardship. That is, they would be aware of which of 'their' factors contributed to the total risk but not what the components of that risk were, beyond those conferred by variables (those factors) within their own domain.

The suggestion from this was that there should subsequently be a joint action plan in respect of, say, the 5 per cent of individuals and households standing at greatest risk. Practical action plans could then be agreed in respect of those most at risk to provide focus for partnership working. One of the benefits of this approach was that all information at the point of use had the personal elements deleted and was therefore entirely anonymous. In spite of this, it was felt that a protocol should be agreed in order to safeguard these issues. This was easily arranged through the data protection manager for Nottingham City Council and was subsequently signed by representatives of the police, the City Council and the Home Office to enable the project to move ahead. A table of risk factors was duly drawn up and some recommendations made which are discussed more thoroughly than is possible here in Moss (2005). There are two issues which are of prime importance in relation to this work. First, although analysis of risk has of course been carried out before – and in this respect, this research is not ground breaking – there has been, as far as the researchers are aware, no other risk instrument developed which combines both victim and location data in this way. As such this would be a useful tool for practitioners to implement. Second, the notion of implementation is important. Practitioners remain to be convinced that they can use this kind of research to good effect and in this sense they too need to take on board the necessity for change which the job of crime prevention and reduction requires. If they do not, they will fall behind the kind of progress that is being made in this sphere.

Using virtual reality: changing the methods for preventing crime

A recent idea which also merits further research is the feasibility of using 'walk through' virtual reality environments for the expert evaluation of urban community and domestic home security. These could be evaluated in terms of the effectiveness of the communication of information given to the perceived urban and domestic security expert and the cost-effectiveness of the technique, with the outcomes leading to the development of a cost-effective design tool for use by all stakeholders.

There is merit in innovative research such as this for a number of reasons. Recent research by Armitage and Everson (2003) strongly emphasizes that home owners and buyers want a secure environment more than any other feature of a home (location excepted) and that domestic home security systems are appropriate and successful in reducing theft and burglary. The average cost of a burglary has been estimated (Brand and Price 2000) at £2,300 whilst the average cost of incorporating enhanced security features into a home is approximately £440 (Armitage 2000). In some cases the perceived security of residents using security systems is that they continue to fear and feel vulnerable to crimes such as burglary. It is already well established (Moss 2005) that certain individuals and locations have heightened risks of burglary victimization and in this sense it is necessary to continue to improve security systems in order that urban environments and domestic homes are geared to the needs of occupants rather than burglars. These factors can have a demoralising effect on the homeowner, causing a reduction in their quality of life (for example, not sleeping at night) and a potential increase in unnecessary call outs of the local police force.

Currently, security experts survey urban communities by walking around the local environment, using their knowledge to identify issues concerning the positioning and layout of street furniture (such as lighting, fencing or even closed-circuit television camera placement). They also review the domestic interiors to identify security issues that require technology product intervention, such as locks, bolts or intruder sensor systems. An engineering drawing schematic can be difficult to interpret by a non-technical stakeholder. The integration of artists' impressions, plans and topographical information requires a skilled individual to be able to interpret all the available information effectively.

The activity of an expert 'walk through' can only be performed retrospectively on an urban layout. However, the use of a virtual environment created by a virtual reality system could be a viable technique, allowing the evaluation to be undertaken on the layout of new buildings and surrounding street furniture or the specification of a building and its interior prior to investment in building. The proposed technique offers an opportunity for all stakeholders to assess the full detail of available information that may be subsequently developed into a design tool.

Using technology: changing the citizenship agenda

As technological capacity increases, it makes sense, as in the case of the virtual reality proposal described above, to use this sort of advance imaginatively for crime-reductive purposes. There is potential here not simply in terms of what might be perceived as more radical approaches but also in terms of more basic, educative and didactic approaches.

A MORI survey on youth crime carried out in July 2004 established that 60 per cent of young excluded people have committed a crime. Of these, 51 per cent carry a knife, 55 per cent take drugs and half deal in stolen goods. These findings would suggest that there is still more work to be done preventing crime amongst the young and this has been highlighted in Chapter 4 by Pease. There are innovative examples of this. One such is the Rizer website (which can be found at http://www.rizer.co.uk/). The site has been designed and implemented by the Galleries of Justice, Nottingham – home also to the National Centre for Citizenship and the Law.

Rizer is a confidential information gateway on the World Wide Web which aims to provide neutral legal information and advice surrounding the consequences of becoming involved in crime. Aimed specifically at 11- to 17-year-olds, it is designed to help young people, reduce youth offending and crime, and communicate information about crime and the criminal justice system as it applies to young people. Rizer also aims to act as a deterrent and as a communications channel, imparting information to young people through a medium with which they are familiar, within a secure and confidential atmosphere and about a diverse range of legal issues. This is an innovative project whose overarching aim is to appropriately inform and therefore empower difficult or alienated young people and thus to help reduce youth offending through the provision of information which can be easily accessed and understood. Rizer has the potential to empower young people by providing them with some of the information which can assist them in developing the skills they need to become more responsible citizens. Alongside this, it also has the potential to be used as a tool to assist the police in communicating effectively with defendants and to assist parents who are increasingly accountable for their dependants. Its further development could provide a forum for partner agencies the better to address young people's offending behaviour and could assist the court process in terms of the speed with which issues are handled and the understanding of those who participate in that process.

The strategies, policies and interventions that are currently employed in relation to youth work and youth offending aim to assist young people to lead law-abiding and responsible lives. Rizer has the potential to assist with a number of these priorities, by providing a comprehensive information service to young people, parents and agencies which is designed to improve awareness and knowledge of the youth justice system. It does this by using the facility with which the majority of young people are so familiar now – the Internet. This is one example of an attempt to prevent and deter young people from committing crime, an issue which was highlighted by Pease in Chapter 4 and which is also one of three strands of the new strategy described by Goode and Brookes in Chapter 9.

Conclusion

Some good practice is emerging. One problem remains, and that is people's attitudes. We have already said that one of the problems with reducing crime is that society is changing all the time and with that change comes the opportunity to commit more and more diverse crime. For example, the most recent trend that we are being warned about is the possibility of having our identities stolen. This is the changing society in which we now live – a society of self-selected environments where we all indulge ourselves more than ever before. The possibilities are endless in terms of what we can do and have in terms of both personal possessions and knowledge. Gone are the days when to have a holiday abroad or a new car you needed to save up. Just take a loan and (hopefully) pay it back later. Gone are the times when to find out something a little unusual it could take days of research at the library. Just search on the Internet and you can find virtually anything. This includes the potential to find out how to make bombs, how to kill yourself or other people and how to indulge any other propensity such as looking at pornography. People no longer live in the enforced environments that they once did and are consequently more selfish and expect more. It could be hypothesized that this in itself could lead to more crime, since young people today appear to feel they have what could be described as a 'legitimate expectation' to possess all the material things which society now tells us we are inadequate if we do not have. Perhaps, if these cannot be obtained by legitimate means then illegitimate means might be employed. The lesson to be learned is that if we continue to work to reduce the opportunities for crime, then the necessity to legislate (with all its attendant pitfalls) will be less.

Bibliography

Armitage, R. (2000) 'An Evaluation of Secured by Design Housing in West Yorkshire', Briefing Note No.7/00, London: Home Office.

Armitage, R. and Everson, S. (2003) 'Building for Burglars?', Crime Prevention and Community Safety: An International Journal, 5(4), 15–25.

Barr, R. and Pease, K. (1990) 'Crime Placement, Displacement and Deflection', in Morris, N. and Tonry, M. (eds) Crime and Justice: A Review of Research, Vol. 12, Chicago, IL: University of Chicago Press.

Barr, R. and Pease, K. (1991) 'A Place for Every Crime and Every Crime in its Place: An Alternative Perspective on Crime Displacement', in Evans, D.J., Fyfe, N.R. and Herbert, D.T. (eds) Crime, Policing and Place: Essays in Environmental Criminology, London: Routledge.

Bayley, D. (1994) Police for the Future, New York: Oxford University Press.

Brand, S. and Price, R. (2000) 'The Economic and Social Costs of Crime', Home Office Research Study No. 217, London: Home Office.

Brantingham, P. and Brantingham, P. (1981) Environmental Criminology, Beverley Hills, CA: Sage.

Budd, T. (1999) 'Burglary of Domestic Dwellings: Findings from the British Crime Survey', Statistical Bulletin No. 4/99, London: Home Office.

Clarke, R., Smith, M. and Pease, K. (2002) 'Anticipatory Diffusion of Crime Reduction Benefits', in Tilley, N. (ed.) Environmental Crime Prevention, Monsey, NY: Criminal Justice Press.

DETR and CABE (2000) *By Design: Urban Design in the Planning System: Towards Better Practice*, London: Thomas Telford Publishing.

Farrell, G. and Pease, K. (2001) *Repeat Victimization*, Monsey, NY: Criminal Justice Press.

Foresight (2000a), 'Just Around the Corner', London: DTi.

Foresight (2000b), 'Turning the Corner', London: DTi.

Gamman, L. and Pascoe, T. (2004) 'Seeing is Believing: Notes Towards a Visual Methodology and Manifesto for Crime Prevention through Environmental Design', *Crime Prevention and Community Safety: An International Journal*, 6(4), 9–18.

Gamman, L., Thorpe, A. and Wilcocks, M. (2004) 'Bike Off! Tracking the Design Terrains of Cycle Parking: Reviewing Use, Misuse and Abuse', *Crime Prevention and Community Safety: An International Journal*, 6(4), 19–36.

Guerry, A. M. (1833) *Essai sur la Statistique Morale de la France*, Paris: English translation: Hugh P. Whitt and Victor W. Reinking, Lewiston, NY: Edwin Mellen Press (c. 2002).

Home Office (2001) 'Tackling Property Crime: An Initial Report from the Property Crime Reduction Action Team', London: HMSO.

Jacobs, J. (1965) *The Death and Life of Great American Cities*, Harmondsworth: Penguin.

Kelling, G. and Coles, C.M. (1996) *Fixing Broken Windows: Restoring Order and Reducing Crime in Our Communities*, NY: Free Press.

Matthews, R. and Young, J. (eds) (1986) *Confronting Crime*, London: Sage.

Morgan, R. and Newburn, T. (1997) *The Future of Policing*, Oxford: Oxford University Press.

MORI (2004) *MORI Youth Survey 2004*, London: Youth Justice Board.

Moss, K. (2002) 'The Good, the Bad or the Ugly? What will the New Planning Out Crime Guidance be Like and What Should it be Like?', *Community Safety Journal*, 2(1) 15–20.

Moss, K. (2005) 'The Nottingham Burglary Risk Index', in G. Farrell (ed.) *Imagination for Crime Prevention*, Crime Prevention Studies Series: Criminal Justice Press.

Newman, O. (1972) *Defensible Space: Crime Prevention through Urban Design*, NY: Macmillan.

Newman, O. (1976) *Defensible Space: People and Design in the Violent City*, London: Architectural Press.

ODPM (2004) 'Safer Places', London: ODPM

Park, R.E. (1921) *Introduction to the Study of Sociology*, Chicago, IL: University of Chicago Press.

Pease, K. (2000) *Cracking Crime through Design*, London: Design Council.

Prison Reform Trust (2004) *Prison Fact File*, London: PRT.

Quetelet, A. (1828) *Instructions Populaires sur le Calcul des Probabilités*, Brussels: M. Hayez.

Quetelet, A. (1846) *Lettres sur la Théorie des Probabilités, Appliquée aux Sciences Morales et Politiques*, Brussels: M. Hayez.

Rizer website: http://www.rizer.co.uk/

Taylor, I., Walton, P. and Young, J. (1973) *The New Criminology: For a New Social Theory of Deviance*, London: Routledge.

Winchester, S. and Jackson. H. (1982) 'Residential Burglary: The Limits of Prevention', Home Office Research Study No. 74, London: HMSO.

Wilson, J.Q. and Kelling, G.L. (1982) 'Broken Windows', *Atlantic Monthly*, March, 29–38.

INDEX

affordance 57–8, 176, 177; *see also* propensity
age of consent 117–120
alcohol-fuelled behaviour 42–4, 95, 141–2, 146
anti-social behaviour 24, 28, 29, 41–2, 74, 187, 189
anti-social behaviour orders (ASBOs) 21, 41
architectural liaison officers (ALOs)17, 22, 25, 28, 30, 31, 84
Association of Chief Police Officers (ACPO) 18, 36, 79, 151
asylum 100
Audit Commission 34, 79

Best Value Performance 30, 38–9
British Crime Survey 42, 67, 75, 76, 161
broken windows hypothesis 57, 187, 190

child pornography 115, 116, 120
child sexual abuse 117, 120
civilianization 78
closed circuit television (CCTV) 15, 27, 190
Cognitive Behavioural Therapy 128–30, 166
command-and-control 140, 142
community penalties 165, 168, 170, 172
community safety 11, 16, 17, 24, 35–6, 44, 47; partnerships 22, 38; *see also* urban safety
Comprehensive Performance Assessment (CPA) 38–9
compulsory detention 90
compulsory treatment 100

cost–benefit analysis 146–7
crime 16, 19, 21, 158, 180; and design; 19; control 135, 152, 159, 169, 175, 182, 186; cost of 146, 147; rates 18, 54, 79, 160, 167; setting 56, 58, 59; targets 71; *see also* pollution
crime and disorder 5, 15, 22, 31, 176; as a material consideration 7–8, 30; reduction partners 8, 9; reduction strategies 25, 84, 160
Crime and Disorder Act 1998 1, 2, 3, 4, 5, 7, 8, 9, 11, 21, 22, 29, 30, 37, 41, 46, 61, 79, 160, 174, 184
Crime and Disorder Reduction Partnerships 11, 40, 44, 46, 61, 75, 84, 160, 162, 175, 191
crime prevention 6, 7, 21, 28, 116, 132, 188, 190; agencies effecting 3, 4, 11, 17, 29, 38, 139; definition of 2; encouraging data sharing 9–11, 175, 191; history of 1–2, 14–17; legislating for 2, 5–9, 11, 12, 18–24, 39–40, 130–2, 137–9; *see also* design, management of places, paedophilia
Crime Prevention Design Advisors (CPDAs) 17, 25, 84
crime reduction xiii, 5, 10–12, 22, 26, 37, 61, 80, 84, 100, 129, 135, 148–51, 152, 156, 161–2, 164, 167, 171, 175, 185; and repeat victimization 82–3, 151; and technology 70–1, 185; and the law 34, 61–2, 160, 180
crime reductive legislation 11, 34, 174
crime reductive tool 7
criminal careers 54–5, 62, 141
criminal justice system xv, 89, 108,